Mental Health Ministry

THE STRUGGLE IS REAL

Dr. Jared Pingleton

TRILOGY CHRISTIAN PUBLISHERS
TUSTIN, CA

Trilogy Christian Publishers
A Wholly Owned Subsidiary of Trinity Broadcasting Network
2442 Michelle Drive
Tustin, CA 92780

Mental Health Ministry: The Struggle is Real

For information about special discounts for bulk purchases, please contact Trilogy Christian Publishing.

Manufactured in the United States of America

10 9 8 7 6 5 4 3 2 1

Library of Congress Cataloging-in-Publication Data is available.

ISBN: 978-1-68556-945-7

E-ISBN: 978-1-68556-946-4

Dedication

Lloyd and Jean Bilheimer, Burl and Berniece Rogers, Ralph and Naomi Houghton, Ron and Rosalyn Prinzing, Bill and Eunice Newby, Mark and Kari Shorey, David and Janice Betzer, Todd and Kelly Hudnall, and Nathan and Jessica Smith are the pastors I have been privileged to be shepherded by in my life. This book is dedicated to them and their examples of selfless commitment, Christlike character, and servant leadership.

Additionally, our four sons had the dubious and (fortunately) very rare distinction of being "double" PKs. Not only were they saddled with the challenges of being a "preacher's kid" throughout much of their lives, but they also had to endure the mantle of being a "psychologist's kid" their entire lives. Both of those labels were difficult and daunting at times. I am very proud of you, Jordan, Josh, Joel, and Joseph of the way you courageously handled those challenges and how you allowed God to use those experiences to shape and mold you into the exemplary young men you are today. I love each one of you very much.

Finally, my dear and darling wife has faithfully labored alongside me in ministry throughout various ministry and leadership roles and positions in my career. Linda, you have been supportive, steadfast, and servant-hearted, and I am deeply grateful. Your mercy heart to hurting people in your own ministries has been impressive, consistent, and giving. I am extremely blessed to have the wonderful wife that you are.

Endorsements

"Mental Health Ministry: The Struggle Is Real" is a wonderful and excellent book on how to practically and directly provide mental health services within the auspices of the church. It includes various diverse models and methods for doing this shared by ten key leaders. This is a much-needed book, especially with the present explosion of mental health needs and problems that the church can and must respond to with caring compassion and wise counsel. Highly recommended as must reading!

—Rev. Siang-Yang Tan, PhD
Senior Professor of Clinical Psychology, Fuller Theological Seminary, Senior Pastor Emeritus, First Evangelical Church Glendale, and Author of over Fifteen Books, Including *Counseling and Psychotherapy: A Christian Perspective*
Pasadena, California

What I love most about Dr. Pingleton is his hot heart for pastors. This book reflects his conviction that a church can only become what the pastor personally practices. Jared gives pastors and ministry leaders a refreshingly practical field guide for creating a church culture that brings hope and healing to their community.

—Rev. Mark Dance, DMin
Director of Pastoral Wellness , Guidestone Financial Services (SBC), markdance.net@markdance
Dallas, Texas

This is a unique, one-of-a-kind, biblically-based, research-informed, and real-world proven collection of practicable ways that Christian ministries that care about and are involved in meaningfully serving hurting people can make a very real difference in impacting those lives. From defining the possibilities and problems to providing models and methods...this is an invaluable resource that you'll refer to many times in the years ahead. It's that practical. It's that relevant. It's that good.

—Gary J. Oliver ThM, PhD
Professor of Psychology and Practical Theology at John Brown University, International Speaker and Author of over 20 Books, Including *Raising Sons and Loving It* and *A Woman's Forbidden Emotion*
Siloam Springs, Arkansas

Practical, sensitive, biblical, and wise, this book offers unique grace-filled strategies that give us answers for the epidemic of mental health challenges in the Church. Dr. Pingleton provides very helpful solutions to implement as we create a healthy Church Body that follows the example of how Christ walked in love with us.

—Julie Ann Rose, MA
Author, Speaker, Trauma Therapist, Minister, Film Producer
Franklin, Tennessee

"Mental Health Ministry: The Struggle Is Real" is a most timely and critically needed resource. All too often, the Church lacks an adequate response to the mental health needs within the church. Many church leaders are ill-equipped to respond effectively. Dr. Pingleton understands that most church leaders desire deeply to see their congregations have health in all facets of a person's life. This resource is an ideal read to help the church minister effectively to the whole person.

—Pastor Philip Dvorak, MA
Author, Speaker, Licensed Mental Health Counselor,
and Founder of the Recovery Church Movement
Lake Worth, Florida

We have an unprecedented mental health crisis in this country. Building on our book "The Struggle Is Real," this innovative resource is a practical toolbox that shows churches how to effectively minister to hurting people. Jared's counsel is biblically sound, clinically solid, and right on time. Every pastor and church leader needs this book!

—Tim Clinton, EdD
President of the American Association of Christian
Counselors, Co-host of Family Talk Radio, Author/Co-Author
of over 30 Books
Forest, Virginia

As a pastor in the local church, I soon identified two realities about mental and relational health. Pastors are likely to be the first someone comes to, even if only "asking for a friend" or testing the waters looking for a safe place to share. Secondly, I recognized my role as a pastor was often best lived out by having just enough familiarity and understanding to recognize, refer, and support the professional clinician who could provide the true mental health care to the parishioner before me. It required networking in my community with Christian clinicians and using helpful resources like the one you are holding so that I could be that first responder in a responsible way, realizing my limitations. I saw myself as a "general practitioner" who would refer to the "specialist" when it came to mental healthcare. This book serves as a solid resource to generally familiarize any "people-helper" with the issues and dynamics of today's mental health. It contains credible information to help you preach sermons and exude understanding that erases shame and removes stigma, extending kindness and grace that people are longing to receive from the Church and its leaders. The ministry you deliver, whether from the pulpit or beyond, should send a message that mental health is an issue you understand, normalize, practice, and promote. Allow this book to be a primary tool as you seek to provide life-giving, freedom-living ministry through the power of the Holy Spirit!

—Donna Barrett
General Secretary
The General Council of the Assemblies of God
Springfield, Missouri

In the past few years, pastors have seen an explosion of mental health and substance abuse issues. Many pastors find their knowledge and experience limited in helping meet this avalanche of human need.

Dr. Jared Pingleton has provided a resource that pulls together best practices and methods from ministers of God serving in the middle of the battle. This resource can assist in enabling pastors and Christian mental health professionals in the ministry of Jesus to heal the broken-hearted and set the captive free.

—Todd Hudnall, DMin
Lead Pastor of Radiant Church
Colorado Springs, Colorado

The stress of addressing mental health issues in the church is real for every pastor. In "The Struggle Is Real," Jared convinced us of the mental health crisis impacting the local church. In "Mental Health Ministry," Jared Pingleton presents us with a toolbox full of helpful and practical resources to address mental health challenges in the local church. Full of helpful insights, Pingleton sets the context for ten mental health experts to share their model for addressing mental health challenges in the local church. I highly recommend this book for anyone seeking a practical understanding of increasing mental health challenges in the midst of a fractured world.

—Rev. Jimmy Dodd
Founder and President—PastorServe,
Author of *Survive or Thrive, Six Relationships Every Pastor Needs; Pastors are People Too; What Great Ministry Leaders Get Right;* and *The Magnificent Names of Jesus*
Overland Park, Kansas

I have had the distinct pleasure of not only knowing Dr. Pingleton as a friend but have also hosted him at many events, and I can honestly say that in over thirty years of pastoral ministry, I have yet to hear a better and more well-rounded practitioner than Dr. Jared. In this new collaborative effort, he and his colleagues get right to the root of the problem, then give us excellent examples to follow as the answer. I highly recommend this book for any pastor or church leader who is concerned about mental health in the Church and is serious about addressing it.

—Pastor Al Stewart, DD
Author, Teacher, and Church Planter,
Senior Pastor , Greater Grace Chapel
Daytona Beach, Florida

Whether or not we would like to admit it, mental health challenges have permeated all of society—including the church. Most church leaders are not equipped to address the complexities that arise in ministering to hurting people. My good friend and colleague, Dr. Jared Pingleton, is uniquely equipped to address such issues in a theological yet real and practical way for pastors and churches. His passion as a pastor and psychologist comes forth in this latest resource to empower other pastors and church leaders. This tremendous manual can be a guide or a "plug and play" outline to effectively address the mental health crisis using the gospel of Christ and through the ministries of the church. There is no other resource like it!

—Robert B. Shaw, DMin, LCMHCS, BCPPC
Professor at Liberty University, Former Clinical Director
and Executive Pastor, National and International Speaker, and
Author of Six Books in the "Created for" Series, Including
Created for Significance, Created for Purpose, and *Created for Love*,
Greensboro, North Carolina

This book is a wake-up call for the church to minister to the mental health crisis currently facing the world. Jared Pingleton calls on ministries and the church to understand that the struggle is real in both their churches and communities. He then shows how churches can do something about it. The book is written innovatively, presenting specific cases of churches that have successfully addressed this issue and offering practical advice for the future. The need within the church is great, but this book provides hope for every ministry that is willing to give the hope of Christ in the midst of their struggle of hopelessness!

—Rev. Brad Hoefs
Author and Founder of Fresh Hope for Mental Health, Fresh-Hope.us, Pastor of Community of Grace Lutheran Church
Elkhorn, Nebraska

A masterpiece for preventing, healing, and recovering from the torments of mental health issues! This is the book that every elder, deacon, and pastor—along with their families—should not only read but heed. Once again, Dr. Jared Pingleton has hit a home run with "Mental Health Ministry." Too often, we attribute the majority of mental health problems to the spiritual world without carefully considering the "natural" adversaries that godly people and their families face daily. This is a genuinely indispensable resource for anyone who serves as, is thinking of serving as, or who serves alongside, a pastor. If you're looking for wisdom, practical help, and scholarship, you'll find all of them in "Mental Health Ministry." So well done!

—Rev. Michael Anthony
Author, Speaker, and Founder of CourageMatters.com
Greenville, South Carolina

Contents

INTRODUCTION

The Struggle is Real

Every pastor dreads that chilling suicidal emergency phone call at two o'clock in the morning. Likewise, it is far beyond most ministry leaders' comfort zone to confront a secretive affair between members of the worship team, deal with a chronic alcoholic in their church, intervene in a congregant's abusive family situation, or cope with a seriously depressed parishioner. When ministering to hurting people, it is easy to quickly get in over one's head and feel overwhelmed.

In addition to the extraordinary stress and the unrelenting demands of shepherding a needy flock (i.e., headaches), most pastors and other church leaders have their own personal and relational challenges and issues (i.e., heartaches). Many pastors grapple with their own and/or their spouse's significant clinical mental health concerns, seasons of unrelenting discouragement and burnout, ongoing marital conflicts, and children's "prodigal" trips. These and other personal and professional ministry challenges can be highly stressful, frustrating, and cumulatively overtaxing to any shepherd—often leaving a pastor to wonder why they ever signed up for this in the first place.

In fact, Pastor Paul Tripp called the minister's life, with its staggering personal and professional demands and often eternally grave responsibilities, a "dangerous calling."[1] Accordingly, Christian psychologists, Brad and William Johnson, conclude that "ministry may be one of the most difficult jobs in the world."[2] The landmark 2014 Lifeway research report revealed that 23 percent of pastors have personally struggled with some form of mental illness.[3] This is indicative of the fact that no group of people is immune from the reality and impact of mental illness and is not surprising given the stressful nature of being a member of the clergy.

Perhaps these cold, harsh realities are why over 50 percent of professionally trained ministers abruptly leave their calling within ten years of graduating from seminary or Bible school, and 90 percent abandon the ministry before reaching retirement age. The burnout and attrition rates in the pastorate are alarming, typically silent, below the proverbial radar, but are nonetheless very real epidemics on their own.

Understandably, the stress partially caused by needing to address and cope with mental health issues in their congregation generates even more mental and relational challenges for pastors and ironically creates or exacerbates their own mental health issues. Tragically, many pastors contemplate leaving their ministry every day. In fact, on April 27, 2022, Barna released a research report stating that 42 percent of American Protestant ministers were seriously considering the ministry.

---

1 Tripp, P. (2012). *Dangerous Calling: Confronting the unique challenges of pastoral ministry.* Wheaton, IL: Crossway

2 Johnson, W. B. & Johnson, W. L. (2014). *The Minister's Guide to Psychological Disorders and Treatments.* New York: Routledge Press, p. 1

3 Clinton, T. E. & Pingleton, J. P. (2019). *The Struggle Is Real: How to Care for Mental and Relational Health Needs in the Church.* Bloomington, IN: Westbow Press

The top three reasons cited were immense stress, loneliness and isolation, and socio-political division.[4]

There have always been people with mental and relational health problems in the church. Unfortunately, we just haven't done a very good job helping pastors to know how to recognize and minister effectively to these pronounced and realistic needs. Bible schools and seminaries generally do a good job of teaching hermeneutics, exegetics, systematic theology, homiletics, and so on—as they must. But specialized instruction regarding the day in, day out demands of practical ministry to hurting people and relationships is seldom provided in pastoral training programs. Distinguished "Pastor to Pastors" Dr. H. B. London put it this way: "There have always been people with mental and relational health problems in the church—historically, we just haven't been properly trained and equipped to know how to minister effectively to their needs."[5]

Interestingly and ironically, clinical research consistently verifies that when people are experiencing a mental or relational health issue, the vast majority turn first to a pastor, priest, or another church leader for help. In fact, "ministers are frequently the first professional that suffering parishioners will allow into their private lives."[6] Pastors and church leaders are truly first-line responders to most people's mental health crises—with all the attendant pressures and responsibilities that go with it.

---

4 barna.com/research/pastors-quitting-ministry

5 Clinton, T. E. & Pingleton, J. P. (2019). *The Struggle Is Real: How to Care for Mental and Relational Health Needs in the Church.* Bloomington, IN: Westbow Press, p. 13

6 Johnson, W. B. & Johnson, W. L. (2014). The minister's guide to psychological disorders and treatments. New York: Routledge Press, p. 175

Pastoral ministry, particularly in a small to mid-sized church (which represents the vast majority of American churches), requires an amazingly diverse skill set. Pastors and ministry leaders are typically expected to creatively prepare and eloquently preach excellent and uplifting sermons, administer and supervise a staff, lead other ministries, visit the sick and infirmed, coordinate volunteer teams, manage a budget, attend to unexpected crises that arise, and superbly do the marrying and burying while they oversee all the rest of church life. In addition to all that and often much more, pastors are expected to expertly counsel their parishioners who are in need—many of whom are likely to be suffering from some type of mental illness.

The horrible reality is that most pastors simply do not have the time and/or training to effectively minister to these serious human needs. Thus, many pastors have had to scramble to learn on the fly or go by the seat of their pants regarding how to care for and cope with people who are in the throes of a panic attack, plagued by an eating disorder, or having flashbacks from repressed trauma, controlled by an addictive substance or behavior or headed to a divorce lawyer. And it is certainly stressful for a pastor or other church leader to have all these responsibilities yet possess very few resources and training on how to address them.

Hence, the reason for this book. This specialized and innovative resource is intended to be a figurative Swiss Army knife or Leatherman Multi-Tool for pastors and other Christian leaders who are not professionally trained to properly address the mental and relational health needs of those whom they serve. Designed as a practical companion to the innovative book *The*

Struggle Is Real: How to Care for Mental and Relational Health Needs in the Church, this volume goes beyond addressing and explaining mental and relational needs to describe how to actually deliver practical mental, relational, and addictive health ministry within and to the local congregation.

It is imperative that we must, with passionate fervor, speak truth, shine light, and spread salt into our deluded, darkened, and decaying world. It is with this focused mindset and heartfelt intensity that this book is prayerfully offered as a consciousness-raising clarion call and catalyst for change. We must exponentially increase the ministry purview and missional parameters of the church to include expertly and compassionately serving the needs of the hurting. Nothing less is acceptable.

Thus, in Part 1, a comprehensive overview of the issues and challenges facing the church in the mental and relational health arena is offered. Pastors and church leaders are provided with a clear outline and broad understanding of what constitutes the major issues and ministry challenges in the mental and relational health of the local congregation.

Part 2 offers some practical, powerful, and profound examples of how to accomplish effective ministry for these needs. An amazing collaborative team of multidisciplinary, specialized experts shares their stories and processes of how they do their vital work of ministering to mental and relational health needs in different ways and in diverse settings. These various models and methods of mental and relational health care are presented along a progressive continuum of care. The examples range from a wonderfully innovative pastoral self-care concept designed to prevent the development of major mental and relational problems from interfering with ministry delivery to various ways in which the local congregation can creatively minister to their own membership directly within the church, to partnering together with local community resources, to regional, national, and even international applications, to specialized residential treatment programs, to partial day treatment, and then to full inpatient psychological and psychiatric care programs. Pastors and church leaders can simply "plug and play" and implement the structures and systems of the ministry methods and models herein to their local church body. Or, churches can be inspired to hybridize and borrow certain of the following concepts or ideas to create a totally unique way of serving their hurting people.

Finally, Part 3 offers simple, practical tools to resource busy church leaders about challenges and questions relating to mental and relational health ministry. Initially, an overview of how to care for those struggling with self-harm and suicidality is provided. Various other practical concerns, including how to understand both the "art" as well as the "science" of making an effective referral follow, along with helpful resources and supportive networks for effectively operating a church-based mental and relational health ministry. Lastly, inspiration, vision, and hope for the future are discussed.

It is time for the church to lock arms, unite hearts, and join forces as we engage in the full calling and mission of the church. Jesus still compels us to embrace those who are brokenhearted, emancipate those in captivity, and enlighten those in darkness. *The church must become a secure sanctuary of safety and a Holy Spirit-infused resource for people's very real and very painful struggles.* Hurting people deserve no less than our very best.

Part 1: Problems and Possibilities

CHAPTER 1

Scope of the Struggle

Life is rarely simple or easy. Sometimes life throws difficult things our way. For all of us, there is often hurt and heartache. Distance and disappointment. Crisis and conflict. Adversity and affliction. Pain and pathos. Setbacks and suffering.

The results of life's trials, temptations, and tragedies can leave us filled with agony, doubt, resentment, and unforgiveness. We frequently feel hurt, alone, confused, hopeless, and scared to reach out for help. Consequently, mental and relationship health issues find their way home. To everyone's home.

Still, some may wonder, "What is the big deal anyway? Shouldn't people just pray more, read their Bible more, and confess their sin more? Shouldn't people just keep a stiff upper lip, tough it out, and quit complaining? Aren't psychotherapy, psychotropic medications, and other mental health interventions just a secular substitute for the gospel and/or a crutch for the emotionally weak? What really is the truth?"

The truth is that people are hurting today in unprecedented ways and in virtually epidemic numbers. The pace, pain, and pressure of modern life have taken over countless people's lives. People are hurting more now and, in more ways, than at any time in history. And yet, the church is frequently silent, unresponsive, and to far too many hurting people and relationships, shame-inducing and/or seemingly uncaring.

The truth is that mental and relational health problems can be messy. And complicated. And costly. They typically require major, labor-intensive investments of time, effort, and attention that consume disproportionate shares of precious and limited church resources. It can be scary, risky, and intimidating to figuratively get one's hands dirty and try to reach out and intervene when needed.

The truth is that tragically, many pressing human needs go inadequately addressed if not ignored altogether. Research reveals that less than half of people with significant mental and relational health needs receive adequate care for them. Statistically, there is no appreciable difference on this grave matter for those within or outside the church.

The truth is that many people do not feel safe to face and discuss their private pain within the public glare and scrutiny of the church. Sadly, many people have experienced painful judgment, criticism, rejection, and betrayal when they disclose their humanness and vulnerability to others in the church. It has been ironically, but all too accurately, said that the Christian church is the only army in history that shoots its' own wounded. Obviously, this further complicates, confounds, and compounds the overwhelming problems of hurting people's mental and relational health. Far too many people have been terribly hurt by the church—in my career, I have worked with thousands of its' victims. It is heartbreaking, unnecessary, and outrageous for people to not experience the church as loving and gracious, merciful and forgiving, and respectful and responsive. The gospel demands no less.

The truth is that the church must become a figurative, if not literal, sanctuary where hurting people can find a trusted safe haven for broken hearts, a refuge for problem-filled lives, and a shelter for damaged relationships. Contrary to much implicit—and some explicit—teaching and preaching, just because we are Christians does not mean we are immune to or exempt from experiencing adversity, anguish, and afflictions. Far too many people who struggle with mental and relational health problems have been scolded, scorned, and shunned for having hurts, habits, and hang-ups. *Safe churches have safe pastors who teach their congregants how to become safe people.*

The truth is that real churches are filled with real people who have real problems and need real help. We should recognize the struggles around us (as well as within us) as potential growth opportunities and redemptive ministry assignments that can reveal and demonstrate God's love, grace, mercy, and transformational power.

Here are some of the latest statistics available (as of 2022) chronicling many of the major mental and relational health issues in America:[7]

- 20–25% of adults in the U.S. suffer from a diagnosable mental illness in any given year; 50% in their lifetime

7 These incidences were compiled from various governmental and other social service organizations, including the Center for Disease Control, the National Institute of Mental Health, the National Alliance on Mental Illness, the National Institute of Health, Johns Hopkins University Medical School, Harvard Medical School, Mental Health America, and several others as of the beginning of 2022.

(worldwide, more than 20% of adults suffer from a mental illness in any given year).

- 14–20% of children and adolescents suffer from a mental, emotional, or behavioral disorder.
- 20–25% of the U.S. population meet criteria for alcohol use disorder.
- 60–80% of adolescent and adult males use pornography on a regular basis; 40-60% of females
- 25% of women (and men!) in the U.S. have had at least one abortion.
- 5–10% of the U.S. population abuse prescription medications.
- Opioid addiction is escalating exponentially (in 2021 there were over 107,000 overdose deaths—293 per day—and those numbers have been escalating dramatically in recent years).
- 130 people commit suicide every day in the U.S. (1 every 11 minutes), those numbers have increased by over 35% since 1999.
- 1 million people commit suicide per year worldwide.
- Over 40% of all marriages end in divorce.
- Nearly half of all live births in U.S. are to unwed parents.
- 1 of 3 girls, 1 of 4–6 boys are sexually abused before age 18.
- 1 of 5 adult women will be victims of sexual assault over their lifetime.
- Only 33% of children in America will be raised to age 18 by both their biological parents.

- Over 30 million Americans suffer from eating disorders; every hour someone dies directly due to an eating disorder.
- Nearly 2,000 children are abused and/or neglected every day in the U.S.; plus, elderly and disabled persons are all too often neglected and/or abused as they are frequently locked up and out of sight.
- 1 of 6 couples are infertile; 1 of 6 pregnancies miscarry—and most couples never adequately grieve or even thoroughly and directly discuss those very real losses. (These are the couples you don't see at church on Mother's Day and Father's Day!)
- 24 people per minute are victims of domestic violence by an intimate partner in America (22% of which are witnessed by children); domestic violence is the leading cause of physical injury to women.
- In 2020, about 600,000 Americans were homeless, the majority of which have severe mental health concerns.

Collectively, these numbers are staggering. They are absolutely astonishing. And again, according to most studies, unfortunately, less than half of persons with the above challenges in America ever receive treatment, and the rates for children getting help are even lower.[8] In Great Britain, those numbers are lower yet: one recent major study found that 75 percent of persons there do not receive the mental health care and treatment they need.[9] The tremendous individual and ag-

8 https://www.mhanational.org/issues/state-mental-health-america

9 https://www.mentalhealth.org.uk/statistics/mental-health-statistics-people-seeking-help.

gregate human pain and suffering of these and other mental and relational health realities are overwhelming. The struggle is real indeed.

But wait—there's more! There is a multitude of frequently overlooked "hidden" costs of mental health issues having to do with a person's diminished ability to function consistently and productively in terms of their capacity to provide for themselves and their family. The economic impact of serious mental illnesses in America approaches $200 to 300 million in lost wages per year. Mental health issues also create significant but difficult to calculate associated "soft" costs and losses such as hospitalizations for emotionally-caused physical illnesses, untold numbers of persons needing to go on Social Security Disability due to their inability to work productively (in fact, *worldwide, mental health issues are the leading cause of disability*), increases in suicide, heightened stress on families and loved ones, and many corresponding often misdiagnosed and/or untreated disorders—which can be and often are generationally perpetuated.[10]

Research has also proven that mental health issues tend to be chronic and shorten one's life expectancy considerably, globally, around ten to twenty years on average.[11] Furthermore, serious relational problems such as unresolved conflict, relational entanglements and estrangements, adultery, consequences of and after-effects from various addictions, divorce, domestic violence, child abuse and neglect, blended family concerns, and other interpersonal issues are equally prevalent, prominent, problematic, and painful.

10 See Exodus 20:5; 34:7; Numbers 14:18; Deuteronomy 5:9, and many other passages.

11 https://journals.sagepub.com/doi/full/10.1177/0040571X20910700

Additionally, the long-term effects of the COVID-19 global pandemic, which began sweeping the world in early 2020, are believed by many experts to endure for many years—perhaps for generations to come. The overwhelming fear, grief, frustration, controversy, and helplessness it brought intensified many people's existing mental and relational problems and created new problems for many others. In addition to the epic numbers of deaths worldwide, the multitude of other losses (e.g., personal and societal freedoms; economic devastation; the ability to go to work, school, and church; individual rights; etc.) was unprecedented and, in itself, traumatizing. Many mental health professionals predict there will be a cascading amount of ongoing issues that will live on like nothing the world has ever seen. COVID has possibly produced more tragedy, trauma, and tribulation than ever in history. The emotional fallout and long-term mental health effects of this pandemic are impossible to foretell.

So, one may ask, "What do all these enormous numbers of terrible problems have to do with the ministry of the church?" Basically everything!

For starters, I must confess a pet peeve and ask your indulgence about the following soapbox rant: I firmly believe the word "Christian" is supposed to be (well, actually is) an *adverb*, not an *adjective* as most believers commonly (mis)use it. Furthermore, the etymology of the term is best understood as "Christ-like" (the suffix "ian" means "like"). Obviously, it is awkward syntax to say one is a "Christ-like," but that is truly more descriptive and accurate—an adverb modifies an action, an adjective describes a thing. Constitutionally as Christ-followers, we are to love God fully and others as ourselves; and love is certainly an action word!

Consequently, what if we in the church truly believed—and lived as though—we are *Christ-likes*? What if we consciously and continuously strived to live our lives like Jesus in everything that we thought, believed, and did? That seems harder to say; could it be that is because it is confrontational to our sinfulness and thus convicting to our hearts to the degree that we do not always think, believe, act, and relate *Christianly*? What if instead of having "Christian" radio stations, bookstores, counseling centers, etc., we had institutions and agencies that conducted themselves Christianly? What if we had churches that ministered to real-life issues, including mental and relational problems Christianly? To reiterate a powerful (albeit to some, hackneyed) phrase, what would Jesus do? And how would he do it? Our identity is to be rooted and grounded in Christ. It should be axiomatic that we endeavor to live our lives in a Christocentric manner innervated by the power of the Holy Spirit.

I firmly believe that Jesus intends the church to be a hospital for sinners as opposed to a museum for saints. And the research corroborates the essential power of that reality. Appropriating the benefits and blessings of biblical faith is simply good mental and relational health. According to the National Alliance on Mental Illness (NAMI), the National Institute of Mental Health (NIMH), and other leading advocacy organizations, the effects of one's personal religious faith exert a consistently positive outcome on a person's mental, physical, and relational health. Thus, the church is perhaps the most natural entity there is to effectively and appropriately minister to hurting people.

One landmark study conducted by the Heritage Foundation[12] found that 81 percent of 99 other studies reviewed found a "[...] positive association between religious involvement and greater happiness, life satisfaction, morale, positive affect, or some other measure of well-being." Other significant positive correlations of Christian values and practices pertained to decreased violent crime, juvenile delinquency, drug and alcohol use and abuse, at-risk sexual behavior, educational dropout rates, suicidality, tobacco use, cohabitation, out-of-wedlock childbirths, divorce, and domestic violence. Interestingly, these findings held true across all ages, races, and denominations. We just need to preach and then practice that which we preach as it pertains to mental and relational health care. Yet the pioneering LifeWay mental health study of 1,000 American evangelical pastors found that 66 percent of pastors never or rarely speak to their church about mental illness.[13]

Additionally, over 3,300 quantitative studies from 1887 to 2010 have consistently demonstrated a positive relationship between religious faith and positive mental and relational health. Thousands more studies from 2010 to 2021 have verified these earlier studies finding a positive correlation between religious faith and positive mental and relational health.

Thus, the church's mission field is truly much larger and perhaps much different than many believe. It seems both natural and necessary for the church to make itself become a safe

---

12 heritage.org/civil-society/report/why-religion matters-even-more-the-impact-religious-practice-social-stability

13 "Study of acute mental illness and Christian faith: Research report," LifeWay Research (2014), http://lifewayresearch.cfom/wp-content/uploads/2014/09/Acute-Mental-Illness-and-Christian-Faith-Research-Report-1.pdf, p.37

and secure sanctuary for all. But for the church to consistently do the work of mental and relational health ministry and for the church to be a viable and valuable resource to its congregants and community, it must offer mental health ministry. And to do that effectively, the church must address the insidious silence, secrecy, shame, and stigma of mental and relational health issues, which all too often precludes it from being a true sanctuary for hurting people.

To reiterate, people are hurting in unprecedented ways and in virtually epidemic numbers. They deserve to be cared for in the best possible ways and with the best possible resources. Most people already go first to the church and its leadership when they need help. Therefore, we must be intentional and proactive about how those hurting people and relationships are treated.

No hurting person or relationship should ever be dismissively treated with pontificated platitudes, pious pomposity, or preemptory proof texts. And they must be cared for well, with the most effective clinically validated practices possible. People with literally broken hearts should receive the best pharmaceutical, medical, and, if necessary, surgical procedures available. Likewise, people with mental and relational health needs and figuratively broken hearts deserve our best loving concern, compassion, and care. Serving Jesus demands nothing less.

Jesus Christ calls us to embrace the brokenhearted, emancipate those in captivity, and enlighten those in darkness. Here in our fallen world, we are never promised a life of ease and Edenic bliss—rather—we are promised that we will indeed have struggles. Jesus promised that "in this world you will have trouble..." But thankfully, He also urged us to "[...] take heart! I have overcome the world" (John 16:33b, NIV). Given the astronomical amount of pain and suffering we do have in this world, that is most assuredly good news—for everyone.

CHAPTER 2

Symptoms of the Struggle

Most major mental illnesses have a fairly gradual onset and rarely appear "out of the blue." Generally, family members and friends will recognize that something about the individual is unusual, odd, or "not quite right" about their thinking, speech, behavior, or social interactions. These concerns often emerge well before the diagnosable indicators of severe mental illness are fully manifested.

I was privileged on my postdoctoral internship to be a resident at the Colmery-O'Neil VA Medical Center in Topeka, Kansas. In conjunction with the world-famous Menninger Psychiatric Hospital nearby, the training I received there was superb. One of the best parts of that yearlong training experience was the wonderful blessing the six of us residents experienced every Friday afternoon. That was when the venerable Dr. Karl Menninger himself would come and dispense a wealth of wisdom to and conduct group supervision for us.

To sit under this brilliant world-renowned pioneer (he actually designed and founded the entire Veterans Administration hospital system after creating his namesake psychiatric hospital) yet humble ninety-three-year-old Christian gentleman was a phenomenal blessing for us. I learned much about our calling, our field, and our work from this amazing leader. One of the many profound nuggets of wisdom he dispensed to us was the axiom "you cannot effectively treat that which you have not accurately diagnosed."[14] Common sense, eloquently articulated.

Directing a reliable treatment towards the wrong problem simply doesn't work. Identifying problems and correctly diagnosing their likely causes is crucial for successful outcomes. Understanding early warning signs and symptom development can lead to appropriate intervention and treatment. Accurately discerning the major issues and key dynamics of what a person, couple, or family is experiencing can often help to greatly reduce the severity and stress of an illness or problem. Consequently, *early detection and intervention can delay or even prevent the onset of a chronic course for many disorders.*

But again, we cannot intervene effectively if we are unaware of or do not properly understand the issues. The challenge and complexity of the prototypical dilemma of many pastors with limited training regarding mental health issues are synopsized well in the words of Christian psychiatrist Stephen Grcevich. He correctly observes that "far too many pastors, church leaders, and attendees within our Christian subculture demonstrate an insufficient understanding of the nature of mental illness and struggle to respond to those affected in a manner that demonstrates compassion and concern and promotes spiritual growth."[15]

14 Personal communication.

15 Grcevich, S. (2018). *Mental Health and the Church.* Grand Rapids, MI: Zondervan, p. 22.

Dr. Grcevich goes on to point out that "fewer still possess a basic understanding of how the experience of mental illness impacts the ability of affected children, adults, and their families to participate in worship services, small groups, educational programming, and service activities through which spiritual growth takes place."[16] *Mental health ministry literally affects all other ministries.* Leaders need to understand the basics of when and how mental health issues affect hurting people—because, as the Apostle Paul wisely noted, the Body of Christ is uniquely and structurally interdependent, with each part affecting all the others (Romans 12:4–8; 1 Corinthians 12:12–31; Ephesians 4:4–16).

As with many medical conditions, early detection and treatment can not only minister to a person's emotional and mental suffering more effectively, but many times the pain and subsequent course of treatment can be reduced accordingly. Being educated about and alert to key early warning symptoms may even prevent more severe distress and dysfunction from developing. Here are some fundamental signs and symptoms a person may commonly display that you, as a pastor or church leader, can identify, which are potentially indicative of mental illness:

Key Indicators of Mental Health Issues

- recent social withdrawal and loss of interest in relationships with others;

16 Ibid.

- intensified conflict and difficulty relating normally with others;
- unusual reduction in functioning at work, school, church, and/or community activities;
- problems with concentration, memory, confusion, and cognitive processing;
- loss of initiative or desire to participate in normal and/or pleasurable activities;
- marked changes in sleep and/or appetite;
- rapid or dramatic shifts in emotions or "mood swings";
- deterioration in personal hygiene;
- excessive and/or unexplained fears, suspicions, worries, and anxieties;
- numerous vague or ambiguous physical ailments and complaints;
- intense and prolonged feelings of sadness, nervousness, irritability, or anger;
- progressive inability to cope with everyday stress and strain;
- heightened sensitivity to sensory stimuli such as sights, sounds, smells, or touch;
- uncharacteristic, bizarre, or peculiar behavior, thoughts, and/or beliefs;
- vague or specific mentions of hopelessness, apathy, despair, and/or suicidality.

Please know that these symptoms in and of themselves cannot clearly or conclusively predict—nor rule out—mental illness. In fact, some symptoms of mental illness may be the result of a medical condition (for example, hypothyroidism typically manifests or mimics symptoms of depression). A person displaying signs of mental illness should be initially screened by a physician to determine if there are any underlying medical issues, concerns, or problems. Each person's situation must be carefully assessed and their treatment individualized.

Barring any medical causes, a person exhibiting even a few of these symptoms is likely to be experiencing significant psychological problems that may be impairing or interfering with their ability to function personally and professionally. (Sigmund Freud famously observed that the essence of mental health is to love and work well.) Accordingly, they are candidates to be screened by a trained mental health professional. Supportively and compassionately encouraging persons who are displaying several of these symptoms to seek help may prove difficult but is essential.

One thing that should be considered is the role of pharmacologic assistance in the treatment of certain mental or emotional problems. There is still a persistent stigma in our culture (and particularly in some realms of our Christian subculture) attached to the use of medication to treat mental illnesses, including depression, anxiety disorders, and even more serious issues. Fortunately, that shame and stigma have diminished somewhat in recent years, but the controversy is sadly still alive and well in many places, including in many churches.

As followers of Christ, we may falsely believe that our emotional and/or relationship problems should miraculously, if not magically, go away if we simply have more faith or trust in God. After all, aren't Christians somehow immune or exempt from trials, turmoil, trauma, and tragedy? Shouldn't those suffering from mental health issues just pray harder, read their Bible more, and go to church regularly? Aren't they just weak or deficient in their faith?

Yet ironically, we would certainly never tell someone with diabetes to just cavalierly go off their insulin, someone with myopia to throw away their eyeglasses or contact lenses, or someone with cancer to not take their chemo due to their perceived or judged faith deficiency. Somehow, those with mental and relational health challenges don't always receive the same grace—which then consolidates, exacerbates, and perpetuates their shame and stigma. Consequently, an individual's suffering and dysfunction are likely to continue, and thus the adversary of our souls is deliriously and diabolically delighted.

While faith and trust may well be at the root of many of our difficulties, there are some issues that aren't caused by deficiencies in our relationship with God. We live in a fallen world where things go wrong with our physical bodies, including one of the largest organs, our brains. For many whose disordered behaviors or thoughts are caused by chemical imbalances in the brain (verified progressively more by recent brain science discoveries), the correct medication can allow these individuals to regain their neurochemical equilibrium, along with an increased capacity to deal with personal issues, problematic beliefs, and dysfunctional ways of thinking. You can do your parishioners an invaluable service by supporting them in their appropriate use of medication along with psychotherapy when indicated and properly prescribed.

To be sure, far from being overlooked in this discussion, spiritual tools, resources, and disciplines have been proven helpful in reducing the symptom severity and relapse rate of mental and relational problems. They can certainly activate and speed up the recovery process, as well as render distress and suffering easier for the person to endure. *Providing hope, health, and healing to the hurting in an informed and capable manner is a valuable and specialized form of ministry no less important than any other way in which a pastor serves their congregation*. Abundant research has demonstrated that strong spiritual supports and beliefs are not only instrumental in preventing some mental and emotional difficulties in the first place but are also highly effective in their treatment and recovery.

People who are hurting, conflicted, and suffering long for help and comfort. Their pain is a potentially redemptive open door for the local church to bend down, reach out, and help them up as the Lord does for us. A healthy church that is lovingly responsive to the pain and problems of others is evangelistic in realistic ways, which are rarely, if ever, emphasized in theological training or at any trendy pastors' conference. Churches that are not afraid to get their hands dirty reaching out to the suffering truly emulate and express the gospel of Jesus Christ in powerful and meaningful ways. The suffering, wounded, and traumatized are vulnerable to isolation and despair, but they are also often open and receptive to the gospel in ways they may not be otherwise.

Although most probably didn't sign up for this honor (and colossal responsibility), it has already been noted that pastors and other church leaders are typically "first responders" for the vast majority of people seeking help or guidance regarding a mental health concern, a suicidal crisis, a severe relationship problem, or a major life trauma. Yet most pastors are not trained in Bible school or seminary to know how to adequately, much less expertly, help navigate their sheep safely through the proverbial rocks and reefs in the storm-tossed waves of their seas of despair and despondency.

Most persons who enter professional ministry do so with altruistic motives. They possess a genuine care and concern for lost souls. They love people. Yet they often feel completely unprepared and unequipped for the often-overwhelming depth and degree of human suffering they encounter on a regular basis in their congregations. The enormity of human need they are confronted with along with the expectation (after all, aren't pastors supposed to be wonderful counselors?) that they are to meet it can be mind-boggling and intimidating.

And because they aren't properly trained to effectively minister to those needs, many feel inadequate, stressed, and guilty. And even for those who have the know-how, few have the time and logistical capacity to deal in-depth with an entire flock of hurting souls and relationships. Tragically, this huge burden of not being able to help everyone ends up creating intrinsically high levels of stress, job dissatisfaction, and burnout for the average pastor.

So how can and do we help those whom we can't help? Realistically speaking, all of us are gifted in some areas, but no one is gifted in every area. While it is a fact of psychology that everyone can help someone, it is a reality of ecclesiology that no one possesses all the gifts and therefore can help everyone. Consequently, we were given the interdependent illustration of the body to describe the distribution of spiritual gifts to the church (Romans chapter 12; 1 Corinthians chapter 12; Ephesians chapter 4). Hey, no one can do it all! Nor should we feel as though we must. That is a burden far too complex and cumbersome for any human to bear.

But in many ministerial quarters, a subtle and surreptitious type of oxymoronic "Lone Ranger Christianity" has implicitly become sort of a glorified ideal to which leaders should somehow strive to aspire. However, even the great Masked Man had his faithful friend Tonto for support, feedback, accountability, and assistance. We need to take off the mask, become honest and transparent, and quit trying to be the superhero believing we can do it all ourselves. Only Jesus can—yet He chooses to delegate!

Therefore, partnering with a knowledgeable, professionally trained, Christ-following mental health professional (or better yet, a multidisciplinary team of professionals) can be a huge relief, help, and benefit for the pastor and their parishioners. In Part 2, many examples of how to get this vital work done will demonstrate the nuts and bolts of how to do this vital ministry. In Part 3, clear guidelines will be given as to when, why, and how to refer to mental health professionals outside of the church as needed.

CHAPTER 3

Sources of the Struggle

Although we can easily become overwhelmed and discouraged in face of all these epidemic realities, we do well to remind ourselves that problems are many times potential growth opportunities and redemptive ministry assignments in disguise! They can reveal and demonstrate God's love, grace, mercy, and transformational power in often amazing and beautiful ways. Accordingly, it seems prudent to understand how all these difficulties have become such an enormous reality in our lives. How do all these problems begin? Where do they come from?

The importance of knowing causation is that it can often lead to knowing how to best intervene. Whereas it would transcend the purpose of this chapter to thoroughly address the full realm and etiology of theodicy and human suffering, we can nonetheless identify several general sources of the above-referenced categories of human pain, pathos, and pathology. What follows is a very brief and simplistic overview of the major sources of human mental and relational health problems. Please also bear in mind that many times there is considerable overlap between two or more of these major origins of mental health concerns:

1. **Sin**. To begin with, we all have a sin problem (Romans 3:23, James 4:1). And as we all know, sin is ultimately fatal. Our sin, individually and collectively, literally and figuratively kills us (Romans 6:23) and others, although hopefully generally and not necessarily immediately. Clearly, since we reap that which we sow (and usually much more than we sow), along with what others also sow, many of our problems are the direct or indirect result of our and/or others' sinful attitudes and actions. Although we know it is thoroughly hypocritical to sow sinful seed and then pray for crop failure, sometimes our problems exist precisely because we have not gotten the sin out of our lives.

   Sins of commission, sins of omission, being sinned against by others, along with general sinfulness per se, all have enormous impact on our spiritual, mental, emotional, physical, and relational health. Sin hurts and kills. It hurts and kills us and everyone else. Some things are our fault, some things are others' fault, and some things don't seem to be anyone's fault at all. In some instances, we can be the victim of a seemingly random and fallen world (in rare instances, our problems are apparently not the direct result or fault of anyone, including ourselves or others specifically—viz., the horrible gravitational impact of the tower of Siloam—see Luke 13:4).

Selfish choices and wrongful actions influence and affect our and others' lives. Not doing the righteous things we know to do (James 4:17) [sins of omission] as well as doing the evil things we know not to do (Romans 7:14–25) [sins of commission] create many of our problems—and often cause problems in others. Our own sinful attitudes and actions certainly create many of our issues.

At the same time, many of our problems are the consequence of being sinned against by others, which then causes our pain. Sexual assault, childhood abuses, bullying, witnessing domestic violence and substance abuse as a child, spousal betrayal, parental neglect, and a host of other problems also create a significant portion of our mental and relational health challenges. Truly the "sins of the parents" can and do produce multigenerational impact, as the patriarch Moses sagely observed (Exodus 20:5; 34:6–7; Numbers 14:18; Deuteronomy 5:9).

2. **Biochemistry/Genetics.** Just as predispositions to physical maladies like diabetes, myopia, hypertension, cardiac disease, and some cancers can result in generational transmission of those health concerns, many brain and mental disorders possess a genetic component. Certain neurochemical factors that are inherited often play a primary role in many mental health conditions. Some of our mental health problems are at least partially biological in nature. The recently burgeoning and fascinating field of neuroscience has greatly increased our under-

standing of the enormous role of genetics and biochemistry in the area of brain functioning and mental health. Just like any other organ, the brain is subject to disease, destruction, and deterioration. Of the ten leading causes of disability identified in the United States and in other developed countries, four are brain and behavioral disorders: major depression, bipolar disorder, schizophrenia, and obsessive-compulsive disorder. Apparently, some people's problems are literally all in their heads! Whereas some of these disorders can often be successfully treated by appropriate medication(s), many cannot, and still, others are difficult to precisely diagnose and effectively treat pharmacologically. Conditions such as bipolar disorder, anxiety disorders, and some forms of chronic depression are best addressed utilizing a combination of counseling, medication, and loving support in specific groups and from a healthy church community.

3. **Environmental Influences.** King Solomon insightfully counseled that one becomes wise as a result of hanging around wise people but conversely suffers harm when they consort with fools (Proverbs 13:20). The Apostle Paul sensibly observed that bad company corrupts good character (1 Corinthians 15:33). Likewise, as was noted above, Moses recognized that the sins of parents filter down multigenerationally and become self-perpetuating and maladaptive. Consequently, children (and adults) are deeply affected by the influences of their primary social-

izing agents. The classic adage that children learn what they live is true.

Pity the poor children's worker or youth pastor who has only one or two hours per week to try to reverse and redeem the effects of the toxic environment of the 166–167 other hours of the child's or teenager's week! A plethora of clinical research verifies the common sense realities that children of divorced parents are themselves more likely to divorce, most pedophiles were themselves molested as children, kids who grow up around gangs tend to evidence higher than average antisocial activity, and kids whose parents abused substances often become addicts, etc. Our environment inevitably and inexorably rubs off on us.

Peer pressures are also real. It has been sardonically said the reason why preachers' kids have so many difficulties is because they hang around with deacons' kids! Anyone knows that it is difficult to soar with eagles when you walk around with turkeys. Therefore, we must be keenly aware of and highly sensitive to *what is going around a hurting person* in order to deeply *understand what is going on within a hurting person.*

4. **Faulty Learning.** Dysfunctional family systems generate their own unique sets of issues and problems. Family relationships comprise the contextual framework within which children originally learn who, what, and how they are. Identity is formed exclusively within the context and rubric of relationship. For example, we know that

children in single-family homes suffer from the absence of their other parent (from either abandonment, death, or divorce) and typically internalize a sense of false guilt and responsibility for the rejection they feel. In turn, this results in low self-esteem and insecurity (i.e., childishly and incorrectly reasoning: "If only I were a better little girl or boy, then mommy or daddy wouldn't have left, not daddy or mommy, but me").

Children raised around substance abuse tend to develop co-dependent personalities and maladaptive coping styles. They are conditioned to subconsciously seek out people with those similarly unstable and distasteful but familiar dynamics and/or themselves become addicts (Proverbs 26:11; 2 Peter 2:22). Many sexually abused children grow up with damaged identities and become promiscuous because that is the primary way in which they receive attention, so therefore falsely believe that is all they are good for. Others may become rigidly prudish, believing even healthy marital expressions and experiences of sexuality to be wrong or humiliating. In my marriage book, I wryly observe that many times the church's implicit (if not explicit) message concerning sexuality is: "Sex is bad, dirty, shameful—so save it for marriage with the one you love!"[17] So much for good news, huh? Negative and inaccurate messages like that cause lots of pain and require a lot of therapy to correct.

17 Pingleton, J. (2013/2022). *Making Magnificent Marriages*. Forest, VA: Redemption Resources, p. 265

Thus, dysfunctional church systems also generate their own unique sets of issues and problems. We must strive to be vigilant and circumspect about how the reality of faulty learning pertains to the teachings of the church. Throughout church history, people have been falsely and erroneously judged, condemned, and even put to death because of heresy and distortion of the scriptures. Legalism, self-righteousness, and false humility, along with a plethora of other inaccurate and unhealthy teachings, have been explicitly or implicitly taught throughout many sectors of the church.

I typically spend several hours each week helping people who have been confused, harmed, and even betrayed by lazy, harsh, judgmental, ignorant, religious, blasphemous, rigid, self-righteous, pharisaical, doctrinally fallacious, and/or otherwise damaging teaching and preaching from the church. It can be very difficult therapeutic work for such persons to sort through, understand, and heal from these theological distortions in order to hopefully eventually internalize the truth. Tragically, however, untold numbers of people end up throwing the proverbial baby (Jesus) out with the bathwater of faulty teaching and discard their faith. Polling organizations over the past few decades have reported an exponentially escalating number of persons who are no longer affiliated with Christian churches and/or adhere to a personal faith. This downwardly spiraling trend is shocking, sad, and serious.

5. **Traumatic Experiences.** Irrespective of our sinfulness, genetic markers, pathogenic factors in our upbringing, or previous dysfunctional learning, trauma can leave an enduring neurological imprint upon us and literally alter our brain chemistries, identities, and relationships. Military combat-related experiences, gruesome accidents, horrific assaults, childhood abuses, and a multitude of other events suffered in our fallen world can create an unexpected yet devastating impact on one's soul and interpersonal relationships, often leaving permanent scars—both visible and invisible. These and other stressful conditions and life circumstances can exert a tremendous toll upon one's mental, physical, emotional, spiritual, and relational health and functioning.

   In my clinical training on my postdoctoral residency, I was privileged to be involved with the creation of the first Post-Traumatic Stress Disorder unit in the Veterans Administration system for Vietnam combat veterans. Unfortunately, that was not until many years after those men had suffered with the excruciating stressors they experienced consequently to their traumatic combat experiences. Typically, those men had gone through dozens of jobs, nearly a dozen marriages, and many other similarly maladaptive adjustments in their civilian life. It was tragic to see the destructive and deleterious effects of their combat trauma, brutal torture, and nightmarish horror on their mental and relational health. Many of those brave men went to war right out of high school, received very little training and support, and suffered unspeakably inhumane experiences with which they had no way to understand, process, and cope. Many of these men had given up trying to function in society, were labeled as hopeless or crazy, and were relegated to spend many years on a locked ward in a psychiatric facility. Watching them heal, grow, and change as they insightfully grasped the dynamics of their trauma when it was presented to them in a therapeutic and supportive manner was both a wonder and a joy. Many of those brave men got their heads, hearts, relationships, and identity back as their brains marvelously and miraculously healed from their trauma.

Recent advances and discoveries in neuroscience reveal more of how truly "wonderfully made" our Creator lovingly designed us to be. The complexity and intricacy of the human brain are indescribable. One of the most fascinating contributions of recent neuroscience research is that we now know that when a person experiences trauma, the brain is literally impacted by it damaging one's cognitive circuitry. However, when a person "knows the truth" of how their trauma literally damages their brain functioning, it can be literally liberating to them.

Understanding the concept of neuroplasticity is a breathtaking breakthrough for trauma survivors. Learning how the brain can often be literally therapeutically "rewired" due to its neuroplasticity is truly amazing. Recent discoveries have shown that brain cells and neurons have an incredible capacity for adaptation and regeneration and are leading to many revolutionary treatments and therapeutic procedures for healing the neurological effects of trauma. Often, new neuronal pathways can be created that can improve cognitive functioning for those who have suffered closed head physical injuries as well as those who have had emotional and psychological trauma. Once more, the Creator's loving, redemptive, and miraculous power and plan are unveiled. *He delights in transforming blessings out of our brokenness.*

CHAPTER 4

Solutions to the Struggle

So, what is the church to do? How can the community of Jesus become a consistently reliable place of refuge, restoration, and redemption? How can churches become centers of and catalysts for ministering help, hope, health, and healing to the hurting? What is our mission to the multiplied millions of broken hearts, lives, and relationships all around us?

Above all else, we must make a concerted and intentional effort to ensure that the church is both a figurative and a literal sanctuary for shattered souls and a haven for fractured relationships. Unfortunately, for many hurting people, the church is not a safe place they can trust and feel free from judgment, criticism, and/or condemnation. We must strive to become emotionally safe, accepting, consistent, and trustable fellow sufferers with secure, reliable, and strong yet flexible boundaries.

We are all damaged, broken, and scarred. As we all know, the ground at the foot of the cross is level. Inscribed on the ceiling of the library of sixteenth-century French philosopher and theologian Michel de Montaigne was his famous declaration,

"I am a man, nothing human is foreign to me." Similarly, Jesus' incarnational experience was that He was "[...] fully human in every way..." (Hebrews 2:17, NIV) in order that He could "[...] empathize with our weaknesses, [...] [and was] tempted in every way, just as we are..." (Hebrews 4:15, NIV) (Hereinafter, brackets added for clarity.) Understanding and internalizing that truth will free us forever from the temptation to arrogance, self-righteous pride, and judgmental contempt of others. No one is intrinsically any better, nor any worse, than anyone else—consequently, no one has a right to throw rocks at anyone for anything (except, of course, the one guy who chose not to).

For hundreds of years, the church was the innovator and initiator of medical care throughout the world. Literally taking Jesus' parable of the Good Samaritan to heart, the church historically applied the gospel to the physically infirmed, diseased, and wounded in direct and practical ways. Good orthodoxy resulted in good orthopraxy. Christians have historically been pioneers and leaders in the areas of charity and care. Even though, in recent times, we have seen the evolution of medical healthcare delivery transition into the big business world of HMO conglomerates and corporate profiteering, to this day, in almost every city throughout the world, hospitals and health clinics are still named after Christian saints, denominations, or other church entities.

Furthermore, abundant research proves that faith-based social service delivery systems are far more efficient and effective than bureaucratic governmental programs. Think of what might happen to "civilized" societies if the church universal actually cared for such "widows and orphans" as homeless, mentally ill, marginalized, traumatized, disenfranchised, addicted, trafficked, and exploited persons? What a dynamic revival of health, healing, help, and hope we would witness!

Therefore, the pressing question is this: *why can't the church be known as the pioneer for and leader of mental and relational health care and addiction treatment and service delivery?* And if so, then why don't we? What is stopping us? As the progressively spiraling epidemic of mental and relational issues and addiction problems encircle the globe, why can't—and why doesn't—the church be Jesus' literal heart, eyes, ears, hands, and feet extended and applied to hurting people and relationships?

Unfortunately, the church's historical track record for ministering to those with mental health needs has been far less than stellar. In fact, in many ways, it has been downright dreadful. While there have certainly been considerable compassionate attitudes and actions towards those suffering with mental health challenges, far too often, the church's stance was either one of denial, demonization, disdain, or denouncement.[18] To be sure, much of this ignoring of and indifference to people's pain resulted from ignorance and fear. But it is inexcusable and unconscionable to not minister with excellence and distinction whenever and however we can to hurting people for whom Jesus died.

Fortunately, there is a recent progressively growing amount of good news in this regard. Many denominations, churches, pastors, and parachurch leaders are taking a contemporary yet thoroughly biblical look at how mental illness is affecting those

18 Vacek, H. H. (2015), *Madness: American Protestant Responses to Mental Illness.* Waco, TX: Baylor University Press

in their ministries and developing programs to address these needs. Several church communities have invested significant resources to develop effective and sophisticated care and counseling ministries that are oriented toward the mental and relational health of their congregations. Although programs such as these require significant financial and human resources, they can be scalable and may be modified to fit the needs of nearly any size congregation or parachurch organization. In Part 2, several examples of how this crucial work is being done are provided as models to adapt and/or adopt in your church.

According to Jesus, His followers are to be identified by one thing: their love for others (John 13:35). *Altruistic attitudes and actions are to be the sine qua non of Christianity.* Love is to have primacy and priority in all that we are and in all that we do. Love is not only to characterize our methods but also our motives and mission. This love is to be supreme—as Peter so clearly put it: "Above all, love each other deeply..." (1 Peter 4:8a, NIV)

Therefore, in order to "do" Christian counseling, one must "be" Christ-like personologically, not just behaviorally. We are most like Jesus, most genuinely Christlike, or Christ-*ian*, when we are committed to love others unconditionally. Christ-like actions flow naturally from a Christ-like identity.

This covenantal commitment is commanded. Jesus declared, "My command is this: Love each other as I have loved you" (John 15:12, NIV, cf. John 15:17). When we compassionately care for hurting souls and relationships, we are functioning as Jesus' ears, eyes, and hands extended.

Therefore, it is imperative that we strive to embrace those who are brokenhearted, emancipate those in captivity, and enlighten those in darkness. But in order to do so, we must confront what I call the unholy quartet of *silence, secrecy, shame,* and *stigma*, which exists in many quarters of the church surrounding mental and relational problems.

I believe there are four basic aspects to biblically loving hurting people, which will functionally *end the silence, expose the secrets, eradicate the shame,* and *erase the stigma* regarding our human mental and relational struggles. God's word is never silent, secretive, shame-inducing, or stigmatizing about human problems. These four key biblically grounded manifestations and demonstrations of Christ-ian love-in-action are:

1. ***Compassion* "Love as Empathy" [ends silence]**
   (Psalm 103:13; Matthew 9:36, 14:14, 15:32; Luke 7:13, 15:20; 2 Corinthians 1:3–5; Colossians 3:12.)

   The first step in solving a problem is to acknowledge it and create informed awareness about it. Silence connotes and promotes denial. As was already cited from the seminal study regarding mental health and the church conducted by a collaborative team from Focus on the Family and LifeWay Research a few years ago, it was discovered that two-thirds of pastors never preach or speak about mental health issues. That's the bad news. The good news is that shining the light of the good news onto people's problems is, again, not just good orthodoxy but good orthopraxy. Knowing truth is liberating. Applying truth is revolutionary. Lovingly and courageously ending dysfunctional silence is compassionate.

Simply talking about our problems acknowledges and therefore validates the reality of one's pain.

One of my favorite books by theologian/Christian philosopher Francis Schaeffer was profoundly entitled, *He Is There and He Is Not Silent*. Words matter. The Creator masterfully spoke the universe into its very existence through his Word (Genesis 1:1–26; John 1:1–3; Colossians 1:15–17). Giving hurting persons a safe environment in which they can tell their story to someone who will compassionately listen will be Jesus with skin on for them. The art of listening is a priceless gift. *People who are silent about their pain will normally open up to someone whom they trust will compassionately listen.*

The prefix of the term "com-passion" (com) means "with"; the suffix (passion) means "deep feeling." When we minister with deep feeling, we put our hearts into it. Jesus' miraculous healings were characteristically motivated by His empathy and compassion. Similarly, when we are "moved" by empathy, we are ministering to the hurting and broken soul very powerfully and very effectively. Simply put, when we exercise compassion, it proves that we care. We must care enough about hurting people and broken relationships to speak the truth in love about mental and relational health concerns. *We preach and practice what we care about.* And when people's needs are discussed openly, they feel—and are—loved.

We simply must end the silent shroud encircling mental and relational health problems. We know that Jesus came to minister compassion and sent the Holy Spirit to continue that essential work (John 14:16). Churches must talk about the reality of people's mental and relational health issues. As Dr. Ed Stetzer put it: "[...] in the church it seems we just don't talk about mental illness. So, people suffer in silence. They feel abandoned by God at times and blame their illness on some kind of spiritual failing. Worst of all, they suffer alone, without the comfort that other believers can offer them. It's time for that to change."[19] Indeed it is.

I often tell my clients there is one fundamental difference between healthy people, couples, families, and churches and unhealthy people, couples, families, and churches. And it is simply this: healthy people, couples, families, and churches *talk out their feelings*, whereas unhealthy people, couples, families, and churches *act out their feelings*. Let that sink in for a moment. Are you and yours healthy? Is your church healthy? Compassionate caring ends the silence.

2. ***Community* "Love as Relationship" [exposes secrecy]** (Psalm 44:21; Psalm 90:8; Jeremiah 23:24; Romans 2:16; 2 Corinthians 4:2.)

In the recovery world, it has been correctly emphasized that we are as sick as our secrets. Why do we keep secrets? It is because of fear and a lack of trust, resulting in feeling unsafe. Yet when we are engaged in meaningful,

19 Stetzer, E. "How to assess the mental and relational health needs in your church." In Clinton, T. E. & Pingleton, J. P. (2019). *The Struggle Is Real: How to Care for Mental and Relational Health Needs in the Church*. Bloomington, IN: Westbow Press, p. 2

connected relationships, we hopefully begin to experience emotional safety. God is omniscient, and everything is already exposed to him—yet he graciously and mercifully loves us anyway. Although we are certainly limited, we are to treat others likewise—without judgment, prejudice, criticism, or disparagement. Again, we do well to realize that "nothing human is foreign to me."

In healthy community, problems are normalized. We must normalize the fact that all humans have problems and that aside from Jesus, there has never been and never will be a perfect person, marriage, family, or church.

We keep secrets because we are afraid. We are subconsciously afraid that our conflict, dysfunction, and psychopathology threaten to expose our own faults, failures, and foibles. Then we will be judged. Then we will be humiliated, rejected, and alone.

The incredible irony is that life is relational. We were designed by the Creator in loving relationship, through loving relationship, and for loving relationship. Without relationship, life itself could not consist or continue. But then sin destroyed, and the curse ensued. Paradise was lost, and so was community. Consequently, we automatically subconsciously hide and keep secrets.

But in true community, we can experience mutual disclosures and exposures without fear of retribution or discrimination. True, trusting community is emotionally and, in every other way, safe. As the penultimate source of safety, God knows us thoroughly yet loves us despite our fear and/or shame-based secrets. The liberating power of the gospel message is that God knows us fully but loves us anyway. It has been profoundly observed that Satan knows our name but calls us by our sin, whereas Jesus knows our sin but calls us by our name! Thus, we are empowered and free to renounce our secretive ways in the sight of God and in the context of safe, caring relationships with other broken people. *Safety supersedes secrecy and results in sanity, security, and stability.*

3. ***Counseling* "Love as Discipleship" [erases shame]**
(1 Chronicles 27:32; Proverbs 11:14, 15:22; Romans 12:15, 15:1; 1 Corinthians 3:5–9, 5:17–20; 2 Timothy 4:2.)

Just as exercising compassion decimates silence and safe relationship defuses secrets, providing counseling dismantles shame. Shame is perhaps the deepest and most painful emotion that humans can experience. Shame is both ubiquitous and pernicious. Shame is best understood in connection with and in contrast to guilt—both of which have clear theological significance and implications. Basically, *guilt is feeling badly about what one does or doesn't do* [actions/doing], *whereas shame is feeling badly about whom one is* [identity/being]. Shame penetrates to the very core of what it means for us to be vulnerable, fallen creatures causing us to reflexively and subconsciously hide—afraid, humiliated, and alone.
Humans have been struggling with shame (and instinctively hiding) since Genesis chapter 3, and it is always

toxic and destructive.[20] Recently we see the incredible power of public shaming, which fuels the so-called "cancel culture." Further back in history, the deleterious impact of "shunning" was intentionally utilized to judge, control, and reject individuals and even entire people groups by fascist government systems and corrupt religious bodies to ostracize and banish those whom a group in power wished to repudiate.

The contextual framework for the original onset of shame was in loving relationship (which sinfulness and our resultant fallenness distorted), so it stands to reason that the Creator designed the redemptive cure for shame to be contextualized within loving relationship. Much like cleansing the dirt out of a deep wound in order to promote healing, it is therapeutic to disclose our shame within a safe, trusting, secure relationship with someone who is able to non-judgmentally listen, support, and competently guide us through the humiliation and excruciating pain of our human suffering. Whether individually or in small groups, counseling connotes caring and thus can make a hurting person or relationship be empowered to reveal their hidden or buried pain, exposing it to be healed with love and truth. In this

---

20 However, an interesting but perhaps rather controversial argument can be made that some sense of shame has some positive purposes and actually contributes to a healthy moral and emotional experience. In his book *For Shame: Rediscovering the Virtues of a Maligned Emotion*, Grand Rapids, Zondervan, 2021, Dr. Gregg Ten Elshoff posits a belief that shame is the opposite of honor but that some people who possess no shame (i.e., they are shameless) are not healthy. He does concur that when a sense of shame leads to self-loathing and a negative self-concept, it is toxic.

respect, counseling is sort of like surgery but without the advantage of anesthetic!

By the default of our sinful nature, humans' reflexive, innate reaction to shame is to hide. And not only to hide but to immobilize. Dr. Curt Thompson helps us understand that shame affects every aspect of our personal lives. It seeks to destroy our identity in Christ and replace it with a damaged version of ourselves that results in unhealed pain, broken relationships, and an ineffective witness. In fact, "Shame is a primary means to prevent us from using the gifts we have been given. And those gifts enable us to flourish a light-bearing community of Jesus followers who work to create space for others who wish to join it to do so. Shame, therefore, is not simply an unfortunate, random, emotional event that came with us out of the primordial evolutionary soup. It is both a source and result of evil's active assault on God's creation..."[21] Love expressed in any form, but specifically as mediated through counseling, is redemptive and transformative because it cancels our shame within the rubric of caring relationship.

4. ***Courage* "Love as Action" [eliminates stigma]**
   (Galatians 5:13, 6:1–2, 6:10; James 1:27, 2:1–8; 1 Peter 3:8–9, 4:8–10; 1 John 3:16–18, 4:7–12.)

Among other things, effective and godly servant leadership requires boldness in both attitudes and actions.

21 Thompson, C. (2015). *The Soul of Shame*. Downers Grove, IL: Intervarsity Press

It takes a courageous servant's initiative to intervene in crisis situations with marginalized, disadvantaged, and/or overburdened people. When we actively love people in their stress and distress, it eliminates their stigma. When we step into their stigmatized situation or circumstance to carry the part of their burden that they cannot and are staggering under (Galatians 6:1–2), they are enabled to walk—perhaps even with a spring in their step. Normalizing and accepting a person's pain, pathos, and pathology liberates and empowers them to heal, grow, and become all that Christ designed them to be.

In his bold and prescient book, *A Call for Courage*, pastor/ speaker Michael Anthony declares, "[...] today's world needs a tremendous, ongoing infusion of courage—the kind of courage mere mortals can't muster. We need the kind of courage made possible by God."[22] Fear, however, naturally paralyzes us. *Fear causes us to close up and shut up; courage emboldens us to stand up and speak up.* To stand in the gap and advocate for those who are unable to do so for themselves encapsulates the gospel in action. The slimy mold and mildew of our psychological stigma cannot grow under the liberating and illuminating light of God's love and truth.

But sadly and ironically, several authors have noticed that stigma for mental health disorders is actually great-

22 Anthony, M. (2018). *A Call for Courage.* Nashville, TN: Thomas Nelson

er within the church than in the rest of society.[23] Due to simplistic and naïve beliefs about sin as well as a fear-based resistance to looking at the realistic complexities of life, people have been marginalized, dismissed, and horribly treated by many quarters of the church. The countless numbers of hurting souls who have been turned away from help, hope, and healing is perhaps the worst blight of all on the modern church. It is forgivable but patently and categorically unacceptable. There must never be even a hint of stigma, even implicitly given to anyone who reaches out to the agents and ambassadors of Jesus for assistance and ministry for their mental and relational health problems.

In Matthew 25:31–46, Jesus starkly delineates the eternal implications of earthly examples of whether or not we also minister to people marginalized and stigmatized by homelessness, hunger, poverty, alienation, and imprisonment. It is a tragic but well-established fact that the primary cause of the scourge of homelessness (along with many other major societal problems) revolves around mental illness and/or relational problems of various kinds. Acting courageously to care for hurting people and relationships in the face of their stigmatizing conditions activates and demonstrates the love of Christ to and in them.

23 Vacek, op. cit.; Grcevich, S. (2018). *Mental Health and the Church.* Grand Rapids, MI: Zondrevan; Johnson, W. B. & Johnson, W. L. (2014). *The Minister's Guide to Psychological Disorders and Treatments.* New York, NY: Routledge

Of course, there is always risk in actively loving those with mental and relational problems. We might be expensed or even hurt in some inconvenient—perhaps even painful—ways. But there is also great reward—here on earth as well as in heaven. Jesus always loved courageously; so should we.

Part 2: Models and Methods

CHAPTER 5

The Refuge Church

Kannapolis, North Carolina (and Three Other Sites)

Rev. Jay Stewart

Jay Stewart grew up in Columbus, Georgia. He met his wife, Melanie, in high school, and they were married in 1983. Together with their five kids and grandkids, they live just outside of Charlotte, North Carolina. Jay is the Founding and Lead Pastor of The Refuge Church, a multi-campus ministry in Kannapolis, Greensboro, and Salisbury, North Carolina, as well as a congregation in Brazil.

He has also authored four books, including *Welded: Forming Racial Bonds that Last*, which was released nationwide in November 2020. In addition to leading The Refuge, he serves on several ministry boards, coaches pastors and church planters, and travels nationally and internationally to speak. He enjoys traveling, riding his Harley, playing basketball and golf, and spending time with his family.

[Note: This chapter highlights some innovative and creative ways for pastors and church leaders to address and enhance the mental and relational health of their own team members and their spouses and families. Tragically, research reveals that 50 percent of all professionally trained pastors drop out of the ministry within the first ten years after graduation from Bible school or seminary. Furthermore, only 10 percent of ministers retire from the ministry—in other words, there is a 90 percent attrition rate among professional ministers in America!

In sharing his own story, Jay introduces two unique and effective ways to get upstream from pastoral burnout and attrition. The first concept outlines the rationale for, need of, and pragmatics surrounding taking a periodic sabbatical. People professionals and leaders, especially Christian ones, often ignore and neglect their own self-care and psychological needs. Accordingly, they are at risk of overinvesting, overextending, and overdoing in their dedicated passion to reaching the lost and serving the needy. But we simply cannot give that which we do not have. If we are running a tow truck service, we must keep our battery sufficiently charged in order to jump-start others. We know intuitively that the laws of physics prove that a stream cannot rise higher than its' source; thus, many pastors on the verge of burnout will do well to utilize this Old Testament concept of sabbatical.

Secondly, Jay discusses a novel and practical way to help pastors, church leaders, and their spouses cope with the challenges, rigors, stressors, and emotional demands of professional ministry. Most professions require ongoing training after college or graduate school in the form of certified continuing education to help them stay up to date and support them professionally. What he proposes is to offer the clinical services of a mental and relational health expert to address the unique and often overwhelming personal and relational demands exacted on pastors, church staff, and their spouses through the course of providing ministry to their congregants. In-service training addressing biblically healthy self-care, appropriate boundaries, and balancing and prioritizing one's own personal and relational needs can prove to be life-giving and sustaining. Additionally, having each member of the ministry team, and if applicable, their spouse, avail themselves of a mental and relational health check-up provides them the opportunity to be ministered to in a caring and compassionate way. This proactive idea of a professional in-service combined with a intensive counseling needs to go viral!

We must come alongside servant leaders in ministry so that they do not keep running on empty, much less crash and burn. We are all broken, wounded, hurting, and vulnerable to succumbing to the enormous challenges, pressures, and demands of professional ministry. Untold numbers of pastors have faithfully tried to lead on empty but struggle themselves with discouragement, stress, addictions, loneliness, anxiety, and more. Many have lost their marriages, their families, their health, and their careers—all sacrificed on the altar of trying to serve God and others in their own strength. But we know it is when we are real about our weaknesses that He is strong. As you read Jay's story, allow the Holy Spirit to speak to your soul about how He wants to lead you—so you can lead others more effectively. Be real—because the struggle is real.]

Personal Care for Pastors, Church Leaders, and Spouses

"Hey, Dad, you better stop and get some gas," my son Caden said when he heard the "low fuel" indicator signal sound in my Ford F-150 pickup as we sped along I-485 on the west side of Charlotte, heading back to Kannapolis. We had just enjoyed some father-son time at TopGolf, and I was scheduled to address a group of prospective students who were visiting The Refuge Church to check out our discipleship school. "I'll stop in a bit once we get closer to the church," I replied. The low fuel indicator light was on, and it also provides a countdown of "miles before empty," which starts at thirty-six miles to go. Every now and then, Caden would lean over just enough to be able to see what that number read, and as it moved into the twenties and then into the teens, I could hear the concern in his voice. "Dad, don't you think we should get off at this next exit?" I assured him we were fine. "These things have a grace period even when it hits zero," I told him. "You can usually go another ten to fifteen miles after that."

Now the countdown was in the single digits, prompting him to suggest we get some gas with a little more urgency in his voice. I passed station after station, exit after exit, believing we still had time before we were really in trouble. When the countdown hit zero, I announced my plan to get gas at our exit, which was still a few miles up the interstate. The traffic filled all four lanes and was barely inching along towards Exit 54. We were in the third lane from the right when our exit came into view, no more than a half a mile ahead. And then it happened.

First, it was a brief sputter, and then...nothing. The engine cut off, leaving us stranded in the third lane, exit in sight, with honking cars and angry drivers behind us. Another pickup pulled over in front of us, and a man immediately began pulling chains out of his cab, offering to pull us over to the side of the interstate. The story gets even better. After pulling us across two lanes of bumper-to-bumper traffic into the emergency lane, as he is unhooking his chains, a member of my church snaps a photo and posts it on social media with a caption about how "my pastor is always helping others." Quite the opposite in this instance! That Sunday, I had our team put the picture up on the screen in the service; I told "the rest of the story," and we all had a good laugh at my expense. Now every time Caden is in my truck and the gas gets low, we joke about how much farther we can go before needing to stop.

I have had the privilege of serving in full-time vocational ministry for nearly four decades now. There have been many times when the real-life scenario that played out that day on the interstate provided a stark parallel to what was going on emotionally and spiritually in my life. There are indicators going off warning of danger, breakdown, or engine failure, and we think we can push on a little farther. I have been guilty of doing so many times, convincing myself that the "grace period" extends beyond reality and then getting frustrated when it runs out and the engine quits, blaming it on a "factory defect" or something else other than my stubbornness and unwillingness to admit that I need to pull over. Maybe you are cringing just a little right now because you know you've been guilty of the same thing. We want everyone around us to think we are the benevolent ones, helping everyone else, when the reality is that we are all in need of being rescued by someone else. Can we talk? Hello?

Get in the Zone

Pastors, leaders, and those involved in ministry or professions that are focused on meeting the needs of others are notorious for neglecting self-care and pushing themselves into an unhealthy place. We typically operate in one of three zones: the *dream* zone, the *drained* zone, and the *danger* zone (cue the Top Gun soundtrack, please!).

The dream zone is that place where we are firing on all cylinders, life is great, we are in a healthy place, our marriage is good, we have minimal staff issues, and the church, ministry, or organization is growing. The drained zone is when the "low fuel" indicator light has come on. We have pushed our schedules to full capacity, we start missing date nights with our spouse, some problems have surfaced, our stress level needle has moved further over to the right, and we have left little or no margins. Let's hit the pause button for a moment and consider a thought. What if the publisher of this book ran the words all the way to the edge of the page and left no margins? Would you keep reading it? Would you have ever started reading it? Probably not. Over sixty percent of every page of a book is white space because books read better, and life itself works better when we have margins.

Notice what the Bible says in Isaiah 5:8–10 (NIV):

> Woe to you who add house to house
>   and join field to field
> till no space is left
>   and you live alone in the land.

The LORD Almighty has declared in my hearing:
"Surely the great houses will become desolate,
the fine mansions left without occupants.
A ten-acre vineyard will produce only a bath of wine;
a homer of seed will yield only an ephah of grain."

This is a clear and sober warning from scripture about running our lives right up to the edge with no room for rest, an arrogant disregard for self-care, and not paying attention to the warning signals. Notice the line in verse 8 that reads "till no space is left and you live alone in the land." There is an old African proverb that says if you want to go fast, go alone, but if you want to go far, go with others. Living our lives on fumes in the drained zone brings loneliness and greatly reduces output and productivity, as we see in verse ten. A bath of wine equals about six gallons, far below what ten acres would normally yield. A homer of seed, or about 360 pounds of seed, is reduced to an output of only thirty-six pounds of grain. Refusing to pull over and refuel, thinking we can stay in the drained zone, inevitably moves us into the third zone, which is the danger zone.

My exit was in sight, only a half-mile away. But there I sat stranded in the third lane over, unable to move, but nonetheless inconveniencing and even endangering the schedules and safety of others. You are so close. You know you need to reach out for help, and that is exactly what you plan to do after just one more mile, one more meeting, one more Sunday, one more week. It is in the danger zone where lives quickly unravel. This is where rational thinking takes a cruise, compromise sets in, affairs unintentionally happen, embezzlement feels justifiable, substance abuse takes over in the form of drinking, prescription meds, or narcotics, self-pleasuring porn becomes the norm, and at times people even resort to criminal activity—all in a subconscious effort to medicate the pain and/or inappropriately soothe the soul.

There are plenty of statistics I could cite that would support the fact that pastors and leaders have many emotional and relational needs that go unmet or unaddressed, and the struggle is indeed real. Chances are you have read many of the stats, so I will spare you from having to ingest them and be confronted with them yet again. I want to focus on a couple of practical things for your consideration that might help move you from the danger zone or the drained zone back into the dream zone. The suggestions I want to present to you are from personal experience and painful but necessary growth and have both been a game-changer for me.

The Fourth Commandment

We are all familiar with the Ten Commandments found in Exodus chapter 20. The first three commandments are related to our vertical relationship with God, and the last six have to do with our horizontal relationships with others. Sandwiched in spot four, right in between these two groups, is this often misunderstood or neglected commandment about the Sabbath. If we are honest, many people don't quite know what to do with this one. It is sort of like the drunk uncle who shows up at the family reunion or the space invader who corners us every Sunday after church. If I am honest, for years, I did not know what to do with Commandment Four.

I am a church planter, and for the first several years of The Refuge, I wore many hats, as do most church planters or pastors. Our church saw explosive growth in the beginning, going from forty people in a basement to over 400 people in our first nine months. I found myself running on fumes many times in those first several years, trying to find times of rest but most often not succeeding. We moved from the basement to a middle-school auditorium and immediately began renovations on a warehouse that had been a fitness facility. We recruited volunteers and, on a shoestring budget, renovated 8,500 square feet in less than five months.

Once we moved into our new church home, the growth continued, eventually requiring the addition of a second service, then a third, and in time a fourth. During this same period of time, we also launched a satellite campus twenty-five miles north in Salisbury. One week later, we launched our first Brazil campus. Just a few months before our seventh anniversary as a church, we closed on thirty acres of prime property and began making plans to build, raise funds, secure financing, and design a building. We moved our Salisbury location into a more permanent location, which required another renovation project. And then, we began construction on our new state-of-the-art main campus after nearly two years of preparations and planning. The ten months of construction were demanding and exhausting, and the normal daily and weekly tasks of pastoring a growing church, preaching, leading staff, developing leaders, and preparing the people for the transition into the new campus never stopped.

The exciting day came when we were able to move into and dedicate our beautiful new building on the ten-year anniversary of our church. I knew I was emotionally, physically, and spiritually drained. I just did not realize how tired and depleted I actually was. There were warning lights going off on the dashboard, and I knew the fuel tank was low. By the prompting of the Holy Spirit, I made a request of my Board of Directors to do something I had not done in over thirty years of full-time ministry. I asked to take a sabbatical. And they said yes. I began making arrangements with my staff and leaders for my wife and me to be away from the church for sixty days. I have to be honest. I was scared! I was afraid I would take this time off, and nothing would be different at the end of it. I was afraid things at the church might unravel. I was afraid I would go crazy if I did not have multiple tasks and responsibilities in front of me. However, God met me during those sixty days and revealed some truths to me that I believe can be a game-changer for you as well.

Say What?

I unplugged from my email accounts, meetings, preaching, and the daily duties of pastoring and began my best effort to rest. Three weeks into the sabbatical, I felt something shift in my body. I do not really know how to describe what happened, but something had changed, and I knew I had finally moved into a place of true relaxation and soul rest.

About this same time, I was reading the story of Elijah taking on the false prophets of Baal at Mount Carmel found in 1 Kings chapter 18, arguably one of the greatest showdowns and victories in the Bible. Elijah went from the awesome thrill of victory in chapter 18 to the adrenaline crash of despair that so many leaders have experienced. Jezebel had threatened to kill him, and we find him in chapter 19 alone, depressed, and asking the Lord to finish him off and take his life. Amazingly, God's servant went from the peak of a literal mountain top spiritual and emotional experience to the depths of a suicidal pit of despondency in a matter of hours.

In verse 5 of chapter 19, Elijah lays down to rest and falls asleep under a tree. An angel awakens him with a message from God. As I was reading this during my sabbatical, I could feel myself sitting up a little straighter with anticipation of what God was about to say to him through the angel. He had just experienced this major victory over the evil Ahab and Jezebel and the false prophets of Baal. He had defended the name of the one true God. The future of Israel was at stake. I knew whatever God would say in this moment would be deeply profound, impacting both Elijah and the nation of Israel. "Get up and eat!" Time out! What? That's it? However, Elijah did just that, and then he lay down and slept some more. In verse 7, the angel returns with another message from God. Surely this will be the moment when Elijah receives the word of the Lord for the nation of Israel. "Get up and eat some more, or the journey ahead will be too much for you."

Elijah gets up from his power nap, eats and drinks, and is supernaturally energized with enough strength to travel forty days and nights to Mount Sinai, the mountain of God. It is here that God gives him instructions to stand before him on the mountain. While standing there, a powerful windstorm passed by, followed by an earthquake, which was followed by fire. But still no instructions, no directives from God. And then it happened. Elijah hears a gentle whisper, the Lord gives him the

GPS coordinates for his next destination along with the name of the person who would be his successor, and the future of Israel is secured.

It was at this point I realized that I was too tired to hear God's voice or to receive His instructions for the future of The Refuge. What I needed more than anything was to rest first and receive His invigorating sustenance. Attending to the physical and emotional deficit I was experiencing would position me to spiritually hear from God, just like Elijah. And it took me three weeks to reach the place where I could begin to hear the whisper of His voice.

That experience and download from the Lord prompted me to do two things that I believe have contributed to the soul care and health of our staff. First, we immediately began working on a sabbatical policy for all our pastors. We make it mandatory for our pastors to take a sabbatical once they have served in full-time ministry for a certain number of years. Practicing this Old Testament concept is healing, restorative, and transformational. A prolonged rest will recharge, reinvigorate, replenish, and even redeem one's ministry. Burnout is a terrible and unfortunate occupational hazard in professional ministry. And the epidemic attrition rates testify to it. Too many pastors give up because they have been beat up and used up.

The second thing we did was to bring in a professional spirit-filled psychologist to meet with our entire staff for a few hours and then, over the next few days, to meet one-on-one with each of our pastors and their spouses to ensure that everyone was healthy. This professional pastoral workshop and then personal and relationship counseling mini-intensive experience was a purposeful investment of finances and time that our staff greatly appreciated and something we will continue to do on a regular basis. After all, it is good physical health to get a regular check-up. Why not be proactive and get a good mental and relational health check-up? Prevention is easier—and far more effective—than cure every time. The more we can get upstream from individual and marital problems, the better off we and our congregations will be. Research demonstrates that the sooner mental and relational health issues are recognized and addressed, the easier and less painful it is to deal with them. The smaller the weed in the flower bed, the shorter the roots, and thus the easier it is to pull. This proverbial ounce of prevention by means of a staff mental and relational health check-up is far more significant than several pounds of cure.

We will never be able to effectively lead others if we are spiritually, emotionally, relationally, and physically bankrupt. We do well to pay attention to the warning lights going off on the dashboard of our souls and to respond accordingly. However, to do so will require three things:

1. *Courage:* Being vulnerable and transparent takes an enormous amount of courage and kicks against the default setting of most leaders. My experience has shown that people respond positively to this type of leadership, and it creates a culture where others are inspired to live authentic and transparent lives, which then leads to health and freedom. It is scary at times to be real, but personal authenticity is a hallmark of emotional and spiritual maturity.

2. *Community*: Leaders are often some of the loneliest people on the planet. If we fail to have the courage to live with vulnerability and transparency, our fears of being judged, criticized, and/or rejected gradually cause us to isolate ourselves from the very thing for which we were created: intimate relationship. The goal of the enemy is to isolate us from life-giving relationships. We thrive in the context of community, but we atrophy and become easy targets for all manner of failure in isolation. Self-protective hiding from ourselves and others ironically results in experiencing the only thing in all of God's Edenic creation that he declared to be "not good"—being isolated and alone.
3. *Commitment*: Most people can do anything once. Effective leaders often become really good at crisis management or damage control and will make changes in an emergency situation long enough for the storm to pass. The key for long-term health, longevity in one's career or marriage, and a thriving relationship with God is a commitment to preventative care and not just making temporary changes to avert a crisis. Make sure your tank is full before your trip, and make sure you plan times and places of refueling along the journey. If your tank is empty and you need to respond to an emergency situation, you can have the assurance and peace of mind that you can make it safely to the hospital at 3:00 a.m. without having to drive around to find a gas station that is open.

In the county in which I reside (Cabarrus County, North Carolina), a mere thirteen miles from where I sit, the first-ever gold discovery in America was made in 1799. Conrad Reed, the twelve-year-old son of John Reed, was fishing in Little Meadow Creek with some buddies when he noticed an oddly colored rock. He took it home and showed it to his father. For the next three years, this yellow rock was used as a doorstop in the family home. In 1802 a friend of John's, a jeweler from Fayetteville, North Carolina, was visiting the Reed family when he noticed the doorstop and recognized that this yellow rock was actually a seventeen-pound gold nugget. John did not understand the value of what he possessed, so when the jeweler asked him to name his price, John threw out what he felt was an audacious figure: $3.50!

I believe there are many leaders who have devalued some of the most important things in life or who have no idea of the true value of certain things. Our culture has slowly but surely redefined many of our morals and societal standards and has attached great value on developing a social media following, achieving personal and professional notoriety, attaining personal identity derived from busyness and activity, and material and financial gain. However, these subtle and surreptitious preoccupations have all the while cheapened true and enduring commodities like intimate relationship, emotional health, identity in Christ, and the freedoms of simplicity. There is no doubt that the struggle is real, life is hard, leadership is not for cowards, and there is an enemy who seeks to rob you of life, kill your soul, and destroy everything of value. But the truth still remains that Jesus came that you might have life, and life to the fullest!

Sabbatical Policy for The Refuge

What is a sabbatical?

- An extended leave from ordinary work;
- a period of rest for the body, mind, and soul;
- a time for renewal and development of relationships with God and others.

> A Sabbatical typically includes time for travel, rest, prayer, and the broadening of one's sense of God's work in the world. It is a time to pause, step back, and behold God and creation from a new perspective. Nourishing one's soul and discovering a new perspective calls for both a change of pace and a change of location.
> More intentional than simply taking a break, the sabbatical consists of more than just a vacation. This is a time for the pastor to distance self from the demands of leadership, to gain fresh vision and energy. It is a time to focus on comprehensive renewing and re-equipping for long-term ministry.
>
> Drexel Rankin, *Ministry Magazine*

1. A sabbatical may be requested by any staff pastor who has served at least seven (7) years at The Refuge.
2. Sabbaticals are not automatic and are considered upon request and must be requested one year in advance with a written proposal to include
   - proposed dates,

- a plan for how the ministry will be covered in their absence, and
- a plan/schedule for the sabbatical.

3. Consideration will be given to the time of the year, the church's calendar, and the condition of the department(s) under the pastor's supervision.
4. Sabbaticals cannot run concurrently with vacation time.
5. Sabbaticals will be three to four weeks in length, with no more than three Sundays missed.
6. During the sabbatical year, no other "continuing education time" will be granted to the staff pastor.
7. Once a sabbatical is granted, the staff pastor may request a two-week sabbatical every three years thereafter.
8. The staff pastor is required to keep a journal during their sabbatical.

CHAPTER 6

Christian Counseling and Discipleship Center

West Monroe, Louisiana

Rev. Trent Langhofer, PhD

- PhD Marriage and Family Therapy (University of Louisiana at Monroe)
- MS Marriage and Family Therapy (Harding University)
- BA Ministry and Leadership (Randall University)

Dr. Trent Langhofer is a licensed professional counselor who has worked with individuals and families since 2010. Presently, he serves as the clinical director of counseling in the College of Adult and Graduate Studies at Colorado Christian University in Colorado Springs, Colorado. Dr. Langhofer is a sought-after conference speaker and teacher. He has lectured nationally and internationally to large audiences on topics that include adjustment following spiritual conversion, the themes perpetuating marital commitment in conservative protestant couples following infidelity, development of authentic intimacy in relationships, and spiritual growth and development in spiritually mature individuals and families.

In his career, Dr. Langhofer has been the founder or co-founder of multiple agencies centered on treating individuals and families from the communities in which he has lived and worked. His clinical expertise is broad and includes but is not limited to the treatment of childhood trauma, substance abuse, sexual dysfunction, marital health, depression, anxiety disorders, and clergy misconduct.

For many years, Dr. Langhofer has also served as a teaching pastor, co-pastor, or lead pastor. His experience in professional ministry helps him integrate spirituality into clinical treatment in helpful, meaningful ways. The leadership experience Dr. Langhofer has gained over the years has been useful in providing leadership consultation to various public and private organizations.

God often calls people to ministry in specific churches for the benefit of the church. This seems to be the case for the vast majority of churches across the United States and the rest of the world. Sometimes though, and this seems much rarer, God calls a *person* to ministry in a church for the benefit of the person. That's my story. In 2010, God called me, my bride of four years, our eighteen-month-old son, and our fourteen-day-old daughter to a church in rural northeast Louisiana, and it changed our lives. This church exists in an area with abundant need and very few resources. Despite this reality, this particular church not only survives but thrives. Thriving is never a perfect process, but this church can testify to God's ability to work within and through a far-from-perfect church to meet real-life needs—especially the mental health needs—of the community in which it exists. According to current numbers published by the Substance Abuse and Mental Health Services Administration, one in five adults suffer from mental illness, and the number for teens and adolescents is even higher. With mental illness as prevalent as it is today in our great nation, how can churches function in such a way that they essentially exist as a place of healing and hope for those struggling with mental illness? Following is a discussion of how White's Ferry Road Church is doing just that.

WFR Church

Whites Ferry Road (WFR) Church is a multigenerational church in the metropolis of West Monroe, Louisiana. A quick search will indicate that West Monroe is a town of about 25,000 people situated on the Ouachita River. (Residents, myself included, are fond of saying it's one of the top ten scenic rivers in the United States!) The Ouachita River was formerly a significant means of transit for cotton, and the Cotton Port historic district still houses an interesting collection of restaurants and boutique shops in burgeoning downtown West Monroe.I ended up in Northeast Louisiana not because I was looking for that specific church but because God led my family and me to Monroe, Louisiana, so I could complete my doctoral degree in marriage and family therapy. It's hard to describe how afraid I was to move my family to northeast Louisiana. My bride, Kearstin, and I literally knew only one person from the area when we moved, and the culture of northeast Louisiana was dramatically different from anything we'd ever experienced in our lives.

In general, Northeast Louisiana presents some unique challenges to church function and growth. Mental illness prevalence rates are high, substance abuse rates seem even higher, and Northeast Louisiana is one of the poorer, if not one of the poorest, areas in the country. It's not the type of geographical location church planters are fighting over for prospective new church real estate. Despite these and many other challenges—for example, the water table is so high that homes and businesses can't have basements, and WFR Church has a huge basement!—WFR Church is changing lives locally, nationally, and around the world.

In the early 1970s, WFR Church housed a school of biblical studies. The White's Ferry Road School of Biblical Studies was started to provide pastors with theological and biblical training so they could be equipped to preach the Gospel of Jesus around the United States and the rest of the world. For twenty-two years, the school of biblical studies existed and equipped ministry leaders—many of whom are still in ministry today.

When the School of Biblical Studies closed, the space previously used to house the school became storage for the church. After a handful of years, a wonderful lady from the church finished her doctoral degree in marriage and family therapy and started a Christian counseling center in the church. Eventually, I became the director of the Christian Counseling Center of West Monroe. Today, the Christian Counseling Center is still housed within the church, staffed by three doctoral-level clinicians and a few master's-level clinicians. The Center is still improving the mental and relational health struggles of hundreds of men, women, and children in Northeast Louisiana every year.

WFR Church is home to one of the largest per capita Celebrate Recovery ministries in the world. Every Friday night at WFR, over four hundred people with hurts, habits, and/or hang-ups gather to worship God, support and encourage one another, and work through the transformational steps of the Celebrate Recovery process. WFR has a thriving recovery home ministry connected to the church and to the Celebrate Recovery ministry that exists within the church. WFR Celebrate Recovery Inside is a ministry of the church that sends men and women into the Louisiana prison system to provide Christ-centered encouragement to incarcerated men and women.

A number of years ago, leaders at WFR church launched a worldwide broadcasting ministry called World Radio. This ministry, which today is called One Kingdom, reaches the world by purchasing radio broadcasting in third world countries and spends a few hours each week preaching the gospel of Jesus in the native language of that particular country. Over the years, One Kingdom has partnered with some of the most wonderful ministers on the planet to host local radio shows centered around preaching the Gospel and teaching the Bible. This ministry is still thriving today.

WFR Church is also the home church of the iconic Robertson family of Duck Dynasty fame. Phil Robertson, patriarch of the Robertson family, has faithfully attended WFR Church for decades. Phil, his wonderful wife, Mrs. Kay, his boys, Alan, Jase, Willie, and Jep, along with his daughter, Phyllis, have impacted thousands of lives locally and millions of lives around the world.

The WFR School of Biblical Studies, the Christian Counseling Center of West Monroe, Celebrate Recovery, One Kingdom, and the Robertsons? How did a mid-sized church from rural northeast Louisiana with very little resources and no support from a national association become a place that influenced the lives of millions of people? How WFR did it and is doing it can provide any church with the means of having a significantly positive impact on mental health in the lives of men and women from the community in which it exists.

The WFR Way

Before I get deeply into how WFR Church and the Christian Counseling Center worked together on the front lines of mental health, I need to share some of the features of WFR's leadership. Years ago, I read a quote that is worth mentioning here, "Everything rises and falls on leadership." That's true for any organization, and it's especially true in churches. The primary way WFR Church was able to integrate mental health counseling into its ministry DNA has everything to do with WFR Church leadership. This is the first and most critical paradigmatic shift churches must make if any church intends on influencing mental health in its community. There are five features of WFR leadership that I would identify as non-negotiable requirements for mental health influencing churches to exhibit.

Relentless Christ-Centeredness

It's hard to describe how WFR Church leadership is relentlessly Christ-centered primarily because church culture in America today is saturated with this phrase. The verses that perhaps most appropriately describe this relentless Christ-centeredness are found in Mark's Gospel:

> While Jesus was having dinner at Levi's house, many tax collectors and sinners were eating with him and his disciples, for there were many who followed him. When the teacher of the law who were Pharisees saw him eating with the sinners and tax collectors, they asked the disciples: "Why does he eat with tax collectors and sinners?" On hearing this, Jesus said to them, "It is not the healthy who need a doctor, but the sick. I have not come to call the righteous, but sinners."
>
> Mark 2:15–17 (NIV)

For a church to be on the frontlines of mental health, this is what the leadership of the church must do. What's difficult about this is that hanging out with broken people can't be simply a box that leaders check on their to-do lists or be a weekly obligation they week to meet week after month after year. People with mental and relational health challenges and addiction issues are not to be avoided or shunned. They are to be loved, accepted, and discipled with grace, mercy, and forgiveness through the redemptive and transformational community that

God offers through the Word of Jesus and the power of His Holy Spirit. Living alongside and loving broken people must be woven into the DNA of church leadership.

Love

What was it that drove Jesus to fellowship with, to live alongside, to sacrifice His very life for tax collectors and sinners? Love. This is where things get tricky. Broken people are usually in really unstable situations that require lots—and I do mean lots—of time, resources, and effort. Often in northeast Louisiana, people are in need of stable housing, consistent food, healthcare, including mental healthcare, and spiritual encouragement. These needs are often chronic—meaning the needs don't just exist for a weekend or a month. Often, hurting people need support for long periods of time. What's tricky about this is that when the church can't or couldn't provide the time, resources, or effort needed at any given moment, the person in need feels a lack of love and acceptance—which ironically and insidiously serves to reinforce and intensify their underlying feelings of shame and stigma.

I can recall many times people were depending on me to help meet some need in their life, and I simply didn't have the resources, time, or effort needed in some of those moments. I know this made some people feel unloved by me over the course of my ministry at WFR Church. These are the moments that keep me awake at night—still. So how can the capital C Church love people without occasionally unintentionally hurting some people? Realistically it can't. We are all fallen, finite, and broken clay pots with our own issues, hurts, and challenges.

If that's the bad news, the good news is that the church, despite hurting people and falling short from time to time, can love people with a love that changes their lives and heals their mental health issues in profound ways. This is happening at WFR Church every single day. I could tell you story after story of people that, honestly, were as good as dead because of a substance use disorder or another mental health malady who are now serving in some capacity of leadership at WFR today—not kidding. It's worth the pain at stake to love people with the love of the Lord.

This is what I sense Jesus' teaching was all about in John 13:34–35 (NIV), which, by the way, I think is the central point of the entire Bible:

> A new command I give you: Love one another. As I have loved you, so you must love one another. By this everyone will know that you are my disciples, if you love one another.

This wasn't a "new" command in the sense that it had never been commanded before. In Leviticus 19:18 (NIV), we read, "Do not seek revenge or bear a grudge against anyone among your people, but love your neighbor as yourself. I am the LORD." So, what was "new" about this command? What was new was the depth of its meaning, illustrated no less by the life and sacrifice of Jesus. Here Jesus essentially says take the risk to love people until it hurts and let Him pick up the pieces when we fall short.

Risk-Taking

Living alongside and loving broken people requires high levels of risk tolerance. Betrayal, abandonment, rejection, and emotional pain, among other things, are all possible outcomes of leading in the ways we've mentioned. Overwhelmingly, it's worth the risk to love people the way Jesus loved people. For people to change, they must be loved with that kind of love, and that love requires risk.

Part of the DNA of WFR Church leadership is a willingness to not only risk loving people like Jesus did but giving people opportunities the way Jesus did too. I don't have the time to do this in detail here, and it's been done elsewhere with excellence anyway, but if we looked at the qualifications of the twelve disciples as far as starting a revolutionary religious movement was concerned, we would all have overlooked them. I know I would have. You've heard it said before that Jesus doesn't often call the qualified, He qualifies the called. This is what risk-taking actually looks like in churches that are impacting the communities they serve.

Influential churches must be willing to take calculated risks in giving broken, unqualified people kingdom-building opportunities. This was one of the handfuls of ways WFR Church—and its leadership—changed my life. They took a chance on me. They didn't really know me—they vetted me, yes, but they didn't really know me. And they've taken chances on people time and time again. I can't quote a statistic on this, but a majority of the time, the risk WFR Church took on people played out not just well but in what I would call miraculously beneficial ways.

Transparency

For leadership to experience the "genetic" transformation required to live alongside and love broken people, they must be in touch with their own brokenness. Rather than having a leadership that looked as if they had "everything put together," the leadership at WFR was and still is open about their struggles and brokenness.

I cannot overstate the powerful and profound effect this had on my life. I'm a former homeless IV-using junkie. To walk in a church for me is still sometimes an unsettling experience. I wonder sometimes, "Would these people welcome me if they knew where I've been?" At WFR, not only did I not feel that way, but I often felt as though I fit in, as though I was "one of them," and like I was genuinely accepted. The most powerful influence of transparency on church culture is in the way transparency creates an atmosphere where anyone feels as though they genuinely belong.

People who struggle with mental illness often tell me—and I've worked with thousands in the past several years—that one of their most desperate struggles is finding a place they belong. What has always seemed unfortunate to me about this is that the church is the one place where *everyone should feel as though they belong*. If we're being honest, what's challenging about this is navigating the balance of helping people feel they belong without giving people a sense that any and all behavior is *affirmed*.

There is a way to strike a balance between providing people a place to belong without affirming behavior that is separating people from God and thus, negatively influencing their mental health. The way to strike this balance is for leaders to embrace transparency while also demonstrating their own surrender to Jesus and communicating about their personal healing journeys. WFR is so healing and life-giving to so many people, including me, because of the transparency of its leadership.

Grace

WFR Church is deeply rooted in the restoration movement. I should say that even though I no longer minister at WFR today, I still consider myself a restoration movement-oriented preacher/teacher and that these roots run very deeply within me. Briefly, and for those not familiar with restoration movement theology, the restoration movement is deeply conservative, heavily oriented to following what it considers the actual teaching of the Bible, and is particularly focused on evangelism. There are so many wonderful things that these tendencies of restoration movement churches create in the churches where restoration movement theology is present. There are also a few things that restoration movement theology complicates.

One of the things complicated by restoration movement theology and its rigorous commitment to "doing" church the way the New Testament—especially the book of the Acts of the Apostles—teaches is that church practice can become a matter of salvific importance. This can, at times, influence restoration movement churches to underemphasize grace and overemphasize other things. Certainly, this isn't only an issue in churches rooted in the restoration movement but is an issue some restoration movement churches face.

What is important about this is that the leadership of WFR Church had to navigate both the wonderful things about its theological heritage and the less wonderful, more complicated things about its theological heritage. I suggest that every single church in America and across the world must endeavor to do the exact same thing. For some churches, perhaps most of their theology is wonderful, and very little is less wonderful and complicated. For others, perhaps most is less wonderful and very complicated. Wherever a church falls on this continuum, the requirement is the same, to sort through theology and tradition in ways that situate any church to better serve its community.

The elders of WFR Church navigated this situation with grace. A type of grace that, based on my front row seat, came across to me as very humble, open to feedback, and was done in an attitude of brotherhood that quite frankly felt like a healthy family. Sure, the process wasn't perfect, and sometimes people were hurt. I suspect it's not possible to navigate this situation such that imperfection and hurt are not present. This willingness on the part of leadership to gracefully consider its theology and traditions was nothing short of inspiring to me. This grace-based approach transcended considering theology and tradition and "leaked" out to every other area of church functioning.

We need churches willing to "spring a leak" in America. What we need churches to leak is Jesus-centered grace. Churches that leak this type of grace wrestle with tough ideas, embrace broken people and take risks on those broken people by giving them kingdom-building opportunities, and see failure as progress and growth. These are churches that don't hide failures or shortcomings but talk through struggles in a way that helps others see the pathway of change and inspires them to walk that path.

Hard Work

There will be no such thing as transformation or the healing of mental illness in churches today without a willingness of leadership to work hard. Hard-working, engaged, present leaders promote an atmosphere of genuine compassion and mercy in the churches they serve within, the families they are a part of, or the businesses in which they work. *People work is always hard work.* It's emotionally expensive to walk with people through the valley of the shadow of death. As such, leaders must be willing to spend time in the trenches and meet the needs of the people they're serving.

At WFR Church, this was one of the most obvious qualities of our leadership. Often, when I was at the church late in the evening counseling a family, as I was leaving, I would notice the vehicles of our leaders at the church. They were either still in meetings, working with families, or tidying up the building after a service. This always helped me feel connected and supported in doing the work God was calling me to do. It's also one way our church was able to use our resources so effectively—when everyone is contributing significant effort, a team can do a lot even if they have very little.

This also helped set the tone for many people's transformational journeys. I've been in the business of treating mental illness professionally now for over a decade. Of the few things that are always required for a person to experience true and lasting transformation, one of the most important is a willingness to work hard. When individuals in need of transformation see hard work exemplified by the leaders in the churches they attend, it's easier for them to "batten down the hatches" and put in the work. At WFR, the results speak for themselves.

The Christian Counseling Center of West Monroe

The Christian Counseling Center of West Monroe is the counseling agency connected to WFR Church. It was started by a wonderful friend and mentor, Dr. Joneal Kirby, in 2002. Dr. Kirby has a heart to help heal the hurt that stands between people and Jesus, and from that inspired vision came the Christian Counseling Center. That said, the Center would not exist if the atmosphere at the church was different than I've described it. But the right vision mixed with the right atmosphere and the right people developed over time into a successful counseling practice that both met and continues to meet the needs of individuals and families in Northeast Louisiana and provided an atypical but highly effective evangelizing pathway into WFR Church for people who were either unchurched or underchurched.

There are some critical things that churches should consider before opening a counseling agency within their church. Among the more critical things to consider are legal and liability issues, confidentiality and ethical issues, personnel and staffing issues, and theological and doctrinal issues.

Liability

One of the most important components of addressing mental health and the church is considering how to appropriately, ethically, and legally integrate the two together. Mental health treatment is, as the name implies, part of general healthcare. This naturally means there are potential liabilities associated with the treatment of mental health. All practitioners, regardless of whether or not they operate within or in partnership with a church and whether they are licensed by the state, should carry appropriate liability coverage.

The Christian Counseling Center exists as its own S-Corporation in Louisiana. The Center leases office space from WFR Church for $1.00 per year. The liability coverage of the Christian Counseling Center was extended to protect the church. This way, the church has as little liability risk as possible. Organizing the partnership between the church and the Christian Counseling Center this way made as clear as possible the distinction between the two, which is important.

Confidentiality

Another important issue that is critical to navigate and uphold is the boundary of confidentiality. Counseling is implicitly protected by the foundational concept of counselor/client confidentiality. It's one of the more important components of the counseling process. For clients to feel safe providing clients with enough intimate information to get the help they need, they must be reassured that counseling is confidential. Exceptions to client privacy are legally required when there is concern about potential danger to a client and/or other persons and when there is suspicion of neglect and/or abuse of elderly persons, disabled persons, or children. In such cases, it is incumbent on the therapist to report these concerns to the state authorities as well as to warn others as appropriate.

Churches need to know if someone in their congregation is struggling with something that could possibly endanger others at their church. Since churches have a need to know when people may be a danger to others in the congregation, and since clients need to be certain their counseling is done in confidence, counselors that practice in church settings can find themselves caught between a "rock and a hard place," so to speak.

What makes this particularly complex at WFR is that the church often subsidizes counseling for church members. Further, I was employed as the teaching pastor, co-pastor, or lead pastor of the church during my tenure in West Monroe. This made clarifying the boundary issues of confidentiality and roles from the outset very important.

We decided to put language in our paperwork clarifying what information we would tell our church leadership should that information be disclosed in counseling. We asked clients to give consent to this prior to counseling. This clarity allowed clients to feel confident about their privacy. We also always clarified the roles of the counselors working with the clients prior to counseling. Should clients feel uncomfortable getting counseled by someone in the church, we referred that client to an outside agency that could meet their needs.

Personnel

The Christian Counseling Center has been blessed with an absolutely incredible staff over the years. The men and women who have worked at the Center have always been highly qualified. Qualification and professional credentialing, however, has not been the most critical component of the staff at the Center. First, each clinician exemplifies character that aligns with the leadership culture of WFR Church. Our clinical staff have always been Christ-centered, loving, transparent, graceful, and extremely hard working. Having personnel with the right character has been the core feature of our staff; without that, the ministry would never have been successful.

The Center has also been fortunate to hire staff with extremely high integrity. At the time of this writing, there has never been anyone on staff that experienced any semblance of a moral, personal, or relational failure. Further, all staff at the center have healthy marriages, are involved parents, and are active in the local community. I have always hired staff that I've known personally. The disadvantage to this is that there has always been very little separation between my professional and personal life, which can be a challenge. The advantage is that I always knew what I was getting when I hired someone.

This process has also been the easiest way for our ministry to maintain a healthy culture. My relaxed leadership style fits well with other relaxed, highly relational people. For people who need every administrative "i" dotted and every "t" crossed, my agency would have been a nightmare. For counselors interested in a highly relational approach to mental health treatment, who are willing to deal with a few administrative tasks left undone, our ministry would feel like a dream come true. It's important to have clarity on which personality types fit well with particular church cultures and work to bring those personalities onto the team.

Theology

Theology is perhaps the most critical thing to consider when integrating a counseling agency into a church or when partnering a counseling agency with a church. While there may be small differences between Christian counselors and counselors who are Christian, ultimately, both must unequivocally see the Lord Jesus as the solution to all human maladies, mental or physical. This has been true of every counselor employed at the Christian Counseling Center of West Monroe since its inception.

The core and center of the theological premises of church-related counseling ministries and staff must be Jesus. From there, the farther we venture theologically, the less important theology becomes. I like Rupertus Meldenius's quote here, "In essentials, unity, in non-essentials, clarity, in all things, charity." So it should be for clinicians practicing inside or in partnership with churches. For a clinician to act in positive regard towards clients and colleagues related to their theological premises is healthy and appropriate, so long as they center around the Lord Jesus Christ.

Among the Tombs

In chapter 5 of Mark's Gospel, Jesus encounters a tomb dweller. This is a term I've used over the years to refer to the person in this story, a person in the midst of one of the most desperate mental health struggles imaginable. In verses 3 to 5, we learn the details of his suffering:

> This man lived in the tombs, and no one could bind him anymore, not even with a chain. For he had often been chained hand and foot, but he tore the chains apart and broke the irons on his feet. No one was strong enough to subdue him. Night and day among the tombs and in the hills he would cry out and cut himself with stones.
>
> Mark 5:3–5 (NIV)

These verses have always weighed heavily on me. I've wondered about this person's backstory. I've wondered what pain this person endured. I've wondered where his family was and what people felt about the fact that he was all alone and struggling.

Over the years, I've applied this man's story to a more modern context. I imagine someone crying out, harming themselves, all alone, feeling desperate and overwhelmed. I imagine that this man and his family had tried everything, and nothing has worked. Medicine didn't work, jail didn't work, and isolation isn't working either. His struggle has been going on for so long that everyone has given up hope.

People like this exist today. And today, they are just as desperate, they feel just as alone, and things seem just as hopeless as they did in this story. I should know, I've met many people like this. Truth be told, I was a tomb dweller nearly two decades ago. The only hope tomb dwellers have, and the only hope they need is Jesus.

Living and working among the tomb dwellers, I believe, is the next great frontier of mission work for the capital C Church universal. For churches that are willing to partner with mental health providers and work on the front lines of this struggle, great will be their reward. Yes, the cost is high living on the front lines, but the reward is even higher. And, when desperate people find hope and healing, lives are not only changed, but entire communities are changed. This is the secret to the success of the Christian Counseling Center's partnership with WFR Church, and it will be the secret to the success of any church that answers God's call to live and work among those serving hurting people in the tombs.

CHAPTER 7

Reid Temple A.M.E/ Restoration Center, Inc.

Prince George's County, Maryland

D. Fredrica Brooks-Davis, PsyD

Dr. D. Fredrica Brooks-Davis serves as the executive director of the Restoration Center, Inc., located in Prince George's County, Maryland. In 2012, Dr. Brooks-Davis began consulting in both the public and private sectors as the founder of Destiny Empowerment and Consulting Services LLC. In 2014, she began serving as the president and co-founder of the Brooks-Davis Institute for Brain Cancer Awareness. This organization was birthed from the personal experiences Dr. Brooks-Davis and her husband gained following the brain tumor diagnosis he received within the first three months of their marriage. Her beloved husband, Teddy, fought a courageous battle until his transition on July 11, 2014.

Dr. Brooks-Davis earned a bachelor of arts degree in psychology from Clark Atlanta University in Atlanta, Georgia. Upon graduation, she moved to Michigan and earned a master of arts degree in community counseling from Eastern Michigan University in Ypsilanti, Michigan. After working in the mental health field and academia, Dr. Brooks-Davis attended Regent University in Virginia Beach, Virginia, where she earned a master of arts degree and doctor of psychology degree in clinical psychology, specializing in program development and consultation. She is a psychology associate in the State of Maryland.

Dr. Brooks-Davis has published articles, presented at numerous professional conferences, and facilitated workshops and trainings in both the public and private sectors. In addition to serving the community via DECS LLC, the Brooks-Davis IBCA, and the RTRC Inc., Dr. Brooks-Davis is an Adjunct Faculty member in the Department of Psychology and Department of Counseling at Bowie State University. She is also an Adjunct Faculty member in the master of arts in Christian Care Program at Capital Seminary and Graduate School.

This chapter offers insights from a mental health professional who partnered with an African American church to provide both paraprofessional and professional counseling services to its church members and the surrounding community. The information shared in this chapter outlines the steps African American pastors, clergy members, and mental health professionals are encouraged to take when either starting a counseling ministry, establishing a counseling center, or initiating a partnership to address the mental and relational health needs of African American parishioners via the African American church. While the content of this chapter focuses on African American pastors and/or clergy members and mental health professionals interested in serving African Americans via the church, the reader will find many of the recommended steps are universally applicable.

The Historical Role of the African American Church

The African American church has a long-standing tradition of serving as a safe space for African Americans to express themselves and receive spiritual and emotional support (Billingsley, 1989; Brooks, 2008; Lincoln & Mamiya, 1990). Swanson et al. (2004) state,

> The Black church has played a significant role in the lives of African Americans in a variety of ways, including providing spiritual guidance, educational programs and services, emotional and psychological support, political advocacy, community development services, financial support, and numerous other roles. The church has also been a significant contributor to the health and well-being of its members, a role, although currently thought to be innovative, has been part of the church from the beginning (p. 79).

Despite the African American church's history of responding to the needs of church members and the surrounding community, research identifying the church as a resource for addressing the mental health needs of its members and those served in the surrounding community is limited (Mattis et al., 2007). Taylor et al. (1987) conducted an analysis of the National Survey of Black Americans data and found 82.2 percent of Black Americans report the church has helped improve the lives of Blacks, 4.9 percent maintain the church has hurt Blacks, and 12.1 percent report no difference made by the church. The research literature concerning the role the African American church has played in improving the mental and relational needs of African Americans shows there is improvement in the lives of those who view the church as a safe space, view fellow church members as family, and attend worship services on a regular basis.

As a result of the many roles the African American church has played in the community, some of the best strategies and community-based programs that have helped African Americans have been birthed in the African American church.

The Role of the African American Pastor

A recent review of the literature suggests that African Americans will seek the support of a clergy member instead of a mental health provider to address stressors impacting their psychological and emotional well-being and daily life. The trust between an African American pastor and the members of his or her church and community is noteworthy. To that end, there has been an increase in the number of studies reviewing the role African American clergy members have played in addressing the emotional and psychological needs of their parishioners (Blank, 2002; Brooks, 2008; Levin, 1986; Mattis & Jagers, 2001; Neighbors, 1985; Neighbors et al., 1998; Rubin, 1994; Taylor, 2000). At the very least, ministers are the gatekeepers for persons seeking assistance for mental and relational health care.

Step One: Building the Foundation—Trust and Respect

Trust and respect are the foundation of a healthy relationship, and this is especially true in the African American church. The shame and stigma associated with mental health issues are primary barriers that have kept many African Americans from seeking the support they need. A congregation may trust their pastor's ability to pray for them, lay hands for healing, and preach the gospel. However, that same pastor may find that members of the congregation may disagree with and challenge them when they begin talking about mental health and the importance of seeking professional counseling services.

There are certain variables that can create a welcoming audience for the discussion of integrating mental health with spirituality. For example, the pastor who historically preached that mental illness is a result of a person's sinful nature and/or a lack of faith and has recently changed his/her views may have a harder time encouraging their parishioners to embrace a new mental health ministry or partnership with a mental health agency. Conversely, a pastor who preaches that receiving a mental illness diagnosis is no different from being diagnosed with a physical illness; therefore, seeking healing from God and a trained professional is the right path to pursue is more likely to find a congregation willing to embrace the vision for a mental health ministry or partnership with a mental health professional.

As pastors, clergy members, and mental health professionals strive to be seen as leaders equipped to respond to the mental and relational health needs of the congregation and community, it would be important for them to begin by acknowledging the history of mistrust, lack of access to quality health care, and the financial barriers that have contributed to the hesitancy and resistance of many African Americans to seek mental health services (United States Department of Health and Human Services). Prior to introducing the vision for establishing a ministry or counseling center, it is important for the pastor to acknowledge and affirm the additional concerns and experiences of his/her congregants. If the pastor previously discouraged his/her congregation from seeking professional counseling services, he/she will need to share why their views have shifted and if the strategies they previously taught have merit.

Equally important is the pastor's ability to share biblical examples of persons who dealt with alcoholism, depression, infidelity, grief, promiscuity, etc. The ability to exegete the text in a way that shows God's ability to use ordinary people with challenges to do extraordinary things will be the first step in laying the foundation for a discussion on the value of establishing a ministry or counseling center that provides people with the opportunity to share their concerns with a trusted advisor who relies on the guidance of the Holy Spirit.

Trust

Are you trustworthy? You may be a pastor, clergy member, mental health professional, or church member; however, the title you hold does not mean the community or congregation you serve or wish to serve can trust you. Consider your current reputation and credibility. Are you a pastor or leader known for using the pulpit or your office to tell a member how you really feel? Are you known as someone who upholds healthy boundaries, including confidentiality? Regardless of the current position you hold in your church or community, once you have answered these questions, consider if you are the best person to lead the discussions regarding the establishment of a program, ministry, or partnership that will address the mental and/or relational health needs of the parishioners and community members.

Allow the spirit of humility to overtake you as you seek to establish trust and credibility with the gatekeepers and stakeholders. If you are a pastor, ask God to guide you as you identify potential partners within your church, faith community, and the surrounding community to help you bring the vision to fruition. Be open to who God will send. God may send those you can trust who do not look like you and may not be of your same faith tradition to establish His ministry, program, counseling center, or partnership.

Case Example: Establishing Trust

The Lord gave me the vision for establishing a center to serve the holistic needs of the African American community in 1991. In December 1998, while attending a New Year's Eve service at Reid Temple African Methodist Episcopal Church (previous location—Lanham, Maryland), the Lord revealed to me that Reverend Dr. Lee P. Washington would be the pastor to bring His vision to fruition. When the Lord revealed this to me, I was living in Ypsilanti, Michigan, completing a master's degree in community counseling, and was considering moving to the Washington, DC, metropolitan area to work for an agency devoted to children and families. I did not have any connection to Reid Temple or to Reverend Dr. Lee P. Washington.

Yet, this is where God instructed me to go. Needless to say, after graduation in May 1999, I moved from Michigan to Maryland, trusting God would open the doors to bring the vision to fruition. You see, in my case (and may I also suggest the same is true for you), the first person to establish bilateral trust with is God. God must know that He can trust you with the vision, and you must believe God will bring His vision to fruition in His time.

I joined Reid Temple in 2000, and the invitation from Reverend Dr. Lee P. Washington to partner with Reid Temple to develop a professional counseling center did not take place until 2007. Although I knew God sent me to Reid Temple and why He sent me, I did not share that information when I arrived. I served in ministry, attended church meetings, remained prayerful, and trusted God to order my steps.

Once the trust was established between Reverend Dr. Lee P. Washington and me, it was time to earn the trust of the parishioners. Although I was active in ministry and attended both Bible study and Sunday worship services regularly, it did not mean I could be trusted. How would over 11,000 members come to know me and learn more about the ministry and programs God was looking to develop at Reid Temple? The senior pastor would have to introduce me to the church and offer his stamp of approval, so to speak.

Homework:

Answer the following questions:

1. Has God given you a vision for a mental or relational health ministry or center? If you answered no, are you proceeding based on a personal desire? In either case, be sure to seek God for direction.
2. Are you aware of godly-inspired partnership opportunities between pastors or clergy members and mental health professionals?
3. Ask yourself the following question—"Am I trustworthy?" Next, write down the evidence to support your response.
4. Who are the gatekeepers and stakeholders in the church or community where you are led to serve?
5. Do you have a relationship with the person(s) you have identified in question 4? If yes, can you trust them with the vision God has either given or approved?

Suggestions to Establish Trust

1. As you share the vision, invite questions, suggestions, and constructive feedback from ministry leaders, members of the congregation and community, and mental health professionals.

2. Meet with the gatekeepers and stakeholders to discuss the vision and develop a strategy to share the vision with the parishioners.
3. Share the mission and vision statements with the leadership of the church.
4. Share how the ministry, center, or partnership you are developing will both add value to the overall ministry of the church and enhance the existing ministries in the church. For example, if your church has a marriage ministry, share how partnering with a mental health professional could enhance the ministry by offering professional marriage counseling for couples who need to learn strategies to address the challenges in their marriage.

Respect

Pastors are often the first-person parishioners who will contact when they are experiencing a challenge (Taylor et al., 2000). To that end, if you are a mental health professional looking to implement a program or ministry with a church, it is important for you to do some initial research to see if the pastor is open to collaboration. For a myriad of reasons, the pastor may not be open to collaboration, which may mean you have to consider partnering with another church. Conversely, if the pastor is open to collaborating with other professionals, it is important for you to understand the pastor's role in both the church and community so you will know the boundaries that need to be honored. When the pastor is on board, it will be easier to show respect to both the people and the institution of the church.

In addition to showing respect to the pastor, gatekeepers, and stakeholders, it is equally important to research the community you wish to serve. For example, what are the ethnic backgrounds of the parishioners, socioeconomic status, culture, religious beliefs, traditions, and views on mental and relational health? Is there implicit shame and stigma in the community related to the programs you wish to deliver, and if yes, why? This is not the time to ask yourself whether you believe or understand the hesitancy that may exist within the community you wish to serve. Remember, you are the vessel God is using to meet people where they are and, with His assistance, take them where He wants them to go. "I have planted, Apollos watered; but God gave the increase" (1 Corinthians 3:6, KJV).

Case Example: Establishing Respect

From birth to 2000, I was an active member in the Baptist denomination. Consequently, I did not know much about the history and traditions of the African Methodist Episcopal (AME) Church. To that end, when God declared Reid Temple would be the first church to manifest His vision for the ministry to which He called me, I had to read, research, and ask questions of my pastor and others who were not only familiar with the doctrines of the AME denomination but were also familiar with the history of Reid Temple. Every church, regardless of the denominational affiliation or nondenominational status, has a history, and educating yourself on the major tenets of the denomination and church you wish to serve will not only show that you respect the people and institution, but it will also provide you with the foundational information you need to conduct a needs assessment and develop appropriate and effective ministry programs.

Homework:

1. Research the demographics of the community you wish to serve. For example, if you serve an African American church, some of the members may be from Africa, the Caribbean, etc., and do not identify as African American. Consequently, you will want to do a deeper dive to make sure you know how these differences are celebrated and experienced.

2. Below are some questions to ponder:
   a. What are the lived experiences of the members of the congregation I wish to serve?
   b. How might their lived experiences influence their openness or hesitancy to seek the services I would like to offer?
   c. Are there any additional courses or supervision I will need in order to serve the church members and community in a culturally competent manner?
   d. For mental health professionals: What are some of the key traditions of the faith community that will need to be incorporated in the services I offer? For example, does the church host a service on Ash Wednesday? If yes, will I offer services on that day or close my practice in honor of the religious celebration? Would the church members want me to close, or would they want me to stay open and offer services?

Step Two: The Needs Assessment

Once trust and respect have been established, it is time to conduct a needs assessment. The needs assessment will assist you with identifying the specific needs of the congregation you wish to serve. With this information, you are able to develop a strategic plan that includes tailor-made programs.

Generally, pastors, clergy members, and gatekeepers are extremely helpful with both developing and disseminating the needs assessment (e.g., survey). Once the data is gathered, it will be important to share the information with the gatekeepers and everyone who completed the assessment. By sharing the data and requesting feedback, everyone involved feels they have contributed to the process, and trust is reinforced.

Establishing a ministry, counseling center, or partnership may be on your heart to do and while it may be inspired by God, conducting a needs assessment to learn more about the needs of the congregation and community is vital to the success of the ministry, counseling center, or partnership. The information gathered will increase the chances members will participate in the services offered. Additionally, by participating in the needs assessment, everyone involved will feel a sense of pride in the development and implementation of what can be a blessing to the congregation and community.

Case Example: Needs Assessment at Reid Temple

When developing the counseling center at Reid Temple, two African American pastors permitted me to disseminate The Personal Life Events Questionnaire (Brooks & Rawles, 2005) to their congregations. The predominately African American congregations are in Maryland (suburban) and South Carolina (rural). While the results of the pilot study were not generalizable to the African American community, the findings from the study suggest the majority of the 550 parishioners surveyed would be willing to speak with a psychologist about their life stressors, and the psychologists' faith tradition did not matter (Brooks, 2008). Additionally, the participants indicated a willingness to seek assistance from a Christian counseling center affiliated with their church. When the study was conducted, the top three services participants were interested in having the counseling center offer were Marital and Pre-Marital Counseling (#1), Abuse Counseling (#2), and Spiritual Direction and Formation (#3) (Brooks, 2008). The results from the instrument were instrumental in the development of the counseling center at Reid Temple.

Homework:

1. Identify the questions you would like to ask to learn more about the group you intend to serve. For example, if you serve young adults, it would be important to research what, if any, challenges young adults are facing now. When serving a specific group, it is also important to learn more about the specific needs of the respective group. For example, what, if any, challenges are African American young adults facing that may be different from those faced by non-African Americans? Once you have the information, move forward with designing questions that are specific to the target audience.
2. Identify individuals within the congregation and community willing to help develop the instrument, review, and disseminate the findings. These same individu-

als may be helpful in developing programs and locating resources to financially support the ministry and programs.

3. Once you have gathered the data, consider if your target audience would prefer Christian-based ministry programs, non-biblically integrated professional mental health services, or both. Refrain from using a one-size-fits-all approach. There are several Christian-based programs that may be able to address the needs of the congregation and community you serve. Partnering with mental health professionals to facilitate workshops and to conduct groups is also worth exploring.

Step Three: Implementation

Once trust, respect, the needs of the target audience, and the services and programs to respond to the needs have been identified, it will be time for implementation to begin. When developing the counseling center at Reid Temple, the services were implemented in phases. Implementing in phases provided us with the opportunity to introduce each service or program to the congregation, monitor the impact, and adjust as needed. The implementation team consisted of members of the congregation and community.

If God has led you to initiate a ministry, counseling center, or partnership with a mental health professional, He will send you the help you need. With the support of Reverend Dr. Lee P. Washington, a meeting for members of the congregation interested in using their gifts, talents, and education to assist in the development of the counseling center yielded forty volunteers who remained faithful in assisting this writer with implementing the five phases of the strategic plan from 2007 to 2013. By the time all phases were implemented, some of volunteers had become members of the counseling center's board of directors, others moved forward with accepting their call to become ministers of the gospel, some decided to return to school to pursue a degree in counseling or ministry, and others are still connected to the one-to-one lay care ministry that remains at Reid Temple but is no longer affiliated with the counseling center.

Case Example: The development of the Reid Temple Restoration Center, Inc.

During Phase One, we introduced a lay care one-to-one ministry. This consisted of a series of Christian-based groups that addressed grief/loss, divorce recovery, single parenting, and psycho-spiritual groups that assisted with spiritual formation and development. Pre-marital and marital sessions and groups were also offered. Subsequent phases involved establishing an internship and post-master's supervision program for those seeking a professional license in counseling, psychology, or social work; professional counseling services to include psychological testing; workshops; seminars; conferences; and partnerships with local hospitals, radio stations, and schools.

April 1, 2019, the counseling center, which began at Reid Temple African Methodist Episcopal Church in 2007, separated from Reid Temple and currently operates as the Restoration Center Inc. in Prince George's County, Maryland. The partnership between Reid Temple and the Restoration Center Inc. remains active, vibrant, and dynamic in the community—serving and ministering to more hurting people than ever.

Homework:

1. Once you know the needs and how you will respond, develop a one-to-three-year strategic plan.
2. Consider who will finance the costs associated with implementing a ministry, counseling center, or partnership. Will the church serve as the sole funder, cover start-up costs, or nothing at all?
3. Include the costs for having professionals on staff on a part-time, full-time, or contractual basis.
4. If you offer professional services, will you accept private pay, insurance, offer scholarships on a sliding scale, or all the above?
5. Before you launch a service or ministry, identify the organizational structure for the ministry, counseling center, or partnership. For example, Reid Temple decided at the very beginning to establish the counseling center as a 501(c) 3 not-for-profit organization. Consequently, it is important for the individuals responsible for birthing the vision to consider the pros and cons of operating as a ministry, an independent organization, and/or partnering with a mental health professional or organization.

Step Four: Establishing Partnerships

Given the influential role African American clergy members have in their parishioners' lives, mental health professionals seeking to improve the mental health and relational needs of African American clients would benefit from collaborating with African American clergy members open to establishing a relationship that fosters support, information sharing, and respect. African American pastors can share the tenants of their faith, offer tips on how to establish trust with members of the African American community, and help reduce the shame and stigma associated with mental health by referring the members of their congregation to trusted mental health professionals and incorporating mental health topics in their sermons, Bible study lessons, and workshops. Mental health providers interested in reducing the stigma of mental health in the faith community could contact African American pastors and offer to facilitate trainings on various mental health topics that speak to the challenges their parishioners are facing and offer solutions that can be incorporated in their sermons, Bible study lessons, workshops, etc.

Final Thoughts

Although additional research is needed to determine if the African American church is equipped to address the mental and relational health needs of African Americans, the existing literature suggests African Americans will speak with their pastor and/or clergy member about the life stressors they face. However, most religious leaders are not adequately trained, nor do they have the time in their busy schedules to competently address most mental health issues. Consequently, pastors and clergy members who serve an African American congregation are in a unique position to both reduce the shame and stigma associated with mental health and help improve the mental and relational health of the congregations they serve by creating programs, counseling centers, and/or partnerships with mental health professionals.

This chapter summarizes the journey a mental health professional and African American pastor traveled to establish a church-based counseling center offering both lay care ministry and professional counseling services. There are additional details that could not be covered in one chapter. Nevertheless, by answering the questions at the end of each section, the reader will be prepared to explore the possibilities of addressing the mental health and relational needs of African American parishioners and the surrounding community.

Billingsley, A. (1989, May). *The Black Church as a Social Service Institution.* Paper presented at A national Symposium for Grant Makers, Washington, DC.
Billingsley, A. (1999). *Mighty Like a River: The Black Church and Social Reform.* New York: Oxford University Press.
Blank, M. B., Mahmood, M., Fox, J. C., & Guterbock, T. (2002). Alternative mental health services: The role of the Black church in the South. *American Journal of Public Health,* 92(10), 1668–1672.
Brooks, D. F. (2008). *An Examination of Help-Seeking Behaviors of African-American Parishioners.* (Publications No. 3308671) [Doctoral dissertation, Regent University]. ProQuest Dissertations & Theses Global Publishing.
Brooks, D. F., & Rawles, P. (2005). *Personal life events questionnaire.* Virginia Beach, VA.
Caldwell, C., Chatters, L., Billingsley, A., & Taylor, R. (1995). Church-based support programs for elderly Black adults: Congregational and clergy characteristics. In M. Kimble, S. McFadden, J. Ellor, & J. Seeber (Eds.), *Handbook on Religions, Spirituality, and Aging.* (pp. 306–324). Minneapolis, MN: Fortress Press.
Levin, J. S. (1986). Roles for the Black pastor in preventive medicine. *Pastoral Psychology,* 35, 94–103.
Lincoln, C. E., & Mamiya, L. H. (1990). The Black Church in the African-American Experience. Duke University Press.
Mattis, J. S., & Jagers, R. J. (2001). A relational framework for the study of religiosity and spirituality in the lives of African Americans. *Journal of Community Psychology,* 29(5), 519–539.
Mattis, J. S., Mitchell, N., Zapata, A., Grayman, N. A., Taylor, R. J., Chatters, L.M., Neighbors, H.W. (2007). Uses of Ministerial Support by African Americans: A Focus Group Study. *American Journal of Orthopsychiatry,* 77(2), 249–258.
Neighbors, H. W. (1985). Seeking professional help for personal problems: Black Americans' use of health and mental services. *Community Mental Health Journal,* 21, 156–166.
Neighbors, H. W., Musick, M. A., & Williams, D. R. (1998). The African American minister as a source of help for serious personal crises: Bridge or barrier to mental health care? *Health Education & Behavior Special Issue: Public Health and Health Education in Faith Communities,* 25, 759–777.
Rubin, R. H., Billingsley, A. & Caldwell, C. H. (1994). The role of the Black church in working with Black adolescents. *Adolescence,* 29, 251–266.

Swanson, L., Crowther, M., Green, L., & Armstrong. (2004). African Americans, faith and health disparities. *African American Research Perspectives*, 10(1), 79–88.
Taylor, R. J., Ellison, C. G., Chatters, L. M., Levin, J. S., & Lincoln, K. D. (2000). Mental health services in faith communities: The role of clergy in the black church. *Social Work*, 45, 73–97.
Taylor, R. J., Thornton, M. C., & Chatters, L. M. (1987) Black Americans' perceptions of the socio-historical role of the church. *Journal of Black Studies*, 18, 123–138.
United States Department of Health and Human Services. (2001). *Mental health: Culture, Race, and Ethnicity. A Supplement to Mental Health: A Report of the Surgeon General.* https://www.ncbi.nlm.nih.gov/books/NBK44243/

CHAPTER 8

Hill City Counseling Center

Lynchburg, Virginia

**Rev. David Mikkelson, MDiv, PhD,
and Suzanne Mikkelson, PhD**

David P. Mikkelson, PhD, MDiv, LMFT, grew up in a Marine Corps family and later served as a Marine Corps artillery officer for ten years and, after completing seminary, as an army chaplain for eighteen years. David was fortunate to be on the original team of six chaplains at Fort Bragg, North Carolina, who started the Chapel Next ministry paradigm in 1996 that later spread worldwide throughout the army. David was later selected to establish a new pastoral counseling training center at Fort Bragg, North Carolina, in 2008. He was responsible to identify, renovate, and furnish a suitable facility, establish a partnership with a local university counseling program, and create all operational procedures and standards for the center. When he retired from the army five years later, he had established a lasting program that was providing over 500 hours per month of free pastoral counseling to the military community and had trained fifty chaplains and civilian interns. As an ordained and experienced minister and licensed marriage and family therapist and clinical supervisor, David sees tremendous opportunity for the gospel to intersect quality mental health care and lead to lasting healing. He earned an MDiv from Reformed Theological Seminary (1995), an MS in counseling psychology from Tarleton State University (2002), and a PhD in counselor education and supervision from Regent University (2015).

Suzanne Mikkelson, PhD, LMFT, grew up in North Carolina and married David upon their graduation from Duke University. She is a former military spouse with nearly thirty years of Christian counseling experience with military members and their families, civilians, as well as with church communities. She is a licensed marriage and family therapist, an American Association for Marriage and Family Therapy (AAMFT) approved supervisor, and an approved consultant and trainer with Eye Movement Desensitization Reprocessing International Association (EMDRIA). Her clinical specialties include trauma, mood disorders, adultery recovery, marital issues, and parenting. As a pastor's wife, she has also experienced the tremendous potential for healing and gospel impact when mental health care practitioners partner with local churches. For two years, Suzanne led a clinical training program for a large non-profit practice where she cultivated a passion for supervising and mentoring developing clinicians. She directed and redesigned the Marriage and Family Counseling graduate program at Liberty University, where she taught for three years before joining David in establishing Hill City Counseling & Consulting. Her previous experience helped her design the current counseling facility as well as establish effective procedures and clinical standards for the complex team of licensed clinicians, residents, and graduate interns. Suzanne earned an MA in marriage and family therapy from Reformed Theological Seminary (1995) and a PhD in counselor education and supervision from Regent University (2015).

Hill City Counseling: A Model of Flexible Services and Community Connection

The ministry model of Hill City Counseling and Consulting LLC in Lynchburg, Virginia (hereafter HCCC), is a practical example of a private counseling practice intentionally connecting with local churches to provide a flexible, faith-friendly counseling resource to the entire community. The ministry of HCCC is a dynamic integration of quality yet affordable clinical care, a biblically-based extension of local church ministry, and focused training and mentoring of the next generation of Christian counselors.

Hopefully, this chapter inspires pastors and other church leaders to pursue creative and effective ways to care for their parishioners while motivating mental health professionals to partner with local churches and clinicians in training to impact their communities with creative, compassionate Christian care. Both churches and mental health professionals can use elements of this model to improve the ministry of local churches and meet the mental health needs of their community.

The primary hallmark of HCCC's approach is a theological distinctive of counseling that is not only integrated with a Christian worldview and guided by biblical teaching but views counseling as an extension of local church ministry. This leads to a passionate commitment to partner with local churches to expand their ministry. The second distinctive of HCCC is a professional one that intentionally and creatively integrates multiple levels of counselors—interns, provisionally licensed residents, and licensed providers—into one comprehensive practice strategy. This directly influences our training methods and results in significant benefits for clients, clinicians, supervisors, churches, the practice, and universities that train counselors. The third distinctive is a financial approach that emphasizes key biblical values of generosity, mutual care, and reduction of greed by setting fees and creating win-win business agreements with staff, which fosters high clinician satisfaction and a stellar community reputation.

Hill City Counseling is a privately owned, for-profit counseling center that operates independently from any local church. It is owned and led by a married couple, both of whom have a PhD in counselor education and supervision, are licensed marriage and family therapists, and are approved supervisors by the American Association for Marriage and Family Therapy (AAMFT). Both have been Christ-followers for nearly four decades, were trained as a pastor (David) and a marriage and family therapist (Suzanne) in a conservative seminary, and have dedicated most of their adult lives to full-time pastoral and helping ministry. While this is an unusual combination of credentials and experiences in one couple, it is not a requirement for the model's success. Two or more licensed mental health professionals, one of whom is a credentialed clinical supervisor, could partner to lead a similar counseling center in many communities across the country.

The Theological Foundation for Counseling

Our foundational belief is that the ministry of providing wise counsel for successful living is an important component of every local church. We view counseling as the personalized application of biblical truth and sound psychological interventions to the daily lives of real people. *In short, the ministry of counseling is where the truth, demands, and invitations of Scripture intersect the wounds, obstacles, and dreams of ordinary people.* Counseling should never be in competition with preaching or any of the other foundational functions of the local church but rather supports and expands evangelism, discipleship, and the journey of sanctification.

Proclaiming biblical truth through teaching and preaching is an essential function of every local church. The sermon is designed to appeal to the entire demographic spectrum of people in the audience: young, old, rich, poor, financially secure, financially struggling, healthy, sick, married, single, divorced, and many others. Effective preaching delivers the good news of God's salvation and empowered living and applies it in an efficient way to fifty or 5,000 people at one time, with the purpose of propelling people into a deepening personal encounter with the relational God of the Bible. In an ideal world, the truth of God's Word directs people to repent and live godly lives. However, one can easily see that we don't live in that world, and many people need time, support, and hard relational work to reflect the character and image of Jesus (Romans 8.29) in the daily reality of their fallen world and painful story.

Godly counseling is the perfect complement to biblical preaching. Counseling is not an efficient ministry in terms of an economy of scale, as a busy counselor will rarely engage even forty people in an entire week, perhaps only half that many. Counseling benefits from good preaching as the comfortable are afflicted, and the afflicted are comforted. We are convinced that good preaching produces more counseling, not less, as lives are stirred to make difficult changes towards godly living, and those who are hurting in private ways are inspired to seek help. The realities of sin within us and around us make life change a difficult process, and most people need far more than a thirty-minute sermon each week to make it happen. They need a safe place to struggle, to explore, to confess, to protest, and to work through the troubling issues in their life. The ministry of counseling is one place where this deep application of Scriptural truth happens, regardless of whether the counselor is an informally trained lay person, a pastor, or a professionally trained counselor.

Biblically, the process of reshaping one's life to conform to the pattern and image of Jesus is called sanctification. Non-Christians also need counseling for life's challenges, even if they are currently just focused on self-improvement. When unbelievers come to believers for counseling, the Christian counselor has an incredible opportunity to enter the sacred space of searching, woundedness, fear, and struggle with the unbeliever in a manner that is rarely achieved in evangelism-based relationships or even friendships. The clinical relationship itself provides sanctified space for life-changing spiritual and emotional exploration.

How Does the Bible Present Counseling?

Counseling is so much more than the five-cent advice-giving at Lucy's counseling window as she tries to tell Charlie Brown how to live. There are at least six different biblical words used to describe the ministry of counseling, with five coinciding in 1 Thessalonians 5:14 (NIV): "And we urge you, brothers and sisters, warn those who are idle and disruptive, encourage the disheartened, help the weak, be patient with everyone." The sixth, shepherding, comes from multiple passages. An essential part of counseling at HCCC is the understanding of how the Bible commissions the ministry of counseling. These six concepts will not only reveal the incredible flexibility and usefulness of the ministry of counseling but will explain our approach.

Parakaleo

Paul models one aspect of counseling to his readers with the very first word of the verse in the original language, and it is the word he chooses fifty times elsewhere to describe a helping or counseling relationship. The Greek word *parakaleo* literally means to call to one's side, often in order to provide help in some way, as the context demands. In 1 Corinthians 16:12, Paul "urged" or "encouraged" Apollos to visit the believers in

Corinth. In Ephesians 6:22, Paul realizes that the Ephesians are unaware of Paul's circumstances and likely feeling unsettled, worried, or concerned, and so he sent Tychicus to "encourage" or "comfort" them with accurate information. Paul sent Timothy to strengthen and "encourage" the Thessalonians in their faith (1Thessalonians 3:2). In each of these cases, we notice the personal interaction that takes place to deliver the encouragement or to urge a certain course of action.

Jesus chose the noun form of the word, a paraclete, to describe the Holy Spirit in John 14:16. The Spirit serves as a helper, advocate, and comforter who teaches us and reminds us of the truth Jesus taught. Later in the same conversation in John 16:7, Jesus said that the paraclete would also convict the world concerning sin and righteousness and judgment, and in verse thirteen, he will guide us into truth and will glorify the Son, always acting in concert with the Father and the Son. In a "coming alongside" ministry, we must be ready to urge, encourage, comfort, advocate, and guide others in their moments of need. The word not only suggests what we do in a counseling ministry, but it also suggests how we relate to hurting people in need—we come alongside them as one might meet and join a hiker on a long journey, sharing the trail and its hardships as stories are explored and progress celebrated and encouragements given. Already we are seeing the broad scope of counseling, and all this from just one word.

Noutheteo

A second biblical word used to describe the ministry of counseling is the verb *noutheteo*, from which we get the adjective "nouthetic" counseling. This word is used eight times in the New Testament and means to warn or advise of coming danger, to admonish, to correct by making direct suggestions. This is a more directive form of relational interaction that is sometimes warranted when helping people. In Paul's farewell speech in Acts 20:31, Paul tells church leaders to be on guard for themselves and for their entire flocks because savage wolves and false teachers will arise. They must shepherd the church of God, which he purchased with his own blood, and Paul concludes by reminding them that for three years, he did not cease to "admonish" or "warn" them of this danger. In this context, it seems that Paul is more pleading with his readers than confronting them.

In Romans 15:14, Paul expresses his confidence that the Roman church is full of people who are enabled to "admonish" or "instruct" one another, a context that suggests more the sense of correction than it does simply adding new information by teaching. The contexts of 1 Corinthians 4:14, Colossians 1:28, and 2 Thessalonians 3:15 all suggest this stronger response of admonishing or warning, a kind of loving but firm correction to do what they already know to do. A ministry of counseling sometimes calls for clearly stated warnings, reminders, or corrections in order to point people to godly living.

Paramutheomai

The ministry of helping others is also described by the word *paramutheomai,* which is also translated as "encourage" and "comfort," though often in the context of grief. In 1 Thessalonians 2:11–12, Paul uses three descriptors of good ministry conducted by himself and his colleagues: they engaged in exhorting (parakaleo), encouraging (*paramutheomai*), and imploring (marturomai) others, like a father would his children. We see in John 11:19 and 11:31 that, after the death of their brother Lazarus, many people came to "console" or "comfort" Mary and Martha in their grief. This word clearly suggests a gentle and compassionate approach when helping hurting people.

Antechomai

The fourth biblical word in 1 Thessalonians 5:14 is *antechomai,* a very straightforward word that means to physically help or firmly support someone or be devoted to someone (Matthew 6:24) in a practical way that is appropriate for the situation. In the church, deacons often oversee a variety of practical ways to help people in need (Acts 6:1–4). In a professional helping sense, social workers in particular often engage in this very important practical work of helping people in need, though all professional helpers should be aware of the practical needs of people they counsel.

Makrothumeo

The fifth counseling concept we see in this verse is *makrothumeo,* which means "to be patient with" or "to wait patiently." It is a word that suggests self-restraint and non-retaliation in the face of provocation and is often associated with mercy and hope. Paul uses this word to describe the persistent patience of love in 1 Corinthians 13:4. Sometimes the counselor is called upon to tolerate slow change in others and to wait patiently for the process of change. Jesus used this word in Matthew 18:26b (NASB), where the man who owed the king a clearly unpayable debt of 10,000 talents fell before him and said, "Have patience with me [all] and I will repay you everything" (the same request is made in verse 29). The man's promise may have been genuine, but vast amounts of patience would be needed for him to repay that enormous debt.

In Hebrews 6:12 and 6:15, the author of Hebrews is praising the readers for their ministry to the saints and urges them to keep doing it with diligence to the very end as others have done before, always showing faith and "patience." Abraham is cited as an example of one who believed God's promises and "waited patiently" to obtain the promise. In James 5:7–10, James used *makrothumeo* four times in his discussion about patience, twice as an imperative to start verses 7 and 8, to describe the attitude of the farmer in verse 7, and to represent emotional calm in the face of provocation or misfortune in verse 10. Peter also uses this word in 2 Peter 3:9, where he says the Lord is not slow in keeping His promise, as some understand slowness. Instead, He is "patient" with you, not wanting anyone to perish but everyone to come to repentance. Most of us know people with whom we have shared the gospel and encouraged to follow Jesus, but for decades, they have not, yet God remains patient with them, granting them more days to repent. We encourage those who help others to show more of this character.

Poimen, Gedeon

The sixth biblical term that guides how we should approach the task of helping others is shepherd, in both noun (*poimen*) and verb (*gedeon*) forms. Shepherding is a vocation as old as the first family on earth, as Abel is said to have been a keeper of sheep (Genesis 4:2). The patriarchs were all shepherds, as well as Lot, Moses, David, and several prophets, including Jeremiah and Amos. The important roles of the shepherd would have been well known by everyone in Israel. Sheep were the primary farm animal, as they thrived in the dry climate and rocky topography of Palestine.

Shepherding is not just a metaphor for people caring for one another, but the shepherd is one of the primary images God uses to help His people understand His relationship to them as well. Shepherds care for sheep and protect them; they ensure the sheep have food and water, moving them around as needed as the shepherd applies information the sheep do not possess. He sheers them at the appropriate time, helps them during the birth of lambs, and protects them from predators, human thieves, and poisonous plants or water. Caring, guiding, and protecting are activities we generally welcome from God, and they often apply in the ministry of counseling as well.

Being scattered on the hills and vulnerable to predators, like sheep without a shepherd, is a frequent metaphor of chaos and danger in Israel. Jesus echoes this in Matthew 9:36 and specifically says they were harassed and helpless, unable to defend themselves. Jesus mentions sheep on several occasions: a man will leave ninety-nine sheep to search for and rescue the one lost sheep and rejoice over it (Matthew chapter 18, Luke chapter 15).

In the end times, God will separate the people like a shepherd separates the sheep from the goats. God sent the angelic host to announce the arrival of the King of Heaven to shepherds, and when Jesus restores Peter in John chapter 21, He commissions him to feed and take care of Jesus' followers, affectionately described as sheep.

Jesus' longest conversation about sheep is in the Gospel of John, where He says, "I am the Good Shepherd" (John 10:11a). What does it mean to be a good shepherd? They know His voice, and they trust Him (John 10:3b–4). He leads them. He knows them (verse 14). He calls them actively seeking. He lays down His life for the sheep (verse 11). He does not turn and run when things get hard or dangerous. We believe such a view of spiritual leadership, pastoral care, and relational perseverance can apply to counselors as much as to church leaders within the context of appropriate counseling ethics.

Lessons for Counselors

This brief review clearly shows that a biblical view of counseling involves so much more than just giving wise advice or urging them to do a better job of obeying Bible teaching. Those who would claim to counsel Christianly must develop a wide spectrum of relationship skills in order to offer hurting and confused people what each of them needs most, whether it is more accurate beliefs, changed behavior, new values, a different interpretation, revised priorities, healthier attitudes, comfort or healing from wounds, or fresh desires. These actions require not just correct biblical information to share with the counselee, but counseling Christianly calls for a relationship of wisdom, trust, caring, honesty, patience, and commitment with a strong dependence on the Holy Spirit in the process.

We see each local church engaging in a spectrum of ministry to support the change process: preaching the application of God's word, putting peoples' beliefs, desires, and emotions into song through worship, sharing the good news of salvation through evangelism, combining teaching, discussion, prayer, and accountability in discipleship, and communing together in God-honoring fellowship. Most of these foundational church functions are conducted in groups, both large and small, while evangelism is generally done one-on-one. The effective church will develop wise and intentional strategies, train leaders, and provide resources for each of these ministries through which people increasingly mature their faith in every context of life (Ephesians 4:29). We believe the ministry of counseling is also a foundational element of church ministry to provide care to hurting people and support the process of life change into the image of Jesus (Romans 8:29). The key question is not whether a counseling ministry is needed but how it will be delivered.

Intentional Partnership with Local Churches

Sometimes smaller churches do not have the resources of space, time, money, or trained people to provide a robust ministry of counseling or discipleship. In most cases, the solo pastor can only dedicate a handful of hours to counseling amidst so many other responsibilities. Even in larger churches with multiple pastors, the need for counseling often exceeds what the staff can provide. A common and effective option in these situations is to connect with a trusted counseling resource in the community that can provide a counseling ministry across multiple congregations and to the community at large. Sometimes these counseling practices or centers fall under the oversight of a specific church, but more often, they operate as a for-profit business or separate non-profit entity. The legal structure may differ, but the goal in each case would be to provide biblically-based counsel to a wide spectrum of people from many congregations by appropriately trained counselors.

HCCC made a commitment from the very beginning to build relationships with local pastors. For decades some pastors have far too easily dismissed the ministry of counseling as secularized nonsense to be avoided (or worse, as antagonistic to faith), while some counselors have criticized pastors for being long on biblical truth but short on compassionate care and understanding for struggling people, especially those suffering from mental health issues.

We believe this ministry civil war reflects sinful pride and judgmentalism, deprives hurting people of effective care, and is heartbreaking to God. No one person or position in the church can do it all; there are many gifts, but the same Lord has distributed them and expects them to work together (1 Corinthians 12:4–6). Our desire to multiply ministry led us to meet with pastors to explore their ministry needs, listen to their theological values and commitments, and discuss practical arrangements that would work best for them. One of the most important elements of an effective church-counseling practice partnership is trust, an invaluable commodity built over time. We taught months-long classes on helping skills in two large churches as a way to help build the ministries they already provided and to let them meet us, hear us, watch us, and build confidence that we would provide quality care to their members. This volunteer time was both an expression of our spiritual gifts, passion, and professional experience over the years and an effort to build trust and accountability with church leaders.

Out of these relationships emerged different kinds of church partnerships. Three churches refer their members to HCCC, and we prioritize their referrals as much as possible. Except in extreme hardship cases, we urge churches to have their members pay $20 per session as a personal investment in the process, while church pays the remainder of the fee. Two churches work on an invoice system where we bill them at the end of the month for all sessions we have provided to their members, while one church chooses to pay for ten sessions at a time up front. Two other partner churches do not provide financial assistance but simply refer members to us when they believe we are the best resource to help. In all cases, if the client has insurance and is seeing a licensed counselor who can assign an appropriate diagnosis, we try to use that insurance in order to stretch valuable church funds.

These creative and customized church partnerships have resulted in a win for all parties: the churches are much better able to meet the counseling needs of more members than they could alone. Busy pastors have a trusted referral resource when counseling demands exceed their capacity. The church member/counseling client benefits by having access to quality counseling at an affordable cost, and they can access that counseling without being seen at the church office or sharing their story with people with whom they have a dual relationship. Pastors, missionaries, and church leaders also have a safe place to receive their own counseling without concern for confidentiality or stigma. The counselors benefit by living out their commitment to help local churches expand their ministry of care and counsel. Finally, the counseling practice benefits by having multiple trusted referral sources that provide a consistent flow of new clients.

The Multi-Level Staff

The second distinctive of HCCC is the multi-level staff comprised of licensed mental health professionals who accept insurance, residents in counseling licensed by the state board who have completed their graduate degrees and are working under supervision towards full licensure, and graduate interns who are in the latter stages of their graduate training program. At each professional level, about half of the staff is a licensed professional counselor or training to be an LPC, and the other half is a marriage and family therapist or training to be an MFT. This has proven to be a very appropriate ratio and combination of skills to meet the counseling requests.

A Commitment to Train and Disciple

The leaders at HCCC are both AAMFT-approved supervisors and Virginia Counseling Board-approved supervisors with a major commitment to train the next generation of Christian counselors to serve in churches, private practice, or the mission field. For us, it is a matter of calling and a source of great joy to coach, mentor, and encourage developing professionals as a service to God and His church. We were both shaped by tremendous supervisors who, in addition to ensuring we learned important clinical skills, invested in our character development and leadership skills that refined us as clinicians, supervisors, and practice leaders. Our commitment now is to pay it forward and similarly invest in the holistic development of future counselors and marriage and family therapists. Our current team has five licensed professionals: two licensed professional counselors, two licensed marriage and family therapists, and one dual-licensed in both disciplines. Our goal is to have about six licensed providers, eight residents, and two interns, the maximum staff size for our eleven-office facility; we believe it is also the best ratio for the counseling requests we receive and the level of fees that clients want to pay.

The multi-level staff is the perfect setting for counselor training as staff at all three levels regularly interact and conduct co-therapy. We create a strong team environment that values interns as much as licensed clinicians and the principles of teamwork, loyalty, integrity, and a commitment to mutual success that permeates the practice. Social interaction outside the office, while never required of staff, is regularly embraced as a fun way to laugh, reduce stress, and build relationships outside the clinical environment, which results in increased mutual care. Inside the building, most offices do not have desks, and many clinicians do their administrative work in the team room, where peer interaction, support, and the exchange of ideas result in valuable learning from one another.

Co-therapy

In addition to team values, relationship building, and intentional office geography, the clinical practice of co-therapy is a major training strategy. While co-therapy seems rare in LPC circles, it is a common component of training for marriage and family therapists, and it is used across the staff at HCCC. Licensed clinicians and residents are expected to conduct about 20 percent of their sessions in a co-therapy setting with a variety of fellow staff. For interns, the ratio begins at 100 percent as practicum students are only allowed to work alongside others as they learn both the logistics of client management and valuable clinical skills. After several weeks of low-pressure transition, practicum students are cleared to be lead therapists, but only with a co-therapist on the case. Eventually, interns are cleared to conduct over half their cases solo.

Co-therapy is simple to implement in a setting where all clinicians can see each other's schedules, with "open" time slots alerting schedulers to perhaps add a new client and also alerting fellow clinicians of the availability for co-therapy. While some same-gender co-therapy is done, most co-therapy is male and female clinicians pairing up to meet with a couple or family. The lead therapist is responsible for the case, writes all notes, and is paid as though they were working solo, while the co-therapist receives direct contact hour towards graduation or licensure. Although licensed clinicians only occasionally serve as co-therapists, they work regularly with residents and interns in both a learning and mentoring role.

The benefits of co-therapy are both numerous and significant. Clients benefit by having two clinicians for the price of one to two perspectives, varied training backgrounds, and increased experience applied to their case. For most couples, co-therapy also balances the room with female and male perspectives. Clients also benefit by the valuable unseen (to them) clinician conversations between sessions that help refine treatment plans and multiply interventions.

Clinicians also benefit greatly by having a partner in the room, helping them directly with planned interventions and spontaneous support, processing tough sessions afterwards, and providing key treatment input between sessions. Additionally, the co-therapist is free to focus more on relationship processes throughout the room when he/she is not responsible to carry the main conversation and benefits by gaining more hours towards graduation and licensure. The only real challenge in the co-therapy process is schedule coordination so that both therapists stay on the case for the duration of care.

On-site Supervision

We believe the training value and level of client care are both enhanced by providing on-site supervision. The three supervisors on the team can supervise through co-therapy, live observation of any room through our closed-circuit high-resolution video recording system, and weekly supervision sessions that regularly include video review. We have found over the course of many years of supervision that less than 1 percent of clients refuse to be video-taped (approval is included in our informed consent) for the purpose of improved quality of supervision, especially when they learn that the system is physically closed from the internet and sessions are automatically deleted after fifteen days. Rooms used by residents and interns have cameras that run all day and pose no interruption to the counseling process; they are hard-wired through the walls and ceilings to a central recorder under lock and key with sophisticated electronic security measures.[24]

We have also realized the immense value of simply being accessible to supervisees for that unplanned encounter that begins with, "Hey, Dr. Mikkelson, do you have a minute?" Such interactions, while brief, help supervisees feel supported in tough situations. Trainees are also offered supervision in a group format two times per month, which encourages clinical presentations, group feedback, and provides intentional time for group instruction in models, interventions, or theological integration.

Appropriate Level of Care

A final benefit of the multi-level staff is the flexibility the practice maintains to assign cases to the appropriate level of clinical care. A brief phone intake gathers sufficient information (nature, longevity, and severity of the main issue, previous counseling, and diagnoses, along with the client's insurance and financial resources) for the practice to assign the case to the appropriate level of clinician from the outset. Less complex and shorter-term issues can be handled by graduate interns and newer residents, while more difficult or longer-term cases can be assigned to licensed staff or more experienced residents. This allows for a more efficient use of staff resources and reduces frustration of getting cases assigned that may be inap-

24 https://www.missionfrontiers.org/issue/article/

propriate or inefficient for the level of staff. Of course, client autonomy is always observed, and sometimes, clients will wait to see a specific clinician if he/she is not currently available.

Financial Approach

The third and final strength of HCCC's model is a financial approach that emphasizes the biblical values of generosity, mutual care, and reduction of greed. While church staff are often salaried and can offer counseling free of charge, counseling professionals earn their living by charging fees. In Americanized capitalism, business owners often pursue any and every means to maximize profit for themselves or their shareholders, with a persistent desire to best the competition. When it comes to living our Christian values in the ministry of helping people, we choose intentionally not to think of our profession as winning over anyone else. Our values drive a deliberate approach to setting fees and business agreements with staff that makes counseling highly accessible to clients and leads to high satisfaction among clinicians. We consistently have a waiting list of clients and often refer people to other practices that are Christ-honoring, effective, and prosperous. The real "win" in our profession would be if every person in our community who needed mental health care were able to receive it.

At HCCC, our financial goals are to earn a reasonable income for the owners commensurate with the risks of significant financial investments in buildings, training, and equipment; maximize counseling accessibility to the vast majority of our community regardless of any demographic descriptor; and to help aspiring clinicians achieve a living wage during their years of professional development that are often financially quite lean. While forces of profitability always search for higher revenue and lower expenses, HCCC leaders strive to push back against this constant increase in profit; just because we could charge more does not mean we should charge more. Instead, focusing on accessibility for clients, community reputation for fairness, and clinician well-being are more ways in which counseling Christianly takes on practical meaning.

While the licensed staff charge rates that are competitive with the local community, most of their clients pay with insurance. The direct pay costs for residents are only about one-third as much as licensed clinicians, or just slightly more than a typical insurance co-pay. Clients pay only $20 per session to see a graduate intern; this fee simply covers HCCC overhead costs, including supervision that interns receive for free. Since residents and interns often cannot bill directly for services due to state regulations, clients simply pay HCCC for the services provided, and the residents are compensated by the practice as independent contractors. The three-tiered rate system and easy access without insurance make counseling accessible by nearly anyone in the community.

This multi-tiered system also keeps expenses lower for our local partner churches, whose cost ranges from $0 to $75 per session based on the credentials of the counselor, with an average cost of about $40 (which is probably less than the cost of hiring a trained staff member to provide the same service). Each church has an internal process to ensure they approve each member who comes to HCCC for counseling, and a confidential invoice process ensures that only a few people know the identity of the clients, likely far fewer who would know if the member came to the church office for care.

In our case, residents receive about 70 percent of the revenue they generate, helping them to earn a reasonable income while going through their months of residency preceding full licensure. Licensed clinicians not only receive a generous split with the practice, but there is a cap on the fees they pay to the practice each month, regardless of their computed percentage. In other words, once their revenue has generated a specified amount for the practice, the clinician keeps 100 percent of revenue earned above that amount. This arrangement enables clinicians to increase their earnings to over 80 percent of total revenue while the amount retained by owners is fixed to help prevent potential profit creep.

Conclusion

We have endeavored to show how this model strongly supports local churches, clients have multiple choices of levels of care and affordable fees, future counselors at multiple levels are effectively trained, and residents earn a good income. By every account, the model has been a resounding success: church partnerships have been strengthened and expanded, the counseling team grew exponentially, and the number of clients seeking care at HCCC continues to exceed capacity.

The only "negative" to this model is the extra work required by the practice owner/managers who must manage the staff changes as interns graduate and residents achieve licensure and either join the licensed team or move on to other settings.

The model requires an unwavering commitment at HCCC to place church partnership, client care, and the training of future Christian helpers above revenue—a strategy that is rewarding in many ways other than the bottom line. We hope that what we have shared about the HCCC model that God developed in us over several decades will inspire you as a pastor, church leader, professional clinician, supervisor, or counselor in training to seek creative ways to partner with others in your community to build effective kingdom care.

CHAPTER 9

Anchor of Hope Counseling Center, King of Kings Ministries

Jerusalem and Tel Aviv, Israel

Katherine Snyder, PhD

Dr. Katherine Snyder is passionate about establishing mental health resources for believers in Israel. There are a very limited number of biblically trained counselors serving the local body of believers in the land. This deprivation led Dr. Snyder to establish Anchor of Hope Counseling Center, Israel, in conjunction with King of Kings Community, Jerusalem, in 2013. This long-standing vision to develop a counseling and resources center came to fruition when King of Kings congregation purchased a former pornography shop across from their sanctuary and dedicated it for God's purposes.

Anchor of Hope Counseling and Resource Center currently has branches in Jerusalem and Tel Aviv, serving believers from all over the land. The center also offers ongoing seminars in mental health training for counselors, lay counselors, and ministry leaders, as well as a thirty-week biblical counseling course. Anchor of Hope is the only ministry in the land of Israel offering believers a twelve-step support group for men struggling with pornography.

Dr. Snyder is a licensed marriage and family therapist ministering to the broken-hearted since 2005. Her involvement in the Mental Health arena includes serving as chaplain in the Spiritual Ministry Department of the National Institutes of Health, Bethesda, Maryland, assessment supervisor at the Psychiatric Institute of Washington, DC, and as an employee assistance consultant in the United States Federal Government.

Dr. Snyder holds a master's in education from the University of Pennsylvania and is trained in both theology and psychology with a master's in theology and a PhD in marital and family therapy from Fuller Theological Seminary.

Dr. Snyder immigrated to Israel in 1982 and holds dual Israeli and American citizenship. She is an avid watercolorist and enjoys creative writing, and her most loved sport is swimming.

Anchor of Hope Counseling and Resource Center

Anchor of Hope Counseling and Resource Center was established in 2013 in a former pornography shop in the heart of Jerusalem. This shop was directly across from the sanctuary of King of Kings congregation, which is located in a downtown mall. At that point in time, I had finished my doctoral training at Fuller Seminary and was ready to return to Israel after a fourteen-year hiatus. I contacted the pastor, Wayne Hilsden, a long-time friend, who knew of my vision to initiate a biblically-based counseling center in Israel for believers. He realized the mental health services for believers were scarce and the need great. Once the shop was renovated, dedicated, and blessed, we began to serve. What was once a gateway for demonic bondage became a portal for redemption and healing!

King of Kings Community was founded by Pastor Hilsden in the 1980s. He took a step of faith in 2013 by pioneering Anchor of Hope Counseling Center as there was no other congregation in the land of Israel with this type of ministry. Pastor Hilsden's successor, Pastor Chad Holland, took the vision a step further and developed a cooperative network of autonomous congregations. This allows the resource of Anchor of Hope to be a conduit of support for several ministries and congregations across the land. There are only 15,000 messianic Jews in Israel (Jews who believe in Jesus as the Messiah), and this was our targeted population along with King of Kings congregation members with ex-patriots working and studying in the land and Israeli Arabs.

Jewish people returned to their homeland after the War of Independence in 1948 from all over the world—creating an extremely diverse and multicultural nation. Many Israeli congregations include Hebrew, English, and Russian speakers. At the inception of our Center, psychology was just newly accepted by local leaders as congregations emerged from their early formation, which focused mainly on survival. The constant possibility of war and the vicarious grief of terror attacks created and perpetuated everyday struggles, in addition to other typical mental and relational concerns.

Many pastors found themselves overextended due to embracing multiple roles and were constrained by limited financial and human resources. Some leaders began to maturely and humbly realize that they could not meet all the counseling demands of their congregants. But who was there to turn to? There were few trained biblically-based counselors. People needed competent, compassionate, and caring help. This combination of factors comprised the challenging situation in which Anchor of Hope Counseling Center was birthed and aspired to infuse hope and healing.

From the onset, the gifted executive leadership team at King of Kings ensured spiritual covering for our Center and has been a rich source of experiential wisdom. Furthermore, the leadership is well-respected throughout Israel, and this enables other congregational leaders and counselees to feel safe utilizing our therapeutic services. Although it is our goal to become financially solvent, the congregation at this time provides our financial support. This allows us to be donation-based instead of fee-oriented, as many believers in Israel can not afford counseling. As a team at Anchor of Hope, we know we do not stand alone but are part of a supportive and caring community that values and encourages our ministry.

Our mission at the Center is to encourage and support healing and restoration through godly counsel and equip and train lay counselors throughout the land, thereby establishing a safety net of counselors in local congregations. Under the covering of King of Kings Ministries, we are able to be a resource for the entire body in the land.

Perspective of the Pastors

The benefit of a congregational counseling center is evident in the perspective of the executive team, as the staff at Anchor of Hope is considered an extension of their pastoral care. Senior Pastor Chad Holland writes:

> The King of Kings Family of Ministries, including all of our connected congregational locations and leaders, are very grateful for the Anchor of Hope Counseling Center. As pastors, we do a variety of things and carry diversified responsibilities. While most pastors are able to give biblical counsel in life issues at an introductory level, there are many cases that need ongoing and advanced level interaction. The Anchor of Hope Counseling Center is our go to partner when we as pastors have taken our members as far as we can. Dr. Katherine and her team of trained counselors are able to partner with pastors and leaders from all of Israel to help congregants become spiritually whole and healthy. We consider Anchor of Hope a vital part

> of our leadership team and how we can better serve our members.

Pastor Daniel Geppert of King of Kings, Herzliya, underscores this and adds:

> We at King of Kings Ministries count it a blessing to have a counseling center within our family of ministries. Very frequently, our team of pastors that are part of our extensive network of congregations refer people to Anchor of Hope to find help and support through counseling sessions, and its accountability groups. However, the help of our counseling center goes beyond helping with the load of needed counseling. With its expertise and experience, the trained staff of Anchor of Hope is only a phone call away for our pastoral team if we seek advice or a second opinion as we help our congregants through their struggles. The counseling center team is well trained and always at the cutting edge of recent developments in counseling. Anchor of Hope also provides short and long-term counseling courses for pastors, leaders, and for every believer who is interested in helping others. As these courses touch very different topics, pastors and lay counselors have the opportunity to continue to grow and sharpen their skills, which helps multiply the effectiveness of the counseling center. We appreciate, and cannot imagine doing without the tremendous work of the Anchor of Hope Counseling Center.

Pastor Ray Ramirez continues:

> As pastors and lay leaders in ministry, at times, we can face situations where a member of the community is experiencing issues that are impacting their mental health, and we can feel inadequate or even unable to assist them. At this point, leaders can be left with limited options; some may choose the approach to say 'I have done what I can' and simply encourage the person in their struggle, or even begin to avoid the individual in order to distance themselves from the situation. Although the heart of most leaders is to see their congregations living in the freedom and health of life in the Messiah, neither of the approaches I have presented will ultimately help struggling individuals enter into that reality.
>
> As a pastor and ministry leader, I can say with confidence that having a counseling center as part of our wider family of ministries has provided me with the following:
>
> - Ongoing training on current mental health and societal issues facing the people in our community and access to valuable resources and tools to help address these issues when we encounter them as leaders. This training is also very helpful in the preparation of lay leaders to assist more effectively in various areas of ministry.

- Confidence that I am not alone when faced with a challenging situation. Knowing that there are trained staff who are ready to assist with complicated situations that would be overwhelming to me is invaluable.
- One of the greatest challenges for pastors can be the efficient management of their time. Having counselors available to assist in situations where a large time commitment is required to see breakthrough and change is a tremendous benefit to the community as well.

The Eternal Value of a Counseling Center Ministry

Anchor of Hope Counseling Center serves families, couples, and individuals. Although our team is small, with only one full-time counselor and four part-time staff members, in the past three years, we have conducted over 1,500 counseling sessions in many different areas, including marital counseling, healing interpersonal relationships, gender confusion, depression, anxiety, overcoming sexual abuse, bereavement counseling, and provided practical ways to apply the spiritual remedies of forgiveness and repentance. We have counseled believers in Jerusalem, the Tel Aviv area, Haifa, and towns as far north as the Lebanese border. Our team provides counseling ministry in English, Hebrew, and Russian.

The work of a counseling center has eternal value as we join Jesus in His mission to mend the broken-hearted. One of our clients shares:

> I came to Anchor of Hope in the most hopeless of conditions. Even as a believer for many years I had completely lost my grasp on reality.
> I was completely dependent upon alcohol from breakfast time to get through the day and kill the pain. None of it really made much sense: I was a partner in a great business, I had years of studying scripture but still I had fallen away from living out my faith and it seemed like there was nowhere else to go but further down. At the point of being literally a few days from living back on the streets I came to Anchor of Hope. Just the shame felt from being a believer in that state was overwhelming. The most incredible transition began soon after beginning one-on-one counselling at Anchor of Hope. That feeling of shame and worthlessness was increasingly lifted as the torment and pain carried for so long was understood from a biblical place. Forever I have so much gratitude for *the love* this ministry has shown this once completely broken soul.
>
> Tamir, age forty, Jerusalem

Psychologist Larry Crabb discussed the parable of Jesus, where He described the house built on the rock and the one built on sand and made this point:

> *You know those two houses? They look exactly the same. If you can't see underground, the same roof, same windows, same porch, until they are tested.* Until the wind, until

> the storms, until the rain comes, both of those houses, they look identical. But one, built on sand, will be destroyed. The other, built on rock, will stand.[25]

Crabb calls this paying attention to the unseen "building below the waterline."[26]

This is the formation that happens in the counseling session as the Holy Spirit penetrates deeply in the heart of the person humble enough to seek help and lower their defenses. The counselor becomes an anchor of hope for that person and a midwife to God's healing power. Furthermore, counseling is a profound form of discipleship as barriers to receive God's love are removed. The person is empowered to apply God's truth in their life in an authentic way, no longer basing their identity purely on performance or some other false or dysfunctional basis. Old wounds, destruction family patterns, disrupted relationships, and misbeliefs about oneself and about God, can surface, be faced, and healed. Counseling is an agent of God's transformational power in the lives of his people. As an illustration of this process, here is the testimony of one client:

> I am a changed person since I started counseling at AOH. The prayerful and insightful sessions taught me how to gain control over negative thought patterns that previously controlled my life. I have been

25 Crabb, Larry (1977). Effective Biblical Counseling. Zondervan: Grand Rapids, United States, 15-mind-blowing-statistics-about-pornography-and-the-church;

26 Crabb, Larry (retrieved 4/24/21); https://livingontheedge.org/broadcast/the-secret-of-lasting-change-building-below-the-water-line/

able to process deep, painful memories and in a very real sense am free from them!

Our Training Model

The Anchor of Hope Biblical Counseling course was created to train lay counselors. From this pool of students, volunteer staff are chosen to help in the counseling center. Then they are supervised every week in order to discuss their cases and receive encouragement and feedback. A trained professional counselor is a necessity to direct the center and guide the volunteers.

The Anchor of Hope counseling course offers a thirty-week course divided into three modules, each ten weeks long. Each class is three hours long. The training is ninety hours cumulatively. Usually, there are fifteen to twenty students. Each student receives a notebook complete with every lesson and handouts that become a valuable resource for review and reference. At the end of the training, there is a graduation that is part of the King of Kings weekly service, and each student receives a certificate.

The training is widely announced throughout the land via local congregations. Potential students are asked to fill out an application form that entails basic demographics, including congregation and pastor, what they hope to gain from the course, and how much ministry experience they already have.

It is an important component in serving well that counselors are well-grounded in counseling theory and techniques within a biblical framework. An extensive course with small group work enables the attendees to build trust, share authentically, immediately utilize tools they are taught, and understand the importance and necessity of confidentiality from their own personal experience. This valuable small group work hones their listening skills, develops community, expands their capacity for empathy, and enables them to experience the vulnerability of being transparent with another person.

Our curriculum

Module 1	*Module 2*	*Module 3*
Theological Foundations	Addiction	Counseling Teens
Theology of Emotions	Motivational Interviewing	Effective Communication
Counseling Tools	Codependency	Depression/Suicide Risk
The Genogram	Attachment Theory	Coping with Illness
Assessment and Process	Pre-marital Counseling	Abuse
Challenging Misbeliefs	Couples Counseling, 1	Crisis Intervention
Anxiety	Couples Counseling, 2	Conflict Resolution
Bereavement, Grief, and Loss	Infidelity	Low Self-Esteem/Identity
Boundaries	Forgiveness	Stress Management
Legal Issues	Family Counseling	Emotionally Healthy Spirituality

This overview of key counseling areas emphasizes the place of the Holy Spirit to bring about transformation in the whole person: cognitively, behaviorally, emotionally, and spiritually. It also aims to usher students into a closer relationship to God with an enhanced ability to love others and themselves with compassion and thereby serve more effectively.

We begin with a "Theology of Counseling" lesson that emphasizes how counseling provides a sanctuary for the client to be authentic and let go of defenses without fear of judgment. We listen with the heart of God to hear beyond the words and understand what the other is experiencing. This establishes a caring relationship that allows for truth to be spoken in love. We embrace the integration of scripture and psychology in what Dr. Larry Crabb calls "Spoiling the Egyptians," which means using concepts from psychology only consistent with Scripture.

Our theology of counseling embraces the Hebraic view that it is the whole person that worships God.

We include a "Theology of Emotions" lecture as some believers are taught not to give credence to their feelings. However, we believe that our emotional life is part of what it means to be made in the image of God. We reflect on the fact that Jesus wept, rejoiced, was surprised, was in agony, was angry, grieved, and was full of joy. He was fully human, as well as fully divine. The question is not whether devout believers have emotions but how to help them understand, accept, and regulate them. Counselors need to accept and understand their own emotions in order to contain those of the people whom they seek to help.

Format

There is a weekly presentation of course material followed by a practical application for students to share in small groups, usually of between three to five people. Our exercises begin with sharing an experience of friendship and proceed over the weeks to disclosing an important event in the lives from their childhood, adolescence, and young adulthood. This personal communication coincides with the emphasis on becoming a trained listener and developing appropriate skills such as reflective listening, asking open-ended questions, learning to challenge without criticism, and the essential task of building trust and rapport. People coming for help need to be understood. This establishes a sense of connection and communion. A common pitfall of lay counselors is the need to "fix" the client. That's God's job. Our purpose is to become His temporary ambassadors. And that means entering the person's story, hearing their pain while building a sense of safety and trust so they can let their defenses melt down. Because of this sacred sense of intimacy, counseling is one of the most profound and powerful forms of discipleship and spiritual formation. It allows people to open up their hearts and creates opportunity for the Holy Spirit to penetrate on a profound level.

The group exercises become more in-depth as students reveal how their family handled various emotions, including anger, their own role in the family system, how family dynamics shape their current interactions, their personal style of being in relationship, their stress patterns, their experience of the forgiveness process, and so on. The counseling course becomes not only an intellectual training exercise but a transformational experience as students become aware of their own identity, behavioral patterns, and coping or defense mechanisms. There is usually deep healing that happens for each one during the course. The pattern we follow is to receive and internalize the healing process, then impart to others what is lived out in the counselor's life.

Recruiting Lay Counselors

In choosing our counselors from the student group, the qualities we look for include: the ability to empathize, listen reflectively, keep appropriate boundaries of confidentiality, demonstrate a good understanding of the course material, contribute insightful feedback, ask meaningful questions, show evidence of spiritual maturity and personal integration, and express a personal calling to counsel. The small group work gives a chance to observe if these qualities are present in the potential counselor. It needs to be stated at the beginning of the course that completing the training is not an automatic assurance of being asked to join the counseling team. This prevents misunderstandings at the end of the training.

The Counseling Process

The counseling process at Anchor of Hope is formal, structured, and organized as compared to "marketplace" counseling, where a congregant and a friend might meet for a cup of coffee to discuss problems. Our brochure and website outline our services and events (https://www.anchorofhope.org.il). The process begins with a short phone intake conducted by the director. Our intake form includes basic demographics, living arrangement, marital status, work situation, congregation, and pastor's name. Then we move on to the presenting problem. A good way to address this is to ask them: "What made you pick up the phone to call us?" Another way to state this is to say: "If counseling was successful, what would that look like for you?" This helps to formulate goals. We found directly asking for goals often was difficult for callers. We need them to be as specific as possible and avoid generalized answers like, "I want to be healed." We ask if there is any history of depression, mental illness, or addiction in the family if they have any physical limitations, prescribed medications, problems sleeping or eating, followed by if they experience any suicidal or homicidal thoughts. If the answer is "yes," we immediately ask if there is a plan and available means to act on the plan, which alerts us to the fact that this person needs immediate psychiatric help. We include a list of basic problem areas such as anxiety, anger, communication issues, depression, emotional or physical abuse, financial problems, family grief, low self-esteem, marital problems, and stress, to which they can reply simply yes or no. We end by asking if they are struggling with questions about their faith. Do they feel that God is close or distant? This gives us a basic sense of how they are coping spiritually. At times, people need to be reassured that in grief or crisis, God may seem far away, or they may feel angry. We normalize these feelings as part of the growth process.

This short intake allows the director to determine if the problem area is within the scope of the counseling center. We are not equipped to manage psychiatric problems or severe mental health concerns. In those cases, we refer the person to their health care provider. Also, the intake allows the director to decide which counselor might be best suited to take the case. The director matches clients to appropriate staff according to gifts and temperament and, whenever possible, to the same gender if that is important to the client.

It is important to have some form of record keeping. Anchor of Hope utilizes the confidential software program TherapyNotes (therapynotes.com) to keep track of our clients and ensure both quality and continuity of care.

The assigned counselor contacts the individual and sets an appointment. Every client must sign a Waiver and Release form, which not only outlines the limits of confidentiality but defines our scope as part of the pastoral staff, not a professional counseling agency. This functions as legal protection for the ministry. We do not charge a fee, but there is voluntary donation.

Duration

We aim for between six to eight sessions in our counseling process. However, we evaluate and adjust this according to the person's needs, goals, and progress. For example, someone who is dealing with childhood sexual abuse usually needs much more time. In general, we try to stay within our limits.

Supervision

Each counselor meets with the director once per week to discuss their cases. This provides support, ongoing training, a place to reflect on their own experience, guidance, and the opportunity to develop their skills. It allows the counselor to become self-aware of their own thoughts and feelings. It's a time for counselors to receive helpful feedback, process treatment challenges, and understand where the person seeking help is in the change process. Sometimes lay counselors struggle understanding why there wasn't a significant transformation in the client. It's helpful to let them know some people come in to vent, and others are really there to heal, grow, and mature. *The emphasis is not on the specific technique that brings healing but the quality of the relationship between counselor and client.* There is also a weekly process group that allows counselors to share their cases with one another, which provides both supervision and accountability.

In summary, choose a counseling training course appropriate for your church, screen applicants, and choose lay counselors from the pool of students who have completed the course based on the criteria noted above. All lay counselors then receive supervision on their cases. The actual process of counseling begins with a short phone intake to determine need and scope and the assignment of an appropriate counselor. Determine the duration of the counseling experience and provide ongoing supervision. It's essential to have some form of confidential record keeping.

Twelve-Step Support Group

COVID-19 has not been the only pandemic to afflict the world. There is a worldwide outbreak in the use of pornography. And it has infested the church. Sixty-eight percent of church-going men and over 50 percent of pastors view porn on a regular basis. Of young Christian adults eighteen to twenty-four years old, 76 percent actively search for porn. Fifty-nine percent of pastors said that married men seek their help for porn use.[27]

Israel is in the middle range of the worldwide pornography pandemic. In Israel, 16 percent of the users are between the ages of eighteen to twenty-four, and 40 percent are between the ages of twenty-five to thirty-four...More than three-quarters of Israelis watch porn on their mobile phones (76 percent) and some (21 percent) on their computers.[28]

---

27 Laaser, Mark. Treating sexual addiction [DVD series]. Available from https://www.lightuniversity.com/product/treating-sexual-addictions/

28 israelis-on-pornhub-what-do-the-chosen-people-choose-to-watch-630341 (2020, June 4). Retrieved from https://www.jpost.com/israel-news/

We wanted to address this growing problem. First, we raised awareness of the problem by offering a fifteen-week course on sexual addiction. This is a topic rarely discussed among believers, especially in Israel. We want to bring light into neglected areas. This course educates leaders and counselors on the challenges faced by those struggling with this addiction and generates a compassionate understanding of the unique issues and dynamics surrounding the allure of the false and superficial intimacy that pornography promises but never delivers. Also, presenting this course prepares the ground for reaching out to those in the grip of this addiction. Most people do not want to admit to their pastor they are using pornography; however, a support group is much less threatening. Addiction brought into the light of God loosens the powerful grip of dependency. Confessing to others relieves the shame and brings motivation for change.

This course is followed by a twelve-week life recovery course explaining the twelve-step recovery program in depth. This program is based on relying on God's power to overcome life strangling habits. It also has built-in accountability. We started a twelve-step group for men in the clutches of pornography addiction. But although the need is great, the participation was limited initially. This was evidenced by the fact that at our first planned meeting, no one showed up! For us, it was a call to action to go to the 'highways and byways' to announce our meetings. To this effect, one of our counselors, who speaks English, Russian, and Hebrew, made arrangements with open-minded pastors to speak for a few minutes on the subject at weekly congregational services. We had leaflets available. This garnered a small group of men willing to open up and change. The group went on online via Zoom in March 2020 when the COVID-19 pandemic brought us into lockdown. The online format proved to be more effective as men from all over the country were able to join. We are now in our fifth year offering this support group. We also conduct one on one counseling in this area.

The transformation one client experienced is exemplified here:

> I am an Israeli man in my early thirties. About two years ago I started meeting with one of the counselors at the center to deal with an addiction to pornography. Slowly but surely, I started to redeem my sexuality, but also gain hope for freedom. Today I am completely free for over a year from pornography. In the process God revealed a lot of things and healed a lot of wounds. Therefore, the process led me to a closer relationship with Him as well.

A more recent development is the growth of people struggling with same-sex attraction. As the moral fiber of society breaks down worldwide, more teens and adolescents are programmed to believe gender fluidity is the norm. This is affecting in the believing community. We have had two seminars on how to counsel those in this category.

Further Education and Training

Anchor of Hope is both a counseling and a training center. Seminars and workshops provide strategies and skills to meet life challenges. They are designed to empower professional counselors, lay counselors, and ministry leaders in their ability to minister more effectively. They are also geared to believers seeking to grow and thrive in stressful times.

Our seminars have been both on-site and via zoom. On-site presentations have included: Counseling Unwanted Same-Sex Attraction; Restoring Hope: Counseling Survivors of Sexual Abuse; Conducting Pre-Marital Counseling; Effective Communication in Marriage; and a three-day conference entitled The Struggle Is Real: How to Care for Mental and Relational Health Needs in the Church. Our seminars presented on Zoom have included: Emotional Maturity: The Heart of Relationship; Making Your Anger Work *for* You; Brief, Solution-Focused Therapy; Overcoming Anxiety; and Pastoral Care: Understanding Depression, Anxiety, and Suicide Assessment.

The Relevance of Seminars and Training.

The COVID-19 pandemic expanded our presentation reach as we provided trainings via Zoom. Our seminar on "Overcoming Anxiety" was particularly well-received during the pandemic as so many were facing uncertainty and struggling in lockdown. The counseling center was able to meet a direct need emotionally, spiritually, and psychologically to many people facing an extremely challenging time. The structure was already in place to respond in an emergency.

Over the past three years, many believers in Israel committed suicide; tragically, two of them were very young. There needs to be an understanding that mental health issues are common and often due to physical problems or imbalance in brain chemicals. Believers often feel like failures if there are not "victorious" over their emotional pain and sorrow.

It's very important for pastors to create a safe place for their congregants to receive ministry for their deepest struggles. A center such as Anchor of Hope provides the opportunity for a church to meet a depth of needs that most pastors do not have the time or training with which to become involved.

What God Has Accomplished Through Anchor of Hope

In conclusion, with a very small staff of one full-time counselor, two part-time staff, and two part-time volunteers, we were able to conduct over 1,500 counseling sessions in the first three years. In 2020 alone, during the pandemic, the number of sessions was over 630, many on Zoom. Among that number were clients studying or working in Israel from eleven different countries, including India, Finland, the USA, France, Australia, and Germany. We ministered to clients between the ages of twenty to eighty in thirteen different areas that included abuse, conflict resolution, crisis intervention, gender confusion, bereavement, PTSD, anxiety, depression, and marital and family therapy. In 2020, our twelve-step group for men struggling with pornography met online over thirty-eight times. Our counseling course has raised up the next generation of lay counselors across the country. To date, we have trained over seventy-five lay counselors, and our seminars have helped leaders, lay counselors, and participants seeking to embrace emotional and spiritual growth.

It has been said that Jesus did not die for an image. A biblical counseling center within the context of a local congregation allows believers to cast off their defenses like the cloak of blind Bartimaeus, overcome shame and find healing for broken hearts and renewal for their souls. This specialized ministry allows for a unique depth of discipleship that releases the person to become closer to God and become a vessel of His love and authenticity to others.

CHAPTER 10

Emerge Counseling Ministries

Akron, Ohio

Rev. Robert Crosby, DMin, PhD

Robert Crosby, DMin, PhD, is a ministry leader and author. He serves as the president/CEO of Emerge Counseling Ministries (Akron, Ohio), a nationally-recognized organization that has served denominations, churches, pastors, and people in need since 1973. His wife, Pamela, is the executive director of communication and coaching at Emerge. Together they have pastored churches in New York, Ohio, and Boston.

The Crosbys are also the co-founders of TeamingLife.com. They write and teach on marriage and parenting. Their newest book together is *The Will of a Man & The Way of a Woman: Balancing & Blending Better Together.*

Robert is a contributing writer to *Outreach Magazine* and *Christianity Today*. He holds a doctor of ministry degree from Gordon-Conwell Theological Seminary and also earned a PhD at Regent University. He has written several other books, including *The Teaming Church: Ministry in the Age of Collaboration*, *More Than a Savior*, and *The One Jesus Loves*. His newest book was written in collaboration with Samuel Rodriguez and is entitled *When Faith Catches Fire.*

The Crosbys conduct conferences and retreats on leadership, marriage, and family life. They have appeared on CBN, Focus on the Family, and several other radio and television programs.

> The Holy Spirit is what I love most about counseling at Emerge.
>
> Matthew Knabe

Matthew Knabe, a licensed clinician at Emerge Counseling Ministries, cites the openness to the work of the Spirit of God as the main reason he wanted to work at Emerge Counseling Ministries, a nationally-partnered non-profit mental health agency based in Akron, Ohio, with recently expanded satellite offices located in Pennsylvania and Georgia.

In 2001, Matthew was doing something quite different vocationally; he was traveling the world playing guitar as a "hired gun" for the Christian band, Sonicflood. While loving the challenge, variety, and opportunity of bringing music to the souls of thousands in new places night after night, something deep within him started to change. Matthew began to ask himself such questions as, "How long can I keep this up? Can I do this type of work and travel on into my '30s, '40s, and '50s? Do I even want to? Can I raise a family and still do this?"

All those questions resulted in a personally life-changing experience for him that counselors deal with in their offices every day—depression. This soul struggle led Matthew to Emerge, not initially as a clinician but as a client. After accumulating a sufficient number of counseling sessions to recognize a new sense of healing and wholeness in Matthew, his counselor made an astute observation. He recognized a more-than-usual enthusiasm about not only the counseling Matthew received but the counseling process itself. Matthew was curious to learn more.

Consequently, after working as an operations manager for Nike, Matthew decided to go back to school and become a counselor. Today, many years later, Matthew works at Emerge and counsels dozens of people every month with a special focus on teenagers and young adults. He also hosts Emerge's podcast—ExEm: Experience Emerge.

Matt is just one of many leaders and individuals helped by Emerge. In the 1980s, Anne Beiler, the founder of Auntie Anne's

Pretzels, and her family were reeling from some painful and abusive experiences she had suffered from a ministry leader. Through a series of events, Anne's husband found out about the specialized ministry help offered through Emerge. As a result of the ministry of Emerge's founder and team, she and her family experienced newfound freedom, which has endured to this day. She says (in a personally authorized public testimonial),

> Emerge not only saved my life, it also gave me a better understanding of sound biblical theology. I went to Emerge broken in body, soul, and spirit and came out on the other side with a healthy view of who God is and who I am. I cannot imagine life without the experience of Emerge.

Emerge's Founder & Counseling Pioneer—Dr. Richard Dobbins (1927–2014)

Emerge is a growing, Christ-centered counseling center, providing confidential, compassionate, biblically-based, and Spirit-empowered outpatient mental health care. The clinical team includes licensed psychologists, counselors, social workers, and interns. But it all started decades ago with one Akron-area pastor and his deeply troubled spouse, Delores.

Dobbins and Delores married very young, and after having their first child, she struggled with a severe postpartum depression. Helping to find a good Christian counselor for Delores proved to be a frustrating and failed pursuit for the Akron-based pastor. Dobbins knew that his wife, Delores, was struggling deeply and that what she felt was stretching beyond the confident purview of his pastoral counseling. Pastoring a growing Pentecostal church in Northeast Ohio had brought an abundance of competing demands and stresses. Dobbins was determined to help his wife find the help she sorely needed, yet he ran into one failed attempt after another. How might he best help her?

"You just need to pray more," some Christian leaders told Delores. "If you would simply read your Bible more, you should improve," others said. When given the opportunity, Pastor Dobbins said, "I don't know anyone who prays and reads her Bible more than my wife." Acknowledging the importance of these faith disciplines, he knew there was something else she needed.

Out of deep concern, Dobbins' oft-failed attempts to understand his wife's emotional pain and no lack of frustration, he decided to go back to school and work on a degree in psychology. Within a few years, he became the first graduate of the PhD in counseling program at the University of Akron and was grandfathered in as a psychologist. From that moment on, Dobbin's life would forever change.

After founding and pastoring a vibrant church, Evangel Temple in Akron, Ohio, Dr. Dobbins, amid significant personal pain, sensed the call of God to transition into full-time mental health ministry. After graduating with his new PhD, "Doc" founded Emerge Ministries. He was a brilliant student, educator, and mental health visionary. Recognized by Dr. Gary Collins and Dr. Tim Clinton (AACC), Dobbins received national acclaim as one of the founding fathers of Christian psychology.

For more than fifty years, God gave Dr. Dobbins the wisdom and strength to counsel with thousands of hurting and confused people and help them discover biblical truths to deepen the Lord's peace and joy in their lives. He counseled thousands of hurting and troubled individuals, couples, and families—many of them pastors and leaders. He helped them discover biblical truths to deepen joy and freedom in Christ. Primarily, he was a praxis-oriented theologian who desired to make God's truths accessible.

Dr. Dobbins had the unique ability to integrate biblical truths with sound psychological principles to help hurting individuals find hope and healing in the midst of painful and difficult personal and family circumstances. One of those individuals, Reverend Jack Strom, wrote,

> 'Doc' partnered with my wife, Barb, and me in a journey of healing and restoration almost twenty-five years ago. It was much more than a moment... he helped me develop an ongoing life attitude and action that still results in our experiencing marriage and family with joy and fulfillment.

At the time "Doc" Dobbins graduated with his PhD, the corner of Christendom in which he served consisted primarily of Pentecostals and Charismatics. These groups in that era had traditionally shunned counseling and psychology, as some described it as "secular" or merely "intellectual," while some others even viewed it as "of the devil." In most of the settings in which Dobbins would have ministered, counseling was viewed with a certain "stigma." It was not unusual to hear gossip-laden comments such as, "Oh, did you hear that they are going to counseling? Can you believe that?"

What began with one hurting man, an inspired vision, and a grace-filled God is now a far-reaching national mental health ministry. Emerge now features 40 Christ-honoring clinicians ministering hope and healing to more than 600 people each week and over 35,000 hours of counseling per year. Over the more than forty-eight years of Emerge's existence in Akron, it is estimated that more than 250,000 individuals and families have been served through the caring counseling of Dr. Dobbins and the many psychologists, social workers, and counselors who have followed him.

Dobbins became a change agent, a rugged pioneer who had a poetic way with words and came to be known as a brilliant pulpiteer and communicator. His intuitive lens led to several biblical psychological models that informed the teaching and counseling of Dobbins and Emerge.

The Emerge Way—The Work of the Spirit and the Healing of the Mind

Emerge counselors embrace a therapeutic approach that is both biblical and spiritual, Christ-centered and clinically sound according to research-validated best professional practice standards. Among people who have experienced counseling at Emerge and for Emerge practitioners, this process is often simply referred to as "The Emerge Way." The Emerge Way evolved from the "Healing of the Mind Model" initially developed by Emerge's founder, Dr. Richard Dobbins. In its simplest version, the following is a point-form description of this model and its principles:

1. *There are two key spiritual influencers of our thoughts* (1. The power of Jesus Christ in this world, which Dr. Dobbins called zoe or eternal life; or 2. The power of Satan in this world, which Dr. Dobbins called sin).
2. *These two influences act upon the mind and are filtered through a person's history* and develop into their interpretations (i.e., narratives) of present events.
3. *Interpretations eventually become an expression of God's presence or Satan's destructive presence* on earth when they are expressed through our choices and behaviors.
4. *Therapeutic interventions are aimed at healing the story we tell ourselves about our past history and/or developing a present awareness of God's voice* so that people can choose the most redemptive interpretation possible and therefore express God's presence on Earth through their choices/behaviors (i.e., "take back dominion"). In other words, we live not with the events of our past; but rather with the interpretation we give those events. Thankfully, these interpretations can, through the Holy Spirit, be "edited" and thereby redemptively transformed.
5. *This process is considered to constitute practical sanctification* (i.e., that of becoming who God originally created me to be; to become more like Christ) through the renewing of our minds. Dr. Donald Lichi, vice president of Emerge, wrote, "Remember, the enemy builds strongholds in secrecy and enforces them by silence. Break the silence and you will break the stronghold" (Broken Windows of

the Soul, p. 96). The Emerge team sometimes refers to this process as "praying through."

6. *In this model, Sin is not simply seen as a behavior but rather as something that is impacting the mind to think in destructive terms to destroy God's image in humanity and on the Earth.* Eternal life (Greek: zoe) is not seen as simply a destiny, but as something that comes from Jesus Christ that impacts upon the mind to develop interpretations that will express God's image on Earth through our choices; to help us reach our original design in relationship with God, ourselves, and others (which Dr. Dobbins called our "divine potential"). Dobbins often said, "Pain is the greatest predictor of change and until the pain of change hurts less than the pain of staying the same, people prefer to stay the same."
7. In very general terms, *the Emerge way is the integration and application of biblical truth with sound psychological principles and current neuroscience to help people live in the "freedom for which Christ set us free" (Galatians 5:1) or to live the "abundant life" that Christ has promised.* This is the key dynamic that each clinician resonates with today.

The Emerge Way of counseling is the integration of biblical truth with proven psychological insights to help people find rest and live free as Christ intended. The life influences we all face, both good and bad, act upon our minds and are filtered through our personal histories. These mental constructs impact our interpretations of present events and result in challenging life patterns. Therapeutic interventions are aimed at healing the story we tell ourselves about these past experiences and transforming our view into the most redemptive interpretation possible. This results in a person experiencing the "life that is really life" (1 Timothy 6:19).

The effect of the Emerge Way is practical applied sanctification (the process of becoming who God originally created a person to be; to become more like Christ) through the renewing of one's mind by God's Spirit. It is the practical "how to's" of the biblical "ought to's." In this transformational model, sin is not seen simply as a behavior but as something that impacts the mind to think in disruptive ways that undermine God's image in humanity and on the Earth. Jesus Christ is our exemplar in the journey of living a life of love and freedom in word and in deed.

This unique counseling framework representative of Emerge's passion is one that originates with the Scripture and the Holy Spirit but unites with best mental health practices.

The AG Connect—AG HelpLine & Partnership

The 1990s were a period rife with stories of ministry scandals, in particular the news-hungry stories of fallen televangelists. These sordid sagas hit several denominations hard, but perhaps none more at that time than the Assemblies of God (AG). Night after night, it was common in that season for AG leaders to appear on national news programs to answer tough questions about fallen leaders.

This season led to the AG taking measures to shore up soul-care practices in the lives of their pastors and leaders. One of these steps was a partnership with Emerge Counseling Ministries to create a free and an anonymous phone call service for counseling help and referrals—the AG HelpLine.

The *AG HelpLine* is an anonymous counseling hotline service that the Assemblies of God contracts with Emerge Counseling Ministries to staff and facilitate. Emerge Counseling is the primary mental health partner of the AG. The HelpLine is also an important part of Emerge Counseling's mission to help ministers live healthy lives mentally, emotionally, relationally, and spiritually. This service is for all AG licensed and ordained ministers, as well as for their spouses and their children.

From the Pacific Northwest Region of the US, Don Ross (superintendent of the Northwest Ministry Network) said,

> The AG Helpline is an invaluable tool and resource for our pastors and credentialed ministers who find themselves struggling with any number of challenges in their personal lives, marriage, or family. Although our District/Network offers other options to help keep our pastors healthy, the HelpLine on the back of the credential card uniquely provides anonymity and a welcome pastoral care option.

From the Northeast, Nick Fatato (superintendent of the Southern New England Network) declared,

> As a Network, we deeply care about the health of our leaders. While we work diligently to serve their needs, we don't always connect in time. The HelpLine assures our ministers that there is always an avenue for

> help. Sometimes the intensity of the situation forces ministers into silence. Making a call to the HelpLine and getting anonymous help/direction/care, can often be easier for them than calling a Presbyter or Network leader. I am grateful for the HelpLine.

From the Southeast, Terry Raburn (superintendent of the Penn-Florida Ministry Network) said,

> The HelpLine staffed by Emerge team members is a 'first responder' for our ministers and their families. Emerge is on-call and there with prayer, help and reassurance at many hours of the week. We depend on that response.

The year 2021 marked the 25th Anniversary of the HelpLine. This service to ministers started in 1996 as part of an initiative to underscore the inner life of pastors and to provide a safe place to respond to soul care and mental health needs.

The general superintendent of the Assemblies of God, Doug Clay, stated,

> The counseling services Emerge provides our ministers and churches is simply outstanding. I regularly hear such great reports from people about lives transformed by these gifted counselors. It is a joy to have Emerge as our primary partner for ministerial health and support.

Pandemic PIVOT

When COVID-19 became the prevalent news in 2020, nonprofit organizations all over the world were asking questions similar to ours: *What will this health crisis mean to our nation, our state, to families, and individuals? How will it affect the type of services we provide? Will we need to reduce our expenditures rapidly? Will we need to downsize our staff?*

It is encouraging to report that Emerge came through this challenging season powerfully, experiencing God's strength and organizational buoyancy. God helped us successfully navigate these turbulent waters. One of the "navigation tools" we developed and found helpful is a simple acronym of P.I.V.O.T. Each letter represents an important part of the process we followed and continue to follow relative to other crises:

Press into the Need—*We are choosing to look for opportunities in the struggle.*
Innovate Solutions—*We are looking for fresh and effective ways to meet needs.*
Vacate the Irrelevant—*We are letting go of projects and processes that aren't producing.*
Optimize Resources—*We are endeavoring to make the most of our team and talent base.*
Team Forward—*We are not just working but learning how to work together better.*

Because of the times in which we live, it seems that the need for Christ-centered counseling and soul care is greater than any other season in our lifetimes. This especially affirms the belief that, as this ministry celebrates its 50th anniversary in 2023, God has raised up Emerge "for such a time as this" (Esther 4:14). The PIVOT organizational model continues to be utilized by Emerge's leadership teams.

Emerge 2.0 Innovations

Since its inception in 1973, Emerge has become a go-to place for people facing all types of mental, emotional, and spiritual challenges and distress. Our clinical team serves adults, adolescents, and children every week. Often entire families utilize the services we provide.

Locally and regionally, Emerge is trusted and respected by people from all walks of life. 35,000 plus hours of counseling occur each year at our Counseling Center in Akron and at various extension sites. People of all ages and walks of life find the help and support they need at Emerge.

Nationally and globally, Emerge partners with various denominations, church associations, and parachurch organizations to serve the lives, marriages, and personnel of pastors and other spiritual leaders.

Emerge embraces a passion for the future, for new generations, and for healthier leaders and families. In order to engage future clients and leaders, Emerge has initiated a years-long strategic plan referred to as "Emerge 2.0." This set of initiatives includes:

Resources and Tools that equip people and churches for wholeness in life through Christ. This includes an engaging, dynamic internet presence that reflects our values and regularly resources our clients and partner churches with helpful tools and ease of access to our services.

Coaching—This new discipline of coaching at Emerge is designed to be a complement to counseling and a rich tool in life. Emerge seeks to develop counselors who are coaching-aware and coaches who are counseling-informed. While counseling assists a person in experiencing healing and a greater sense of wholeness, coaching seeks to help a client engage their life potential with their heart, mind, and soul.

Ministers Enrichment Counseling Team—Emerge is intentional about growing a team of counselors who are especially oriented towards the needs of ministers, pastors, missionaries, and various church leaders and their families.

Emerge Endorsed National Referral List—We have begun to connect to local counselors throughout the United States as a way of highlighting opportunity to collaboration. We affirm their ability to counsel and provide their name on our resources, thus giving pastors and other local leaders confidence in using their services. It also gives them a practice marketing platform and reference point to give and receive clients.

Tele-counseling—The pandemic season required certain immediacies in innovation, most prominent being the move to telehealth. Emerge is engaging ways in which this can help the ministry build on its national brand and serve the needs of more people in more places.

Emerge-at-a-Glance—Seven Things to Know

- *Emerge has a local, regional, and national reach through ministry and church partnerships.* From the Christian counseling that started through Emerge in Akron, Ohio, to the dozens of licensed mental health clinicians and psychologists that practice with us today, Emerge's reach has grown and spread across the nation. Emerge is the primary mental health partner of the Assemblies of God, the largest Pentecostal denomination in the world. Emerge's founder, Dr. Richard Dobbins, was an ordained AG minister. While working with many additional denominations today, Emerge is still the primary mental health care partner of the AG.

- *Emerge is theologically conservative and yet therapeutically innovative.* A biblically-based Christian practice, Emerge values and incorporates many current therapies that fit within our Christian worldview and a high view of Scripture. We have found that there is no contradiction between innovation and biblical orthodoxy. On the contrary, the biblical tradition affirms and enriches meaningful innovation. Simply put, God's Word and God's world never conflict—all truth is God's truth.
- *Emerge has a history of educational partnerships.* For several years, Emerge offered a master's degree program in clinical counseling in conjunction with Ashland Theological Seminary. While that partnership no longer continues, Emerge is developing new educational partnerships for the future.
- *Emerge was originally founded by a local pastor and psychologist whose wife encountered severe mental health issues.* There is no shortage of people today within the local church encountering mental health challenges and crises. The

power of biblical theology and praxis with sound psychological care allows the Holy Spirit to birth new thoughts, new dreams, and new hopes within those in our care.

- *Emerge is a soul-care center for church leaders.* This ministry is perhaps best-known nationally for the mental health care it provides for pastors, missionaries, and other church leaders. We stand ready, like never before, to assist pastors and leaders with their mental health needs through Christ-centered care and performance-improving psychology.
- *Emerge is developing a national Emerge Endorsed Clinicians page on its website*—Our goal is to develop a national network of clinician counselors for spiritual leaders to reference in every community.
- *Emerge strives to function as a Teaming Organization* that accomplishes its mission via strategic and nimble internal collaborations and partnerships. The president of Emerge, Dr. Robert Crosby, also founded Teaming Life and consults and trains on The Teaming Organization, Teaming Leadership, and The Teaming Church. A key value at Emerge is not only doing our work but doing the work together.

To learn more about Emerge or to contact them for professional mental health ministry, please go to their website: emerge.org, or call them at 800-621-5207.

CHAPTER 11

Ministering to Mental Health Needs in Youth Ministry

Rev. Jeremy Smith, MA

Jeremy is a Christian, husband, and father to three. Raised as a pastor's kid in a small Baptist church, he has a history of working as a youth ministry director for Youth for Christ for eight years in rural Ohio, at the Air Force Academy in Colorado Springs, and then at the YFC Headquarters. He has a bachelor of science in computer engineering at Ohio Northern University, master of arts in family ministry at Winebrenner Theological Seminary, as well as a master of arts in clinical mental health from Denver Seminary. Since 2014, he has worked as a mental health and substance use counselor in Colorado and Ohio. Specifically, he has worked in outpatient treatment with domestic violence offenders; he started up an Opioid Residential Treatment Center in Colorado, as well as founding and leading a new adult co-occurring outpatient program at a community mental health center in Ohio. His passion is to bring hope and restoration to those hurting as well as build resiliency and discipleship in God's kingdom.

When not serving as a husband and father or at work, Jeremy writes for his website churchandmentalhealth.com in assisting churches and Christian counselors to connect better and serve their communities. He has spoken at several conferences, created resources for churches and counseling centers to connect Christians struggling with mental illness or substance misuse to get into counseling, and consulted with churches and ministries. He has also served in several church-based technologies and mental health inclusion ministries as well as premarital counseling ministries alongside his wife. He loves cooking with his wife, playing video games with his children, rooting for Ohio State football, and creatively expressing himself through many different mediums.

Introduction

From 2007 to 2015, while working for a Christian parachurch youth ministry called Youth for Christ, I learned a tremendous amount about ministry, relationships, and what is most important in life. I did outreach to teenagers who had never stepped into a church, discipled youth into leaders, empowered volunteers to develop relationships with students and families, and helped instill a passion and purpose for God into countless teenagers. It was a joy to watch students dedicate their lives to Christ as they navigated the awkward stages of being a teenager while they progressed through the psychosocial stages of development, found their role within their family, and then branched off to start their own journey into adulthood.

I found myself not aspiring to be the best youth pastor who had a catchy sermon or the perfect game that students would be talking about for years to come. My heart was constantly drawn to helping that student who did not sit with the crowd and was disengaged. I wanted to see student leaders take personal ownership of their faith. I wanted to see students turn their hearts towards Jesus and honor God in their relationship with their parents and community. Those moments when I was in the hospital because someone attempted suicide or in the principal's office because they were caught using drugs, I found where I could help. It was there, ministering to mental and relational health concerns, that I discovered my calling into professional counseling. As any dedicated youth pastor will tell you, you never really stop thinking about those students who are hurting.

Here is what we do know about teenagers with mental health challenges:

- 1 in 6 U.S. youth aged 6–17 experience a mental health disorder each year. [29]
- 50% of all mental illness begins by age 14, 75% by age 24.[30]
- Prevalence of diagnoses for those under 18:
    - o ADHD: 9.4% (6.1 million),
    - o diagnosed behavioral problem (oppositional defiant disorder, conduct disorder, etc.): 7.4% (4.5 million),
    - o anxiety: 7.1% (4.4 million), and
    - o depression: 3.2% (1.9 million).[31]
- Suicide is the 2nd leading cause of death among people aged 10–34.[32]
- Only 50.6% of U.S. youth aged 6–17 with a mental health disorder receive treatment.[33]

It is imperative that youth pastors and churches begin to take an active role in getting trained on topics of mental illness, having conversations with their community, and reducing shame and stigma within their youth ministry. Working within the church and now alongside it as a counselor and volunteer for a mental health inclusive ministry, I find youth

29 Whitney, D. G., & Peterson, M. D. (2019). US National and State-Level Prevalence of Mental Health Disorders and Disparities of Mental Health Care Use in Children. *JAMA Pediatrics*, 389–391

30 Kessler, R. C., Berglund, P., Demler, O., Jin, R., Merikangas, K. R., & Walters, E. E. (2005). Lifetime Prevalence and Age-of-Onset Distributions of DSM-IV Disorders in the National Comorbidity Survey Replication. *Arch Gen Psychiatry*, 593–602

31 Centers for Disease Control and Prevention (2021, March 22). *Children's Mental Health*. Retrieved from https://www.cdc.gov/childrensmentalhealth/features/anxiety-depression-children.html

32 National Institute of Health. (2021, May). *Suicide*. Retrieved June 9, 2021, from National Institute of Health: https://www.nimh.nih.gov/health/statistics/suicide

33 Whitney, D. G., & Peterson, M. D. (2019), ibid.

who are longing to be personally invested in and are struggling with biological and psychological change. Yet many are unable to verbalize their depression, anxiety, trauma, substance dependence, or suicidal thoughts and are often overlooked and/or dismissed with various superficial messages.

Many church leaders feel unequipped or misinformed about what they can and must do; consequently, many teenage mental health problems fall through the cracks. One Baylor study that surveyed youth pastors found that "only half of the pastors stated that they had received mental health training in their education... three-quarters of the pastors did not feel qualified to work with adolescents experiencing significant mental health issues."[34] Many times, pastors experience barriers of well-meaning parents who do not want to see mental illness within their child, who minimize the symptoms, or who perpetuate the problems through hidden or dysfunctional relationships within the family. The crucial work of youth pastors does not stop at the door when pizza and scripture-filled teenagers leave.

Below I am going to offer some basic crisis implementation procedures that need to be considered, two models for ministry to youth with mental illness (trauma-informed care and family systems), and finally, how prevention can help make a positive impact on the mental health of students in youth ministry.

34 Hunter, W., & Stanford, M. (2014, October). Adolescent mental health: the role of youth and college pastors. *Mental Health, Religion & Culture*, 957–966

Reporting Abuse, Neglect, and Suicidality

One of the few unique components about youth ministry is a high prevalence of needing to report child abuse and neglect. The Federal Child Abuse Prevention and Treatment Act (CAPTA), as amended and reauthorized by the CAPTA Reauthorization Act of 2010, defines child abuse and neglect as "any recent act or failure to act on the part of a parent or caretaker which results in death, serious physical or emotional harm, sexual abuse or exploitation (including sexual abuse as determined under section 111), or an act or failure to act which presents an imminent risk of serious harm" (42 U.S.C. 5101 note, § 3).

As of 2019, clergy are mandatory reporters in twenty-eight states in America, with another eighteen states where it is required of anyone in a position of authority to report.[35] Note that each state's limitations to privacy between pastors and individuals are not absolute and may vary from scenario to scenario with testifying in court or informing the parents. Training should be conducted with church staff and all leaders on reporting mandates.

Mandatory reporting is also required for a student who discloses suicidal thoughts or if there is reasonable suspicion about their risk of self-harm. We need to be direct in our questions, asking, "Are you thinking about killing yourself?" and understand you must not only report to the proper authorities but also contact a legal guardian. No promises should be made. I

35 Children's Bureau (2019, April). *Clergy as Mandatory Reporters of Child Abuse and Neglect.* Retrieved from Child Welfare Information Gateway: https://www.childwelfare.gov/pubPDFs/clergymandated.pdf

offer a free church suicide prevention policy that you can put right into your church's policy handbook.[36]

It is my recommendation that you work alongside a local Christian counseling agency, county social workers, or mental health board with this training for reporting abuse, neglect, and potential risk of harm to oneself and/or others since you will want an established relationship with the counselor you are calling during a crisis. Seek out the director of a local counseling agency or connect with congregation members who are counselors to discuss getting training for all staff and leaders, including security that may be necessary for a teenager who becomes manic at Sunday school and volunteers who may go to youth camp with a student who has a history of suicidal ideation. Identify possible de-escalation techniques you can be trained in, what the referral process is for getting someone evaluated by a mental health clinician, and how to follow up with the youth if they are hospitalized or need professional counseling.

Trauma-Informed Care

Beyond mandatory reporting, understand that you may have several children who are at risk of mental health and substance misuse due to adverse and traumatic experiences. This can include the previously mentioned abuse and neglect, death of a loved one, life-threatening injuries in a car accident, prolonged hospitalization, divorce of parents, parental incarceration, or intense bullying. A trauma-informed care approach to

36 https://churchandmentalhealth.com/product/church-suicide-prevention-policy-free-digital-download/

youth ministry is not a different way to do sermons, worship, and games, but instead, the intentional way you speak, interact, and keep the individual student in mind.

Many churches have a foster care ministry where the local church becomes one of the main partnering agencies with Child Welfare in fostering and adoption of local children (Psalm 68:5, NIV). Other churches have made a priority to serve homeless women and children, urban and underserved populations with children in poverty or gang-related activities, or children who have been trafficked. For many children, this will require significant work with long-term mental health recovery along with the support of family, friends, and their church.

Within the clinical setting, research has been done to help youth who are at risk, called Adverse Childhood Experiences (ACE). The research conducted by Kaiser Permanente and the Centers for Disease Control and Prevention found a high correlation between childhood trauma and environmental instability before the age of eighteen, which leads to life-long problems in the areas of mental health, medical, social, academic, and career problems. This is recorded through a simple ACE assessment that gives an ACE score with questions that ask if the individual experienced verbally, physically, or sexually abusive adults in the home, neglect, severe poverty, household members who were in prison, family substance misuse, mental illness, suicide, or parents who are divorced or separated.

Churches can help with prevention of trauma and promote healing for people who have high ACE scores. Some areas to assess your church's areas to grow include:

- *Strengthen economic supports to family.* Some churches look to financially help offset bills for those in poverty. Other churches do skills training to help adolescents and young adults gain employment.
- *Promote social norms that protect against violence and adversity.* Some call this social justice, which many churches have theological problems with. I will simply state that we need to be more proactive in our words and actions about what Jesus did for sinners and the lowly. Your leadership team should not be promoting violence, lack of boundaries, or youth ministry games that are degrading and demeaning.
- *Ensure a strong start for children.* The first part of youth ministry prevention starts not with the students but with the parents. Parents are often struggling with their own trauma and instability. Some churches host MOPS groups, host after-school tutoring, and have gone as far as having parenting classes that look to assist new parents or single mothers. Youth pastors need to know the name of every parent, stepparent, and legal guardian in the student's home.
- *Teach life and social skills through safe mentoring and discipleship.* Some of the best discipleship programs do not happen in churches. Often they occur at the pond fishing, at the local food bank, or out in the community. We cannot completely prevent ACE events, so we must also help teach and model resiliency, using scripture and Christian practices. Note Paul's time in jail, Nehemiah's time rebuilding Jerusalem, or Timothy as a young adult

attempting to learn from those older than him. Teach scriptural resiliency.

- *Offer support for additional treatment and resources.* Some churches will make a referral to a Christian counselor, help pay for services, and help get the individual to these initial appointments. Reach out and schedule to meet with them.
- *Reduce stigma, promote awareness, nurture relationships, and improve the responsibilities of families.* Regular, appropriate self-disclosure by pastors or church leaders of their honest experience with mental illness and substance misuse is important. Empowering parents with God-centered family teachings and trainings will develop more resilient families during small groups or Sunday school. But then move into the kids' environment: at school and at home. Have activities in the church that are for the whole family to come and live healthy lives together. Include food and activities that require parents to talk with and listen to their kids. Be in the school as much as possible, but also go to the school board meetings and regularly talk with the principal and teachers about concerns with teens and how your ministry can help improve school life.

One additional note regarding trauma-informed care. Understand that what we say and do as a church can be helpful or harmful, despite good intentions or normal church traditions. I do not mean trying to appease someone because they feel bad, but instead understanding that people who experience something that is a trigger for post-traumatic stress response can re-traumatize them. We must be careful of how we influence others (1 Corinthians 10:31–33). Some examples that might be triggering for trauma and further exacerbate mental illness include:

- A popular youth ministry game is to see how many clothes pins you can put on your face. Some people with trauma avoid physical pain, and if a person was physically abused, this might be difficult for them to experience.
- Using incendiary phrases like "you're so crazy" or "I'd die if I couldn't have that."
- Another popular game is racing to see who can shave a balloon the fastest with a razor and shaving cream. But popping balloons may startle someone with trauma.
- Telling people to "just pray about it more" or "have more faith" when talking about mental illness. Specifically, for teenagers, youth pastors should be aware of pejorative labels such as "my ADD is so bad" or "she just always acts like that."
- Social anxiety (or agoraphobia) can make it difficult for anyone to stand up front, do an upfront game, or have a discussion in front of a crowd.
- Taking away a cell phone at camp of a student that has been sexually abused.

Does this mean we have to know every diagnosis of students that attend and just give up on some games? Certainly not. It is not reasonable or possible to know everything. Nonetheless, do not force people to participate, be cognizant of what someone is saying and respect their wishes, and always be upfront with people about what is happening (Ephesians 5:1–2).

Difficulties with Differential Diagnosis

Diagnosing people under the age of eighteen for mental health concerns is vital but can also be difficult. For a person under the age of eighteen who presents with symptoms of a mental disorder, it is critical to correctly identify the problem and initiate early intervention and appropriate treatment. Many times, what sets a professional apart when identifying a mental illness is differential diagnosis, a method of analysis of a patient's history and symptomology to arrive at the correct diagnosis and rule out other diagnoses.

For teenagers whose brains are still developing until their mid-twenties, going through hormonal and physiological changes for several years, and transitioning from being part of a family to separating and finding independence, this can be hard. Furthermore, many adolescents are unable to fully articulate or understand the emotions they are feeling.

Youth pastors who are involved in a student's life may have great influence with them as sensitive and key topics of life, death, salvation, purity, grace, and so many other topics are discussed. Consider how you may support students who are in treatment. As a therapist, obtaining a release of information so I can speak with the youth pastor provides me valuable data as well as a specific support if a client experiences a crisis or if a specific component of a treatment plan needs to be implemented by the youth pastor.

Family Systems Focused Youth Ministry

From my experiences leading youth ministry, when we talk about youth ministry, there are some models that work and some that do not. Some ministries are stagnant, doing what has always been done. Other ministries may be focused on the number of kids there, but it's less about the relationships with teens and more about popularity or giving a performance. You reference the Bible, but does your teenager actually read it themselves outside of the church walls and internalize their own faith?

I want to suggest a model of youth ministry that is not just about teenagers but instead focuses on families. There are models like Mark DeVries' *Family-Based Youth Ministry* or Timothy Paul Jones' *Family Ministry* that complement this idea well, though I will be noting how Family Systems Theory, teenagers with mental illness, families, and the church can come together. Dr. Stephen Grcevich says in his book *Mental Health and the Church* what we do for someone with mental illness should also serve the whole church.[37]

A counseling model called Family Systems Theory explains that human behaviors, beliefs, and identity develops within of a complex network of relationships and interactions. One example that often occurs is where the "identified patient" comes in for counseling because they are seen as "bad" and negatively impacting the whole family. Coping skills and behavior modification techniques are discussed and taught, leading the individual to make positive choices, yet often the family is still hav-

37 Grcevich, S. (2018). *Mental Health and the Church: A Ministry Handbook for Including Children and Adults with ADHD, Anxiety, Mood Disorders, and Other Common Mental Health Conditions*. Grand Rapids, MI: Zondervan

ing negative experiences. This would imply that the problem is only in part the "identified patient," and the whole family system needs to change. Many times, the family pulls the "identified patient" back into negative behaviors or at least perception in order to have someone to blame. True change happens when the individual makes changes that improve them as well as their established relationships; thus, the whole system can move forward.

We often see this when teenagers graduate. Mom and dad want them to successfully and independently launch, yet may find they are overly involved and regularly try to pull the young adult back home. Youth pastors may fall into the trap of "they are a good kid from a bad home," which vilifies the family. And when we attempt to lone-wolf the spiritual walk of a teenager to "when they are with the youth pastor," we find ourselves wondering why teenagers run away from the church in college or young adulthood.

A family systems-focused youth ministry empowers the family to take charge of their home, much like Joshua proclaimed before all of Israel in faithfulness that he and his whole household would serve God (Joshua 24:15). Ministry is not just for individuals but for the whole family and their context. Crucial things to understand when using a family systems approach:

- *Differentiation of Self*
  Within counseling, this means that we want the student to be their own self, understanding their own thoughts and feelings. For someone who may have a mental illness, this can be powerful as they may feel distant from

God or ask questions that you normally would not hear until later in life. Meet the student where they are at, celebrate their spiritual development, and challenge them to rely more and more on God.

- *Avoid Triangulation*
  Triangulation in counseling is when one person attempts to gain support from a second person against the third. We see this in parenting when a child will say to the mom, "But dad said I could," when the child had first received a no from mom. Youth pastors experience this too. What if a parent grounded a kid from youth group or the back-to-school event? Do you take sides? We suggest instead joining the conversation if allowed but supporting the parents' authority within their home. Don't get caught in the middle of a family dispute—the crossfire can be dangerous!

- *Family Emotional Process and Multigenerational Transmission*
  We know that teenagers develop core beliefs initially based on what they were taught. As they grow, they create new ones for themselves. Sometimes this may challenge what they previously believed. But we know that while mental illness is often biological, it is also in many ways environmental. Is there a student causing problems in youth group with disruptions? How do you address them when you know that their parents are going through a divorce? Family emotional process understands that when mental and relational health problems exist in the system, it affects everyone individually. Mul-

tigenerational transmission process understands that families tend to repeat previous generational patterns into our own. And as the psalmist says, give mercy to our current need because of our parents and grandparents (Psalm 79:8).

- *Church Is Your Family Too*
  If we believe that the body of Christ is one family after salvation and we have been adopted along with our brothers and sisters in Christ (Ephesians 1:5), then we as a church are part of this family system. Our health, negative or positive, will influence many other parts, and so we must take care of ourselves in order to improve the health of others, growing along with them (Proverbs 27:17).

Empowering Parents

We need to empower the parents outside of church activities to have more theological discussions and how mental health interacts with their spirituality. Parents can—and perhaps should—be the primary spiritual leaders of the youth group. As we discussed, most youth pastors feel like they are not well enough equipped. So how do you go about empowering parents?

- *Bring a Counselor*
  If you ever have meetings where the parents stay to hear about summer camp, new student orientations, or any kind of family/parenting meetings, invite a counselor to

discuss mental illness. Make it a panel discussion with church leadership and have an open discussion.

- Recommend Books or Further Readings

Hopefully, you are reading about mental illness within youth ministry. If you have a newsletter that you send out, put in recommendations of books parents could read.

- *Get Your Own Resource Book*

Many times people will come to you in crisis with questions. One book you really need to investigate getting is *The Youth Worker's Guide to Helping Teenagers in Crisis*,[38] which covers a lot of mental health topics from eating disorders to suicidal ideation.

- *Let Them Know There is Always Help*

This starts and ends with God through prayer, worship, fellowship, and Scripture. If your church is equipped to address mental health issues or has an on-site counselor, help should include a mental health ministry, youth leaders, available pastors, and yourselves. Beyond that, there are crisis services locally and nationally (Suicide Prevention Lifeline at 1-800-273-TALK or RemedyLIVE's crisis teen text line to text your concern to "494949") and counseling. For your list of referrals for local area counselors, make sure you have a great youth counselor and

38 Van Pelt, R. (2007). *The Youth Workers Guide to Helping Teenagers in Crisis.* Grand Rapids: Zondervan

family counselor who you would send a teenager to if they needed professional clinical help.

- *Separate the Person from the Problem*
  A wise therapist might say, "You struggle with schizophrenia," rather than "You're a schizophrenic." Do not define the person by the problem and encourage the parents to do so as well. This may be hard for parents to do—many times, people see bad behavior as a result of bad parenting or their inability to compartmentalize a child's mental illness symptoms to the choices and behaviors their kid makes. Walking alongside the parents will support them daily in seeing the whole child and not just their negative behavior.

Respite

Working with youth in a clinical setting can be difficult because many times, the parent needs to be present for clinical work, and traditional talk therapy is not effective with younger children. Yet if a family has more than one child, getting into counseling feels impossible because they either have to pay for a babysitter to go to the session, bring all of the children into a counseling session (which can be distracting and take away from the person being helped), or cancel the appointment. Too often, it is the latter.

Further, families with a child who struggles with mental illness, a developmental disability, or behavioral issues are exhausted. These children typically require full attention much more than others. Respite allows the parent to take time for themselves and encourages them to do activities they want to do, go on a date with their spouse, or simply go home and take a nap.

One Christian ministry that fulfills this is Nathaniel's Hope, specifically through their Buddy Break program. The family brings their child, who they label as the VIP kid, but their intention is to serve the whole family and invite siblings who may not have a developmental disability or mental illness to also come. This is important because typically, the siblings of someone with a disorder feel left out. Nathaniel's Hope intentionally serves everyone with the same attention and love. Your church could investigate starting your own ministry for your community.

Prevention

One of the most effective tools we have as a society working with teenagers and families is prevention. Mental health and substance misuse prevention does not require a master's or doctoral degree. Therefore, a compassionate and driven church that has a youth ministry willing to care for individuals and families struggling with mental illness can do amazing things. Prevention is something we can do for every student, whether they are presenting with any mental health symptoms or not. This creates a stronger resiliency, the ability to cope with and adapt to stress brought on by a difficult life event.

Early intervention and prevention are more effective for students than adults since youth are physically, emotionally, and mentally developing more rapidly than adults. Further, the behaviors learned and attempted at this age, coping skills (whether positive or negative) they try out, and relationships they are forming will leave an impact for decades to come. Adults tend to have to unlearn negative coping skills they had established previously as they learn new, positive skills.

You have already seen some ideas within the ACEs section identified specifically for those who may have an ACE score, but prevention says what is good for mental health for one may be great prevention for all. Going to counseling should not be just when we are deeply distressed, just as we should not seek out a relationship with a youth pastor as a teenager or parent merely when we are having a spiritual crisis.

Youth groups and churches that focus on the family unit can produce significant strengthening of resiliency—which is the heart of prevention. One study found significant positive correlations with Christian practices being preventative for mental health symptoms.

Compared with never praying or meditating, at least daily practice was associated with greater positive affect, emotional processing, and emotional expression; greater volunteering, greater sense of mission, and more forgiveness; lower likelihoods of drug use, early sexual initiation, STIs, and abnormal Pap test results; and fewer lifetime sexual partners. It was also possibly associated with greater life satisfaction and self-esteem, greater likelihood of being registered to vote, fewer depressive symptoms, and a lower risk of cigarette smoking.[39]

---

39 Chen, Y., & VanderWeele, T. J. (2018, November). Associations of Religious Upbringing With Subsequent Health and Well-Being From Adolescence to Young Adulthood: An Outcome-Wide Analysis. *American Journal of Epidemiology*, 187(11), 2355–2364

This requires youth groups to focus on the spiritual needs of adolescents and the relationships you create with them, not that youth group numbers grow larger, that everyone is playing the latest youth group game, or having the best lights and sound on stage.

- When you have that summer slip-n-slide game at the local park with pizza afterwards, get to know students' names, take pictures to share on social media or to hang up in the youth group walls to let them know they matter, and go hang out with them to read Scripture or pray with them at McDonald's or a coffee shop. The adolescent is heard, shown value, invested in, and spiritually cared for, all with the mission of evangelism, discipleship, and growing future leaders.
- On your way to all-night skiing, bring up hard conversations like mental illness, the responsibilities that come with being an adult, and substance misuse in the van. Hear what the students think, have them ask hard questions, and be open and vulnerable when it's appropriate.
- Have sermons on topics of mental health, noting about the hope, grace, and redemption of Jesus (Isaiah 41:10). Share that God is our Wonderful Counselor (Isaiah 9:6), God of gods and Lord of lords (Deuteronomy 10:17), and knows the number of hairs on our head (Luke 12:7).
- Make sure the school has your personal cell phone in case there is a crisis so that you can be there immediately to talk to students who need to process. Long before you are called, talk with the principal about what

> you can do so they know you are a support if that time were to ever come.

It really is that simple. Get involved. Be there personally with the student.

To reinforce the family system, consider investing time to be not just with the teenager but the whole family. Some of my most impactful and formative memories were sitting in a living room with my family and a couple of other families every Sunday evening, eating dinner, singing some worship songs, and reading and discussing Scripture. I heard from my father about his theological views, which would strengthen our relationship, and from another parent from another family who we are friends with to this day. I was able to gain my own voice as a Christian and leader where I could ask hard questions, share my own thoughts on the Bible, and pray for others as I was prayed for myself.

Train up youth ministry volunteers who gather with the same two to four families every week or every other week. Invest in those volunteers during the week corporately to conduct Bible studies or small groups. But make this where the whole family is together in homes—adults and youth. The intent is to go beyond Sunday church services and youth group, more than a couple of hours where "we play church," and instead towards a time where we meet the spiritual needs of an individual, which will translate to so much more.

Conclusion

My heart for my fellow youth ministry pastors swells. I love to hear when they take teenagers to summer camp where they get away from the distractions of life, hear their pain and worries, and show them the love of Christ. I have so many stories about how a teenager came to know Jesus and, through their innocence as a youth, was bold enough to invite all their friends and family where many also accepted Christ. And to see a teenager find a home at youth group where they are loved and accepted after living more than a decade in a home that was dysfunctional or even toxic and to know they have a new family that loves them despite their mental illness or home life makes it all worthwhile.

My prayer is that your church will grow towards this. For churches that are just getting ready to become trauma-informed and integrate the family, I pray a hedge of protection because these changes within the church can be hard. People like simple and easy, so to ask them to take an active role in the spiritual life on a teenager can be hard. To actively change your language and become an active listener takes time and intentionality—and you will mess up.

For the church that is already doing these things, I pray you find success but always continue to grow. In a true family system theory model, we never actually "arrive" because when one person in the family does better in life, we all have more growing to do. When one individual has a setback or relapses in their mental health recovery, this is when the family can come in to support them. May your elders and youth ministry leaders be ever-present, and may you see Jesus in the wonderful work that you do.

CHAPTER 12

Adult & Teen Challenge

(Over 200 Locations Nationwide and Over 1,400 Worldwide)

Rev. Gary Blackard, MA

Gary Blackard is the tenth president and CEO of Adult & Teen Challenge (ATC), a faith-based addiction recovery organization founded in 1958. With more than 266 locations in North America and more than 1,400 worldwide, Adult & Teen Challenge is the largest addiction recovery network in the world.

Gary gained extensive global experience while serving Xerox Corporation as vice president for client operations and strategic services delivery. In that role, he led teams as large as 700 plus people and managed annual revenues of $540M. Immediately prior to accepting the position at ATC, Gary served as vice president for strategy and innovation at Evangel University, a position that prepared him for the challenges of working within the nonprofit realm. He gained important organizational insight as a committed member of the National Board of Directors for Adult & Teen Challenge from 2014 to 2018.

Gary is currently an adjunct professor for the graduate program in healthcare administration at the University of Southern California, a certified Lean Six Sigma Black Belt leader, and an executive consultant. His past clients include several Fortune 500 companies such as Kaiser Permanente, WellPoint, University of Pittsburgh Medical Center, Goldman Sachs, Microsoft, Cisco, Northrop Grumman, IBM, and many others.

Gary earned his BA in business administration with emphasis in organizational management from Vanguard University and his master's in health administration from the University of Southern California. He is a veteran of the United States Marine Corps.

Gary and his wife, Debra, have been married for over thirty years and have two married children and four grandchildren.

Adult & Teen Challenge and Ready Now Recovery

I vividly remember meeting a girl several years ago who, from the age of seven, was raped by a family member. After this abuse continued for many years, she numbly and instinctively sunk into survival mode. As a teenager, she used alcohol and several drugs daily to cope with the pain. All the while, the abuse continued, now from multiple family members. She did not receive any help, support, nor was she rescued by those who may have been able to do so. Both of her parents were addicts all throughout her childhood, and they still abused drugs at the time we spoke. Her traumatic situation was heartbreaking, outrageous, and senseless.

As I stood there looking into her eyes and hearing her voice, I found myself hurting not only for her but also for so many like her. Several questions raced through my mind. How many thousands of other grade-school or teenage girls and boys are being raised in these conditions and going through such shame, trauma, and pain? How many are attending churches while living in these unsafe, dysfunctional environments? What is the church doing about it? And most importantly, how and where can these marginalized and exploited children and young adults receive competent, caring, Christian help? These disturbing questions frightened me but also made me angry.

My wife and I prayed with her as we stood in the living room of a lovely, renovated Victorian home that served as a small women's center for those struggling with addiction, now commonly called substance use disorder. She had been a resident in the center for several months, and though she was blossoming in her recovery, she knew she still had a long way to go in the healing process. Now in her early twenties, she is a transformed young woman who is currently working on her undergraduate degree and is becoming well-versed in theology, philosophy, and other scholarly subjects. For most of her life, she was encased in a dark, deeply dysfunctional environment with no human hope, but now, fortunately, she is filled with hope of Christ.

Millions of people with stories similar to this young woman's walk the streets of every city and community around the world. Lonely, even when not alone, afraid, lost, ashamed, desperate, and hurting, these individuals struggle with the effects of a life filled with self-destructive choices and desperate actions that led them to places of seemingly no return. Most function in what outwardly appears to be normalcy within society, but they secretly battle with addictions and other mental health issues nonetheless. Life-controlling issues, including pornography, alcohol and substance abuse, gambling, and digital/internet gaming disorders, have taken over key areas of their brains, creating surges of dopamine followed by withdrawal cravings, perpetuating a never-ending cycle of use and abuse. The church is certainly not immune. In fact, research suggests the church sees the same rates of addiction and mental health disorders as those who are not believers. That is why our ministry exists.

Adult & Teen Challenge (ATC) is dedicated to helping those struggling with substance use disorders and other addictions. Our vision is that all people would be freed from life-controlling issues through the power of Jesus Christ. We believe the answer is not *what* will cure one's addiction but *Who* will cure one's addiction. Through the power of Holy Spirit-led recovery, we have seen tens of thousands of lives marvelously transformed over the six decades since our inception.

We believe the Lord has given us many effective tools in the fight against addiction. Our programming consists of spiritual disciplines (like Bible study, prayer, fasting, chapels, and personal devotions); group and personal studies education (including topics like anger management, emotional intelligence, life skills, and healthy relationships); physical fitness; biblically based licensed counseling; meaningful work; family engagement; community service; church testimonials; and fun activities.

Our programs range from thirty days to fifteen months, with nine to twelve months being our standard model. We have over 260 locations across North America and serve between 11,000 and 13,000 students annually. We have centers specifically designed for women, men, women with children, and adolescents. Globally, we have over 1,400 programs in 129 countries. We are serious about putting hope in front of every man, woman, girl, and boy in the world who struggles with a life-controlling substance or behavior.

In a 2019 outcomes study commissioned by the Department of Behavioral Health at Evangel University in Springfield, Missouri, we found that our one-year sobriety success rate (one year after graduation from our programs) is 78 percent. We are proud of this number, giving all glory to the Almighty Answer behind the programming.

A Brief History

In 1958, God called Reverend David Wilkerson to begin Teen Challenge Evangelism, ATC's original iteration. Wilkerson enjoyed his life as a country preacher in Pennsylvania, and the church he pastored was growing in many areas. Still, he felt a spiritual discontent. God was calling him to something different, a pulpit of a broader and eventually national scale.

One evening while in his prayer time, the Lord led Wilkerson to open a recent copy of *Life* magazine. An article on the murder trial of teenage gang members in New York City caught his eye. Burdened by the story, Wilkerson felt the Lord calling him to the inner city of New York to help the boys, and he obeyed. Through many miraculous interventions and hard ministry work (which are all chronicled in Wilkerson's powerful book *The Cross and the Switchblade*), the Lord used him and others to bring the Gospel of Jesus Christ to New York City. As a result, thousands of the toughest and most notorious gang members there were dramatically and miraculously impacted by the gospel.

While ministering to this rather unconventional population, Wilkerson realized that alcohol and drug addiction was rampant in the streets and created a vicious, violent, and victimizing cycle in the lives of those it affected. Working with other churches and community leaders in Brooklyn and the surrounding boroughs, Wilkerson established the first Teen Challenge Center at 416 Clinton Avenue in Brooklyn, a center that is still active and operational today. This series of events began ATC's journey of organic growth over the decades as God continually calls women and men to faithfully serve and lead in this amazing ministry.

Adult & Teen Challenge Partners with the Church

After years of looking for fulfillment in all the wrong places, one of our students became deeply dissatisfied with his life. To cope, he began drinking excessively. In his five tumultuous years battling alcoholism, he left behind a massive wake of destruction, including a marriage on the rocks, a fractured relationship with his daughter, the trust of a business partner erased, and a sickened body that sent him to the emergency room twice. The son of missionaries, he grew up in a Christian home, attended church services regularly, and knew the word of God. Despite this upbringing, he began to chart a selfish course through life, seeking to do his own will rather than God's.

However, he soon learned that what the world has to offer does not satisfy because it only leaves a person empty, broken, and lost. He grew bitter and blamed God and the church for his insecurities and disappointments. He despised who he had become and believed he had no power to change. Through ATC, God brought him back home, and he is answering the call of the Lord on his life. He is a godly husband, father, son, brother, and friend. By following God's will, he is now serving at Teen Challenge of the Ozarks, directing a juvenile boy's program in Branson West, Missouri, and pursuing a master's degree through Global University.

Readers may be wondering, why are people in the church hurting? The answer is simple and complex at the same time. Christians face the same temptations and sin in the same way as every other human being. When facing these challenges, believers sometimes make the wrong choices for various reasons, and the consequences affect the larger church body. In Matthew chapter 13, Jesus tells the story or parable of the sower. The sower plants seeds, and some are eaten by birds, scorched with the sun, or choked out by thorns and weeds. However, some of the seeds fall into good soil and generate fruitful produce. In explaining this parable, Jesus states the seed is analogous to the word of God. Some people who hear the seed quickly reject it, while others accept the word and permit it to take root in their soul, thus becoming fruitful and nourishing to many around them.

But unfortunately, many who are struggling with trials, temptation, and crisis, hear the word yet tragically walk away. Then there are who are choked by thorns of being caught up with the cares of the world, and the seed does not produce. The reasons for the failure of these seeds are the same reasons the church is hurting. We have some who are "playing church" with no real and relevant relationship with Jesus Christ. We have some who are weak in their faith, and every time life becomes a struggle, they fold and falter. We also have many in the church who are so caught up in life on Earth that their growth in Christ is stagnant or declining.

Moreover, many in the church today are stuck in the mire described in Psalm 40:2. In this chapter, David expresses how the Lord brought him out of a pit. Addictions in the church have become a quagmire that reduces or limits the changes of one's sanctification in Christ and the overall influence and effectiveness of the church body. In a recent study on restoring relationships, Barna Research Group released data showing that 14 percent of adults in the United States acknowledge that alcohol and/or drug addiction impacts their most important relationships. Fifteen percent of practicing Christians reported this same result. Additionally, pornography affects the most critical relationships for 8 percent of US adults. For practicing Christians, that statistic is 13 percent. These percentages are alarming and should be a wake-up call to all believers.

ATC partners with the church in many ways. All our centers engage local churches to attend services, give testimonies, and bring awareness to our ministry identity. We also work with churches to complete community projects like back-to-school events where we can supply backpacks and other school items necessary for those who cannot otherwise afford such amenities. Our primary focus in recovery ministry is life restoration through evangelism and discipleship.

Another way churches partner with us is by being a primary source of referrals for our ministry. Local pastors and staff members hear about an addiction need or some other form of life-controlling issue and contact our centers to see if we can help. Most of the time, we can quickly provide assistance, sometimes in the same day. ATC gives the pastor and his or her leadership team a helpful and reliable resource to share as they counsel and coach those sitting within their congregations and communities.

A powerful example of this partnership can be seen through ATC choirs, which are often invited to participate in a portion of a church service. The congregation hears direct testimonies from those struggling with life-controlling issues and the ways in which Jesus Christ radically changed their lives. They also hear worship songs sung with passionate voices. There is a supernatural element about the worship of Jesus by someone who has been delivered from a fifteen-year heroin addiction that fills the heart with joy and the eyes with tears. These outreach services serve multiple functions. They bring immediate awareness of the ministry to people in the church who may desperately need help. Likewise, the choir trips bring overall awareness of the ministry and the gospel message through song and testimony, often leading to decisions for Christ. Finally, they provide an opportunity for local church members to give to and/or volunteer with the ministry.

Another powerful example is the recent launch of our new non-residential, small group ministry called *Ready Now Recovery* (RNR). This ATC ministry addresses the 90 percent of individuals who will not or cannot enter a residential program. These small groups are designed to focus on five core areas: spiritual development, emotional intelligence, social development, addiction education, and life skills development. RNR incorporates resources from a variety of well-respected organizations, including the American Association of Christian Counselors, Living Free, Right Now Media, and ATC itself. Please see https://www.readynow.org for more information. In one of our pilots, a nine-person group, we saw two salvations and an invitation of a friend within the first four weeks. We believe that God is moving mightily through this new ministry.

Adult and Teen Challenge Partners with Communities

In his early years, one of our students regularly attended church groups and traveled with his parents on mission trips. His life seemed like that of a typical evangelical churchgoer. However, like so many thousands of young people in the church, trouble began when he aged out of youth ministry.

Hanging out with the wrong crowd soon led to drinking and partying late into the night. That grew into drug-fueled get-togethers, where he consumed prescription meds and psychedelics. These activities led to a burgeoning addiction in this young man's life. A few years later, he moved away from home and tried to straighten himself out, but he continued using drugs on the weekends. One night, he drove home from a concert while high, fell asleep at the wheel, and sideswiped a semi-truck. He wound up in a ditch, and miraculously, he and his passenger walked away unharmed. It would not be the only time he escaped death during his years of drug addiction. Finally, fed up with his life and the mess in which he found himself, he had a conversation with his father, who shared his own testimony. That night, the young man fully committed his life to Christ and found hope and purpose for himself. He is currently attending a Bible college and plans to enter the mission field. He feels God's calling on his life and desires to build Christ's kingdom.

The Bible states that King Solomon was the wisest human who ever lived. In Ecclesiastes, Solomon writes that two are better than one, and he uses the metaphor of the strength of a three-strand rope to indicate the power of togetherness and tight-knit community. Loneliness and isolation can lead to anxiety and depression, which sometimes results in substance abuse in an ill-fated attempt to self-medicate an individual's pain and anguish.

Dr. Vivek Murthy, the 19th and 21st surgeon general of the United States, is credited with producing the nation's first surgeon general's report on the current addiction crisis. Murthy's book *Together: The Healing Power of the Human Connection* is a heavily researched exploration of the overwhelming and deleterious impact of loneliness on humanity and the benefits of interpersonal interaction. Loneliness continues to plague humanity in many ways. Consider the following statistics and trends:

- Twenty-two percent of all adults in the US say they often or always feel lonely or socially isolated (represents over 55 million adults).
- One in three American adults over the age of forty-five is lonely.
- One in five adults said they rarely or never feel close to people, and
- people with strong social relationships are 50 percent less likely to die prematurely than people with weak social relationships.

Truly the Creator was correct when He declared that it is not good for humans to be alone (Genesis 2:18). There is immense strength in community. However, in our individualistic, "lone ranger" society, everyone is conditioned to believe that they are the gods of their realities and have no need for others. This arrogant and narcissistic mindset sets us up for failure. By engaging with others, we gain support in many ways. Iron sharpens iron, as King Solomon observed (Proverbs 27:17).

ATC recognizes the need to partner with communities, and we have taken steps to foster engagement in various ways. Many of our centers host outreach events, including concerts in parks or collaborations with food banks and local grocers to give away food to those in need. We engage with community centers, public schools, and other entities to facilitate drug awareness campaigns and prevention. ATC center staff and students also assist disadvantaged community members by doing yard work, painting, and other chores. Our teams go out into the community through both Center-directed and church outreach. We believe this engagement helps us to stay focused on needs and bring vital solutions to the growing epidemic of alcohol and substance use disorders. Psychological research also reveals that giving and volunteering helps us take the focus off of ourselves and our own pain in order to sensitize our attitudes, actions, and outlooks to address the needs of others.

A Personal Word on Hope

One of our students grew up in a loving and supportive home, but when he was seventeen, his father died after a battle with HIV/AIDS. He also suffered from migraine headaches and was prescribed OxyContin for the pain. With both the physical pain and the internal torment from the loss of his father, the young man began abusing the prescription medicine and eventually turned to heroin. Soon, he found himself stealing to support his addictions. He was arrested numerous times but did not care; all that mattered was getting out and getting high yet again.

One night, after acquiring enough stolen merchandise to trade for a bag of dope, he was walking to his truck when he suddenly felt something pushing against the back of his head. He heard a man say, "Give it up!" He thought to himself, *What if I don't? What if I just give up right here? I will no longer be a burden and disappointment to anyone.* He finally turned around, feeling the gun move from the back of his head to his face. With tears streaming down his face, he told the gunman, "No... I can't do it."

After what seemed like an eternity, the assailant lowered his gun and let the young man go. Still shaking from fear, he went to sit in his truck. Overcome with hopelessness and despair, he inserted a needle into his arm. Tears streamed down his face as he pleaded into the darkness for someone to take his pain and loneliness away.

The next day, God answered the young man's prayers. He was arrested, which allowed him to clear his mind while in jail, and after doing his time, he went into rehab. He met Christ, was baptized, and after almost four years, he became the director of a Teen Challenge prison team. He is now married and has a son, and he thanks God each day for his family and their continual love and support.

Hope is the belief in something better and the result of transcendent faith. It is a strong predictor of positive emotions and helps increase productivity and healthy functioning. Individuals struggling with a life-controlling issue will have a much better chance at successful transformation if they have hope. For the Christian, this is game-changing. The Apostle Peter wrote of a living hope, the hope we find in Jesus Christ knowing that He loves us, cares for us, encourages, strengthens, emboldens, and literally transforms our minds and hearts. That is the power of the living hope found in Jesus. Redemption revolutionizes us and leads to recovery.

Believers err when we allow the enemy of our souls to cloud our hope, replace it with fears, doubts, selfish ambitions, pain, and/or pleasure. We seek things that we believe will give us hope but were never meant to satisfy. How do we rectify this issue? By practicing discipline and obedience, including daily reminders to ourselves of who our Hope is.

Recently I was up early one morning, headed to work, and stopped in at the local Starbucks for a cup of coffee. As I walked out of the store, I noticed a very bright light in the far horizon and used an app on my phone to identify it. It was the planet, Venus. I immediately thanked the Lord for His creation and His incredible, creative power. This was a practice of hope. I know I serve the God of all creation, and He loves me unconditionally, no matter what I have done or will do. This relationship with Him fills me with immense hope. No one should be hopeless, but many feel hopeless. The great, life-transforming news is that our Hope lies not in anything humanity or worldly systems can offer. Think about who Jesus Christ really is. The hope He gives transcends anything you know, feel, or experience on your own. Deep down, you know there is more.

Think about the hopelessness felt by an eleven-year-old girl who is raped daily. This girl stayed at school as long as possible, not wanting to go home. In middle school, she experienced weight gains and subconsciously pushed people away. Fear of the unsafe world and predatorial males became this girl's driving force. When she reached high school, the girl actively pushed people away and refused any form of physical touch from others. As she entered college, she was considered by others to be quite beautiful, but inside she was still broken. She learned how to manipulate her peers and used drugs to escape her pain-filled reality.

Now an adult woman, she left college feeling lost and empty, but she is intelligent and found a good job and a caring man. They got married, but both brought many issues and dysfunctions to the relationship. The woman later underwent spinal fusion due to chronic back issues and was prescribed Percocet to help with the pain. Her life went downhill from there. She lost her job, her marriage, and everything else due to the throes of opioid addiction.

However, with the help of Christ's transformational and redeeming love, the woman experienced recovery and now lives a whole and fulfilling life. She currently has a dream teaching job at a Christian school, she is a health coach, and her marriage and family are thriving and healthy.

Psalm 103:1–14 (ESV) is a powerful passage on the sweet tenderness of God. The verses read,

> Bless the LORD, O my soul,
> and all that is within me,
> bless his holy name!
> Bless the LORD, O my soul,
> and forget not all his benefits,
> who forgives all your iniquity,
> who heals all your diseases,
> who redeems your life from the pit,
> who crowns you with steadfast love and mercy,
> who satisfies you with good
> so that your youth is renewed like the eagle's.
> The LORD works righteousness
> and justice for all who are oppressed.
> He made known his ways to Moses,
> his acts to the people of Israel.
> The LORD is merciful and gracious,
> slow to anger and abounding in steadfast love.

He will not always chide,
  nor will he keep his anger forever.
He does not deal with us according to our sins,
  nor repay us according to our iniquities.
For as high as the heavens are above the earth,
  so great is his steadfast love toward those who fear him;
as far as the east is from the west,
  so far does he remove our transgressions from us.
As a father shows compassion to his children,
  so the LORD shows compassion to those who fear him.
For he knows our frame;
  he remembers that we are dust.

The last verse should be a resounding statement in our minds: God remembers that we are dust. He knows our frailties, our weaknesses, and our shortcomings. He understands the ugliness of a heart filled with sin. To fix our fallenness, He sent His Son, Jesus Christ, to be the ultimate sacrifice for all human sin—past, present, and future.

Adult & Teen Challenge exists to serve everyone, especially those of the household of faith—the church. We are a phone call, text message, or web click away—ready and willing to provide solutions to leaders who need resources for their churches and communities. You can find us at https://www.teenchallengeusa.org. The harvest is plentiful, and we are poised and equipped, ready to help.

CHAPTER 13

Meier Clinics

Richardson, Texas (and Eleven Other Locations Nationwide)

Paul Meier, MD

Paul Meier, MD, is the founder of the non-profit national chain of Meier Psychiatric and Christian Counseling Clinics, consisting of twelve locations across seven states. Dr. Meier trusted Christ at age six and began meditating on scripture daily at age ten and has continued that for over sixty-five years. In two intense dreams at age sixteen, Jesus called him to become a physician and use that career to serve Him and to teach and spread "Practical Christianity" throughout the world. God blessed him with the opportunity to do those through a national daily live broadcast on 400 stations to an average of two million people a day for over twenty years. Dr. Meier was also given the opportunity to spread Christian psychology by writing over hundred published books that have sold well over 8 million copies in thirty languages. He has discussed his books on many Christian and secular TV and radio programs. Dr. Meier also does a monthly secular podcast, *Mental Health News Radio*, to 171 nations.

Dr. Meier has traveled throughout the world on mission trips to train pastors, missionaries, lay counselors, professional counselors, and many others about how to integrate the Bible with up-to-date psychological research and medications to treat psychiatric illnesses. "Christian psychology" and "Christian psychiatry" are helpful tools to reach people around the world who would normally not come to churches or pastors for help. He has spread Christian psychology in unexpected countries like Russia, Israel, and Cuba and throughout Europe and South America. In 2021, Dr. Meier was seventy-six years old, and he has turned over many of these opportunities to younger psychologists, psychiatrists, missionaries, and pastors he has personally trained. He continues to see psychiatric patients and administrate his national chain of non-profit Meier Clinics, with no plans to ever retire as long as God enables him to continue to fulfill the two dreams God gave him at age sixteen.

Fulfilling My God-Dreams

> For God does speak—now one way, now another—
> though no one perceives it.
> In a dream, in a vision of the night,
> when deep sleep falls on people
> as they slumber in their beds,
> he may speak in their ears
> and terrify them with warnings,
>
> Job 33:14–16 (NIV)

The Bully

In Psalm 139, we are taught by King David that God designed us in our mother's womb to have certain strengths and weaknesses. With one arm, God hugs us, and with the other, He leads us through life (but often in behind-the-scenes ways that we don't recognize). David ended that psalm, my favorite chapter in the Bible, with a prayer that God would reveal His innermost thoughts that David did not yet see, so David could walk in ways pleasing to the Lord. David talked about our "innermost thoughts" (unconscious thoughts and motives) thousands of years before Freud or any other psychiatrists discovered the concept.

In Hebrews 4:12, we are taught that one benefit of meditating on scripture is that God's word is quick and powerful and sharper than any two-edged sword and able to reveal to us our innermost (unconscious) thoughts to help us grow spiritually—sanctification. An early sign, in hindsight, that God designed me in my mother's womb to become a psychiatrist someday occurred when I was about seven years old. My mom was sitting on our front porch, and I was about fifty feet away, playing in the snow by our front sidewalk. A ten-year-old neighborhood bully walked by and, for no obvious reason, pushed me down into the snow. I suspect he was hoping I would either cry or try to fight him, either of which would give him a false sense of power. But I followed my natural instincts and got up, looked him in the eye to analyze him a moment, then walked off toward my mom. I'm glad she said nothing to the bully, although I know she would have rushed to my side if a fight had broken out. When I got to my mom, I calmly asked her, "I wonder why he did that?" I was a mini psychiatrist even in my youth, always curious about human behavior, including my own. Even in my "older" age now, in my late seventies, God continues to reveal to me both positive and sinful aspects of my innermost thoughts, with "no condemnation"—as Paul revealed in Romans 8:1.

Spiritual Guidance and Inspiration of My Parents

I am very thankful for my mom and dad. They loved God, and they loved each other. Both are with God now. I remember seeing them most days, growing up, spending time studying their Bibles. I was the third of four kids and remember my dad sometimes having fun with us by letting us open up a Bible with him facing the other way so he could not see us. We would take turns picking out a verse from any random chapter of the Bible, from Genesis to Revelation, and he would almost always know the book and the chapter, and sometimes even the verse. Every night at the supper table, when we were through eating, I would want to rush off to play a little baseball with my friends before dark, but dad would make us wait long enough to have brief family devotions. He would read a short passage of scripture, we would discuss it briefly, then he would ask if we had any special prayer requests, and he would pray for us, or mom would. As we got older, we got to pray for our needs as well. It only took a few minutes altogether, and as much as I resented it occasionally because I had to wait to join my friends, I look back and thank God for that golden opportunity in my life. My parents were not perfect, and I wasn't either, of course. Nobody is.

The Power of Psalm 1

When I was ten years old, my mom sat down with me one day and explained to me how meditating on scripture daily had helped her and my dad, even through tough times. Then she patiently helped me memorize Psalm 1:1–3 (KJV):

> Blessed is the man that walketh not in the counsel of the ungodly, nor standeth in the way of sinners, nor sitteth in the seat of the scornful.
> But his delight is in the law of the LORD; and in his law doth he meditate day and night.
> And he shall be like a tree planted by the rivers of water, that bringeth forth his fruit in his season; his leaf also shall not wither, and whatsoever he doeth shall prosper.

I'm glad she never insisted on me reading my Bible daily because that would make me want to rebel and not do it. She helped me memorize those verses, convinced me of the benefits of it, and then left it up to me what to do about it. But that day, I did decide to read my Bible daily, and I have done it most days ever since. There are days that I look forward to it, and there are days I must force myself to do it.

When I was in high school, I was listening to my pastor give a sermon on this subject. He said something very interesting that I wrote in the inside cover of my Bible and have thought about often ever since: "This book will keep you from sin. Sin will keep you from this book." It's really true. During times in my life when I had yielded to temptations, I really hated to read my Bible that day. I knew it would be convicting. But I made a commitment to myself to when I was ten, so I forced myself to read it anyway. And it was convicting! Yet it brought me back and kept me from getting too far down the wrong paths in life.

Most of the time, I really look forward to it, though, and every time I read through the Bible, God shows me new things I had never seen before. I have memorized many hundreds of verses, often writing them down on little cards to pull out occasionally. As I go through life and have a wide variety of experiences and hear about many that my clients have as well, verses come back to mind that I memorized forty or fifty years earlier.

The Elderly Widow at Church

Mrs. Arnold was a very kind, always smiling widow in her late eighties who attended our church when I was growing up. She was a real prayer warrior but never sought personal attention for doing so. I often wonder, "When we get to heaven, who will receive the most rewards, someone like Billy Graham, who led millions of people to Christ, or an elderly prayer warrior like Mrs. Arnold who gets in her prayer closet daily to pray for his crusades?" I think both.

I like old people. It's a good thing since I am one now! I like people of all ages. Most people, anyway. But I always enjoyed saying hello to Mrs. Arnold whenever our paths would cross, walking in and out of church. When I was thirteen, she walked up to me one time after church and surprised me by putting her hands on my shoulders, looking me right in the eye, and saying, "Paul, someday God is going to use you in a very special way to help lots of people." I felt the impact of that. It sent shivers up and down my spine. I thanked her and went on home with my parents and just pondered silently on what that meant. I never forgot it and still think of it often, more than six decades later. But as time went on, I knew. I still think about it often. I want to remind those of you reading this book right now to remember that. There may be a word God gives you to go and share and encourage or inspire someone. Maybe even your mate or child. Perhaps even your pastor. But the right word at the right time, with God inspiring it, can have a powerful impact on someone's life. King Solomon was inspired by God to write in Proverbs 25:11 (KJV), "A word fitly spoken is like apples of gold in pictures of silver."

Dr. Bob Schindler

Bob Schindler was an MD and surgery resident who attended our church growing up. I had no idea that I might be a physician someday too. I was still planning on becoming a carpenter like my father and hopefully going into business with him—"Meier & Son, Contractors." I held doctor in such high esteem I felt really honored if he would pass me in the halls of the church and say, "Hi, Paul." *Wow—he actually remembers my name!* When I was sixteen, Dr. Schindler surprised me when he came up to me after church after a Sunday night service and asked me if I would come over to his home briefly to have a cup of coffee with him and his wife. I was honored and, of course, said yes. (I didn't really like coffee yet back then but would keep that to myself!)

When the three of us sat down in their living room twenty minutes later, he said, "Paul, I have no idea what career you will eventually choose, but I want you to memorize Proverbs 3:5–6 and think about it a lot, and God will guide you into the right career choice—one where you can serve Him. I really think God is going to use you in a special way someday. Don't see your career as your ultimate goal. See your career as a way God can use you to help other people. Your dad is a carpenter, but I know he witnesses to lots of people that he works with. He serves God here in the church, too, as our song leader (worship leader in today's terminology) and in other ways. It doesn't mean you have to go into full-time Christian service, but God may want you to be a missionary of some sort. In fact, when I finish my surgery residency, I am going to be a missionary surgeon in Africa."

And Dr. Schindler did do that when he eventually finished, and served God in that capacity for decades, then returned to America and became the president of the Christian Medical Society. I got a kind letter from his wife when he died of old age.

He didn't try to talk me into becoming a doctor, but he told me about the field—how hard medical school was and the trials along the way, but the rewards upon graduation and the freedom to become whatever kind of doctor you wanted to and to figure out ways to use that for God. Then he drove me home, and I thanked him. It reminded me of when Mrs. Arnold laid hands on me three years earlier, at age thirteen.

I had shivers up and down my spine and memorized the verses he told me to memorize and meditate on—Proverbs 3:5–6—the same night. They have been my life verse ever since: "Trust in the LORD with all thine heart and lean not unto thine own understanding. In all thy ways acknowledge him, and he shall direct thy paths" (Proverbs 3:5–6, KJV). I didn't have to worry about what career to eventually choose or any major decision in my life. I needed to follow Jesus and just go where He sent me. I have dwelt on that passage thousands of times over the years. Often at book signings, even today, I write my name on the book, and under it, if I have time, I add "Proverbs 3:5–6," hoping some of them will look it up and learn it themselves.

Twenty years later, I had a very pleasant follow-up to that passage after one of my "God-dreams." About once or twice a year, I have what I call a "God-dream." (To qualify, it has to be a dream where God is in it, telling me something, and there has to be a verification the next day or two afterwards or else, being a psychiatrist, I will just think it was a cool dream but not an official "God-dream.") I will tell you about a few of them in this chapter. Back to my true story about what happened twenty years after Dr. Schindler told me to memorize that verse: It was the night before a big Super Bowl party with friends to watch the Super Bowl that year. I am an avid football fan. I am six feet four inches and 270 pounds and played a little defensive line in my youth. I liked playing defense better than offense because (I used to say, jokingly) "It's better to give than to receive!" LOL.

But in spite of falling asleep thinking about the big game the next day, I had a totally unrelated "God-dream" where Jesus was in the dream and told me to get up out of bed and dig out my Bible concordance to look up the meanings of the word "acknowledge" from my life verse, Proverbs 3:5–6. In twenty years of it being my life-verse, I never really thought about it meaning anything other than doing what He wanted me to do.

So, I woke up from my dream and quietly slipped out of bed without waking my wife up and went into the other room to grab my Bible commentary. I looked up the word "acknowledge" to see what its possible implications were in the original Hebrew. One of the meanings that stood out to me and gave me the "shivers" was the implication to be aware of the many ways that God is present in our everyday activities—behind the scenes—in ways we never even know that He is guiding us.

I thought about my favorite chapter in the Bible also, Psalm 139, where we learn that, behind the scenes, God hugs us with one arm while leading us with the other. I thought about how awesome that concept is and that from now on, when I thought about my life verse, I would be on the watch for the many ways God is bringing "coincidences" into my life. Then I went back to sleep.

The next day I was getting dressed for the Super Bowl party and decided to grab an old pair of jeans I had not worn in a year or more. When I started to put them on, a little piece of metal fell out of the pocket. I had no idea what it was or where it came from, but I picked it up, and to my total surprise, it had an engraving on it, saying, "In all your ways acknowledge Him." I really got the shivers and knew, without a doubt, it had been a God-dream. I will never forget it.

My Two Most Significant, Life-Changing God-Dreams:

Not long after my Dr. Bob Schindler experience, I had the two most significant God-dreams of my life. In fact, they determined the whole direction of my life from that night forward. In the first dream, Jesus simply said the words, "I want you to be a doctor." I woke up from the dream and knew it wasn't just a random dream. It was so intense I knew it was God calling me to change all my previous plans and become an MD. I remembered what Dr. Schindler said, too—not to become an MD just to become an MD but to use the MD to find unique ways to serve God. It was a means to an end. I immediately said okay to the Lord and went back to sleep. Then that same night, I had the second God-dream, in which Jesus was showing me myself as an adult, traveling around the world teaching pastors and Christian leaders and others about "practical Christianity." Those were the exact words Jesus used. I woke up and pondered that, wondering what he meant by that, but again told the Lord, "I don't know what that will be like or what that means, Lord, but when the time calls that you make it clear to me, I will do it." The second dream about traveling the world training pastors and others came true twenty-eight years later. We will get back to that later in this chapter.

The Hard Work That Dr. Bob Schindler Warned Me About

Dr. Schindler had told me how hard it was to get through med school and residency. I remember him telling me, halfway joking, that it would take lots of coffee and late-night studying. He was right. If I was going to use my medical profession to be a platform, somehow, to spread "Practical Christianity," much like Johnny Appleseed went around the country spreading apple seeds, then I better have knowledge and professional credibility. I went to college, medical school, psychiatry residency, and finally obtained a seminary degree from Dallas Theological Seminary, becoming an ordained minister.

Dr. Bill Wilson at Duke

In the early 1970s, the closest thing to a Christian psychiatrist was my mentor at Duke Medical School Psychiatry Residency, Dr. Bill Wilson. He was an enthusiastic, dedicated Christian who also happened to be a great scholar in psychiatry. In the '70s, most psychiatrists and psychologists had a very low opinion of Christianity, so logically, pastors and other Christian leaders thought psychology and psychiatry were all evil concepts.

All good psychiatric and psychological research backs up the Bible, often to the dismay and even disgust of psychiatrists and psychologists doing the research because the Bible is truth. Most evangelical pastors didn't like psychiatrists either because of that hostility, so Christian leaders tended to throw out the baby with the bathwater. Many thought all psychiatry and psychology must be evil and anti-biblical and anti-God. The book of Proverbs is the best book of Christian psychology ever written. Dr. Bill Wilson had two residents he personally mentored, teaching us to integrate psychiatry and the Bible—David Larson and myself.

Dave had a calling from God just as strong as mine. His calling was to help psychiatrists be less hostile toward Christianity and more open-minded about it. Dave wanted Christians being treated by physicians or psychiatrists to be treated with dignity and respect. My calling was to somehow spread "practical Christianity" throughout the world if my second dream would eventually come true.

In 1975, my final year of residency, I learned that most of the counseling in America at the time was done by pastors, priests, and rabbis, and a minority by professional therapists, psychologists, and psychiatrists. God convicted me that if I became a full-time psychiatrist, I might help a thousand people in my lifetime, but if I helped train pastors now and fulfilled my second dream of doing so internationally later, I could potentially help millions. I knew that was the route God wanted me to go—if I could persuade a seminary to allow me to teach!

I wanted to train pastors and Christian leaders to become better equipped to meet *all* the needs of the people they minister to—and to know where to refer the ones who needed professional mental health help from a Christian perspective. I wanted pastors to be able to separate anti-Christian psychological theories from the helpful psychiatric facts that would help Christians with various mental illnesses, whether lifelong genetic, mental illnesses, or just a temporary but severe depression.

Dave and I became prayer partners for the next twenty-five years, calling each other up and confessing our sins to each other but also encouraging each other and spurring each other on to have the best possible effect on the cause of Christ in the world. Dave became a full-time psychiatry researcher, studying the benefits of religious faith in physical and mental health and proving it. Dave lived in the Washington, DC, area to have an impact there, and I moved to Dallas to teach pastors full time at Dallas Theological Seminary. We both accomplished our goals.

The Bible says that one person, with God's help, can put a thousand to flight, but two, with God's help, can put ten thousand to flight—5,000 each! I encourage everyone to have a prayer partner because of that. When Dave died of a ruptured aorta, the US Congress dedicated a Chair in the US Library of Congress to him, honoring him for the integration of physical and mental health with the value of spirituality. I received the 2019 "Great American" award from a conservative group of politicians for the same integration.

Kenneth Kantzer's Prayer "Coincidence" and Trinity Seminary

When I finished my psychiatric residency at Duke University Medical School, Duke was ranked second in the nation to Johns Hopkins, with Harvard third. Consequently, I had job offers to immediately come and run clinics in Maine and in Wisconsin for well over $100,000 a year, which was really a lot of money in 1975!

But I listened to the calling I had in the two dreams I had at sixteen and instead decided to call a couple of evangelical seminaries to see if they would consider hiring a committed

Christian psychiatrist to teach biblical psychology to their pastors. I called Trinity Evangelical Divinity School in Chicago first because they had such a great reputation and trained pastors from different evangelical denominations.

When I called, the call was passed to the assistant of Dr. Kenneth Kantzer, the academic dean. She told me that Dr. Kantzer was at home but that she knew he would love talking to me and gave me his home number to call immediately. I did, and Dr. Kantzer told me, "Paul, I don't know anything about you yet, but I am telling you the truth, Paul. I was just on my knees praying for God to send us a psychiatrist who is a committed Christian, so I want to meet you as soon as possible because that is such a coincidence it makes me want to at least get to know you to see if you are the one."

I flew there the next day, and since I had been meditating on scripture since I was ten, when Dr. Kantzer asked me various theological questions to see where I stood, I shared passages of scripture on every topic. He said he thought I knew the Bible better than some of his profs! I think he was joking, but he was pleased with my beliefs and my attitude and offered me a full-time job there for about $13,500 a year, a big drop from $135,000 in Maine. I found a part-time psychiatric practice in Milwaukee, Wisconsin, an hour's drive from Deerfield, Illinois, where Trinity Seminary is. I used that to keep up my skills and earn enough to pay down my medical school loans.

Mentoring Graham Barker

I loved teaching at a seminary, and I took courses right away to hopefully eventually get a seminary degree of my own. I was fulfilling my two dreams even though I was not yet traveling around the world to teach practical Christianity. I was teaching pastors and future missionaries who would be traveling around the world to teach practical Christianity.

One of the things I loved about teaching was finding special students to mentor, much like Dr. Bill Wilson had mentored David Larson and me. One student really stood out, with a great heart for God and great desire to integrate practical psychology research and scripture. His name was Graham Barker, a student from Australia.

We ended up having meals together, and he took several of my courses. He ended up feeling led, upon graduation from seminary, to go to graduate school and get a PhD in psychology to become a Christian psychologist to have an impact in his home country of Australia. And he did.

I continued to stay in touch with and mentor Graham over the years, and he got his postdoc training under me years later before returning to Australia, where he was a leader for many years in the Christian psychology movement there. He taught at a seminary, did missionary work with Young Life and other groups, had a private practice, wrote books, and did radio broadcasts there on Christian psychology.

The Death of Fellow-Professor Paul Little and Funeral Sermon of Leighton Ford

The professor in the office next to mine at Trinity Seminary was a great Christian leader, Paul Little, author of many books, including *How to Give Away Your Faith*. Paul had a real impact on me since I wanted to give away my faith through psychiatry.

When Paul died in 1975, Leighton Ford, Billy Graham's brother-in-law, spoke at Paul's funeral. Leighton Ford really struck a chord to me in his funeral sermon when he talked about what Paul Little accomplished in life and what we want to accomplish in our lives. He talked about being a pioneer for Christ, going places no one had gone. I certainly felt like that was my calling, but Trinity already had a counseling program when I went to teach there.

My cadaver-mate way back in medical school, Dr. Frank Minirth, had also gone into psychiatry and also felt the same calling I did and also went to teach at a seminary—Dallas Theological Seminary—that had no counseling program before Frank arrived in 1975. Frank and I had stayed in touch with each other and really felt way back in med school that we would probably have a ministry together someday.

Frank wanted me to come and join him at DTS to build the program from scratch. After the sermon by Leighton Ford, I knew that is what God wanted me to do. I love Trinity Seminary—an awesome school, but I wanted to be a pioneer in Dallas. In 1976, I moved to Dallas and took a pay cut—from $13,500 a year to $12,800 a year—to teach full-time at the seminary.

Frank and I had started a part-time psychiatric practice together that we named The Minirth-Meier Clinic. Dallas had 1,800 students, a much larger seminary, and all of them had to take our required course. Others could take our other courses. There were no Christian psychology textbooks at the time, so for each course Frank and I taught, we had to write our own textbook. His first was *Christian Psychiatry. Mine was Christian Childrearing and Personality Development.* Then together, we wrote *Happiness Is a Choice.*

Between them, there was such a thirst in America for an integration of true biblical psychology with Christian living and mental health that the books sold millions of copies. God turned our sacrifice into a financial blessing but much more so into an opportunity to spread practical Christian living throughout the USA. I also maintained a part-time psychiatric practice with Dr. Minirth, and as our books sold throughout the world, we sometimes even got patients from other countries who needed our professional help. They come to our Day Program for seven hours of therapy daily, five days a week, for three or four weeks.

I remember one day when two people came the same day all the way from Jerusalem, and neither of them knew the other was coming. One of them was a wonderful lady in her early thirties who had obsessive-compulsive disorder. She hated herself and felt all her life like God could not possibly accept her. She was suicidal all her life despite having very nice parents who were believers in Yeshua (Jesus). I knew that lifelong OCD is genetic and that almost any serotonin antidepressant at double the normal dose would cure her.

Her messianic synagogue had tried to cure her for years and was disappointed that she was coming to see me because they thought all psychology and psychiatry were sinful and that anyone should be curable just by using the Bible and prayer. They failed to see that God allows some people to have diabetes and need insulin to live. Without it, they die. Others inherit severe hypothyroidism and would die without thyroid meds. What they failed to see is that God also allows many people to inherit low serotonin levels, causing lifelong depression and often OCD that is curable only with serotonin meds.

God can heal anything, of course. But if your engine fails in your car, do you pray for God to supernaturally replace it? If you get cancer, God can and sometimes does heal it, but usually, you can either get surgery or radiation and cure it or die. Everyone Jesus healed during His personal ministry on earth died of something else later. Death is part of life. So, God allows mental illnesses also.

We put the young Israeli woman on a serotonin med, and within a few weeks, she was totally normal for the first time in her life. She was happy, at peace, and felt loved by God. But she went back to her legalistic messianic synagogue, and they told her she had to quit taking the meds and just rely on prayer and the Bible. So, she quit, went back into despair, and hung herself. After that, the church realized the truth and contacted me, and I sent them copies of my book Blue Genes, which describes genetic, mental disorders, and now they pass out copies to other people there. That has been my goal—to help believers see the value of legitimate Christian psychiatry and psychology.

The Delight of Mentoring

Of all the variety of things God has led me to do over the years, one of the most rewarding has been the opportunity to mentor a few people in a very special way who God has brought into my life. I already mentioned my good friend, Dr. Graham Barker, who retired in Australia in 2021. In 1976, I came to Dallas Theological Seminary to teach pastoral counseling full time for the next twelve years before God led me on to other ministries when others were able to carry on the counseling training at DTS. Did national radio with Dr. Minirth an hour a day live to two million people a day the same way?

One of the first students who really stood out to me at DTS was a young man who had a deep heart for God, Tony Evans. Tony was also brilliant. He was a man of many God-given talents, which Tony worked hard on to improve. He was a scholar but also won awards for his outstanding preaching ability. He was humble and shared private things with me when we had an opportunity to get to know each other. He took my courses and loved them and got 100 percent on every test. I ended up taking Tony out to lunch almost every Thursday at an inexpensive Chinese restaurant near the seminary for the next three years. Tony did not become a psychologist, but he did become one of the best pastors in America, with an international ministry, books, training of other pastors, and a host of other ministries.

Another student that I really felt God was leading me to mentor was Abede Alexandre, a Haitian student who was my top student academically despite getting most of his education in Haiti. He had and still has an outstanding love for God and for helping people. I spent lots of time with Abede, and when he finished his seminary degree, he felt led to become a psychologist. By then, I was no longer living on my meager DTS salary but had money coming in from millions of book sales, so I paid Abede's way through PhD training, including living expenses. Then he did his postdoc work at our Chicago clinic and went on from there to teach at Harvard for several years. He also pastored a large Haitian church in Boston, where he continues in 2021 to do three sermons every Sunday—one in English, one in French, and one in Creole. He has also written books and had other ministries. He now serves on the board of directors for Meier Clinics.

A few years after I started teaching at DTS, Dr. James Dobson started his ministry, Focus on the Family. I read his books and loved what he was saying and doing, so I volunteered to go there three days every six months for the next twenty years or so to assist him in his ministry in an association of Christian physicians that included my prayer partner, Dr. David Larson. I would not consider myself a mentor to Dr. Dobson, but I was blessed to assist Focus on the Family as they spread and continue to spread practical Christianity and Christian psychology to millions around the world.

There are many outstanding students I could write a whole book on who I got to mentor. Ken Hendren ended up becoming a messianic rabbi in Tel Aviv with a writing and teaching ministry throughout Israel. I was blessed to mentor John Townsend and Henry Cloud when they were just young students—John at DTS and Henry, who I got to know when he did a practicum under me in a hospital when he was a student at SMU. John and Henry both went on to become outstanding Christian psychologists and have written the Boundaries series of Christian psychology books and many others that have sold millions of copies. I also chose them to run our California clinics when we grew into a national chain, then had them do radio with us daily because they were so gifted by God. Now I have retired from doing national radio, but they have continued that program.

Finally Fulfilling My Second Dream

My first of two God-dreams I had that night at age sixteen was to become a doctor and somehow use my MD degree to serve God in a ministry. I had fulfilled that throughout my career. My second dream was to travel the world teaching practical Christianity, which I later labeled Christian psychology for my own books and teaching. My books are sold in thirty languages all over the world, including Arabic and Hebrew. I never took a penny of royalties on any foreign books because the publishers could sell them less expensively without me getting any royalties so they could reach more people for Christ.

Somehow that second dream of actually traveling the globe to train pastors and missionaries and professional counselors and lay people around the world in person had not been fulfilled yet by the late 1980s. But I got to be the team physician on a mountain climbing expedition led by astronaut Jim Irwin to climb Mount Ararat in search of Noah's ark in the late 1980s.

Our preliminary team got captured by terrorists on the mountain and were lined up in a firing squad but allowed to run down the mountain. Turkish soldiers rushed in helicopters and found the terrorists and killed them on the spot. No long trials there. Jim Irwin came after that and went up accompanied by Turkish soldiers but was never allowed to go to the spot he believed the Ark to be based on classified photos he was aware of—at the 16,500' level above the Ahora Gorge. Jim died of a heart attack a few years later, having never fulfilled that dream he had of showing that to the world.

But after that experience, I developed an urge to write a Bible prophecy novel to wake up people as to things to come.

I loved Bible prophecy all my life and took courses on it from Dr. John Walvoord and Dr. Dwight Pentecost at Dallas Seminary. Before writing the novel, I also memorized verses from every single chapter in the Bible that had anything to do with prophecy.

In final preparation for my novel, based on the best guesses I could make from my studies, especially of the book of Revelation, I traveled to Israel to learn street names and as many facts as possible to make the novel accurate when I described the seven-year Great Tribulation. The name of the novel is *The Third Millennium*. It ended up selling nearly a million copies. More importantly, in God's scheme of things, it led to the beginning of fulfilling my second dream. Here is how.

The Messianic Synagogue

While in Jerusalem, I decided to go to a service on a Saturday evening at the largest messianic synagogue in Jerusalem. Messianic Jews are Jews who have accepted Jesus (Yeshua) as their Messiah. I slipped in the back row of the messianic synagogue quietly, having gotten there a few minutes late. Nobody there knew me, but they could tell I was a tourist, so they gave me earphones to hear an English interpreter since the rabbi spoke in Hebrew.

As I sat down, the first thing I heard him say was, "Here in Israel, we have over ten thousand believers in Yeshua now but not a single professional Christian counselor, so let's pray right now that God will send someone to train our lay people to be able to help people with special mental health needs, maybe even an American Christian psychiatrist or psychologist." I almost fainted, and my mouth gaped in disbelief. I got those special shivers again. I knew God was calling me to start fulfilling my second dream that I had decades earlier at the age of sixteen.

I went up to the rabbi afterwards and said I was Paul Meier, a Christian psychiatrist, and when would he like me to come to train other messianic rabbis and people interested in becoming lay counselors there. I ended up going back to Israel to teach Christian psychology for five years in a row for one to two weeks each time. Some of the students went on since then to become professional Christian therapists and psychologists, and that was the beginning of the Christian psychology movement in Israel.

The French Lady

On my way home from Israel after my synagogue shock, I had three flights. One from Tel Aviv to Paris, one from Paris to Chicago, and the final leg from Chicago to Dallas. I had the most unbelievable trip home anyone could imagine.

On my first flight, nobody sat next to me who spoke English, so I was bored for about five hours. The second flight from Paris to Chicago was going to be about eleven hours long, so I prayed, "Dear God, please put somebody beside me who speaks English so I won't get bored to death!" LOL. God knew I was joking with Him but also serious about my request. "I will try to minister to whoever it is, Lord."

Then a young French lady came and sat beside me and seemed kind and spoke English fairly well. I thanked God, and we shared our first names only, and I asked her where she was going. She said she was from Lyon, a suburb of Paris, and going to Little Rock, Arkansas, for vacation. I told her Little Rock is a really nice place, but why would someone from Paris go on vacation to Little Rock?

She said since I asked her, she would tell me. She said ten years earlier, she had been a college student in Paris and went through a broken engagement and got very depressed and had lost hope in life. But a missionary at her university from Little Rock helped her out and gave her a copy of a book called *Happiness Is a Choice* by Dr. Paul Meier.

She asked me if I had ever heard of that book, and I hid my shock and told her I had heard of it but didn't tell her I wrote it. She went on to say that as a result of that book, she became a believer and got over her depression and that now she is a missionary to college students in the Paris area. She was going to Little Rock to visit the now-retired missionary who had given her the book and was also going to Little Rock to "hunt down Paul Meier."

I asked her why she wanted to hunt down Paul Meier, and she said that Paul Meier has a branch clinic in Little Rock and thought she could find out how to reach Dr. Meier through them because even though the Bible addresses most of life's problems, they have students who come to them with bulimia, mood swings, genetic things that affect mental health, etc., and the missionaries in Paris had asked her to ask me what they could do to get some training in Christian psychology to better help the students they minister to.

At this point, I could no longer contain myself, and I told her, "Well, I am Paul Meier. When do you want me to come to train you all?" She thought I was joking, so I pulled out my passport and showed it to her. She almost fainted.

A couple months later, I was in Paris training pastors, missionaries, and even one man who had three doctorates, one in psychology, who helped me teach them. His name is Jean-Luc Bertrand, a very committed Christian with many talents, and we became good friends.

Years later, when my first prayer partner, Dr. David Larson, died, I called up Jean-Luc and asked him if he would be my prayer partner. He was a little surprised and asked me why I would want someone from Paris to be his prayer partner. I told him there were three reasons: 1. He lives a couple thousand miles away, so it is easier to confess very personal sins without worrying about everybody finding out! 2. He is a psychologist, and I am a psychiatrist, so we can analyze each other why we were tempted in the specific areas we would sin in when we did. 3. My first prayer partner, Dr. David Larson, was such a genuinely godly man that it seemed like it was always me confessing my sins to him.

"You're French, Jean-Luc, so I know you probably sin as much as I do!" We both had a good laugh, and he said those things all qualify him, so he accepted. We have been prayer partners for about twenty years now and even visit each other sometimes, confessing everything from birth on that we can remember. Like Dave and I had, we have encouraged each other to achieve things neither of us would by ourselves.

We wrote a book together, *Blue Genes*, and he has written several more since. He is a wealthy man and the former owner of a Paris professional soccer team, which is like owning a pro football team in America since soccer is their most popular sport. Jean-Luc used his money and time and raised funds from others to start Generation Africa, where they raise and educate 2,000 children now in South Africa whose parents died of AIDS. Jean-Luc even made a documentary about his AIDS kids, and it won an academy award here in America for best foreign documentary. One with God's help can put 1,000 to flight, but two can put 10,000.

Other Countries

After training pastors and missionaries in France, thus fulfilling my second dream at age sixteen, I had many callings to other countries. I never once picked out a country to go to. I waited for more opportunities like my Jerusalem experience, the "French lady" experience, and opportunities—sometimes very surprising opportunities—opened up to me as I was "acknowledging Him" by looking at all the signs around me since God promised to direct my paths. I could write an entire book of my experiences, but I think you get the picture by now.

I will tell you one more unique way God allowed me to start the Christian psychology movement in Sweden. A Swedish evangelical Lutheran minister in Sweden and his wife had read one of my books together, and she had become very so depressed that somehow her brain had actually swelled, and doctors there could not find a way to stop the swelling and told her she was going to die.

Dan and Joyce Rosendahl called me from Sweden and explained her situation to me. Lutheran nuns had given her last rites already, expecting her to die soon. I told them if they could fly her to Dallas, I would treat her for free and probably as least relieve the depression, but that I had to ability to treat the pressure in her brain.

They came, and I treated her in our Day Program (Catalyst). In Catalyst, we can help most people with depression in a few weeks using our techniques and God's word and the best new meds to help them restore their happy and peaceful chemicals in their brains (serotonin, dopamine, etc.). So, Joyce came, and we dug and probed and helped her see and resolve even childhood issues that had eaten away at her for years, and she completely recovered, and the swelling went away also, thank God.

When they got back to Sweden, newspapers wrote articles about the "Miracle Cure in Dallas." Dan and Joyce decided God was leading them to spread Christian psychology across Sweden, so they had me come and train pastors, missionaries, and they even invited non-Christian professionals to come.

I trained them all day, every day for a week, and by the end of the week, some of the secular professionals even trusted Christ and wanted further training in Christian psychology. One psychiatrist became a believer and gave up half of her income to develop Christian psychology in Sweden. Sweden is very liberal socio-politically, and yet they developed a Christian Day Program like ours, with the help of Dan and Joyce.

When Yeltsin took over as leader of Russia, the doors opened for a few years to spread Christianity there. I got an invitation to go teach secular psychologists in St. Petersburg, Russia, for a week, so I went almost immediately.

My parents both grew up in a German community in Russia. Their families were friends. My paternal grandfather owned a large farm machinery production place there, and he was so wealthy he had thirty servants living in quarters behind his house. He also served as pastor of a Baptist church there. My great-grandfather had started the first Baptist church in that entire area near the Volga River.

My mom's family were evangelical Lutherans. My grandfather was a friend of the czar, who even traveled to my dad's home when my dad was seven years old to visit with my grandfather. But in 1917, when my parents were ten-year-old neighbors and friends, the communists came and killed many of their relatives all over the city, right in front of their families. My parents were both fortunate that their parents were able to bribe their way out of their town to St. Petersburg and from there to Germany, where they would live several years before moving to America but settling in different States. At age twenty-seven, they were both still single and visited each other and fell in love and got married.

So, I pounced on the opportunity to go to St. Petersburg to train secular psychologists, nearly all of whom were atheists. By the end of the week, half of them had trusted Christ and pledged to further their training and become Christian psychologists, which was the beginning of the Christian psychology movement in Russia.

But on the last night there, in a hotel overlooking the Baltic Sea, I fell asleep with a very prideful attitude. I was arrogantly thinking how lucky God was to have me there to do those things. In the middle of the night, God woke me up with a nightmare, though.

In my dream, Jesus showed me sin after sin after sin I had committed in my life that I had overlooked and not confessed to myself or to God. In the dream, Jesus reminded me that He chooses the weak of this world to show Himself strong. The main reason I was qualified to be called by God at age sixteen was because, deep down, I was spiritually weak without God's saving grace. I wept and asked God to forgive me, and He comforted me and gave me total peace.

I knew that was God convicting me, but for me to classify it as a definite God-dream, I would need some follow-up evidence, and it came the next morning. It was our last breakfast together before departing to return to America. The missionary chosen to do our breakfast devotional knew nothing about my dream the night before. Nobody but God and I knew. But he said that God spoke to him in a dream last night, and he felt led to change what he was going to share about how God chooses the weak to show Himself strong. First Corinthians 1:27 says that God chooses the weak things of this world to shame the strong, and elsewhere, He says it is also to show Himself strong. I got chills and shivers and knew that was my confirmation.

My Cuba trip was two years after my Russia trip, so I had gone to two or three countries a year between those trips. One of the most unusual mission trips I ever went on was a unique invitation from a group of Christian physicians to go to Cuba.

In Cuba, political leaders or soldiers who became Christians were killed. Being invited by Castro to come to Cuba and allowed to teach Christian psychiatry to 1,000 physicians in Havana and several hundred more in Cienfuegos and to lead 700 Cuban children to Christ using clown shows followed by gospel presentations—had to be an act of God to trick Fidel in such a way. Castro even somehow allowed my talk on Christian psychiatry to be broadcast on radio in Havana.

The doctors did it by raising more than a half-million dollars worth of medical equipment donated from US hospitals that had been replaced with better equipment. The Cuban dictator bragged about free medical care in Cuba, and the media here bought it hook, line, and sinker. They don't mention that they can't afford anesthesia, and whiskey is used for surgery or all the host of other shortcomings.

My ticket from Mexico to Cuba got lost by them somehow, but as I was almost ready to give up and go back to Texas, a man in a suit came out of the plane and gave me his ticket, which they allowed me to use. Other miracles happened that I don't have the time or space to tell here. I stayed at the home of one of the leading cancer specialists in Cuba, whose family lived on $40 a month. His wife had to get in line to get a loaf of bread. His son played with a scooter with only one wheel as his main toy.

I bought the doctor a coke to drink, and he sipped on it slowly for many hours, then wrapped the empty can in a newspaper page to take it out to the trash because if his neighbors saw him with a coke can, they would be jealous. Many of the Cuban doctors were in tears as I told them story after story about the healing of patients I had treated using Christian psychiatry.

When I heard that hundreds of kids were coming to a clown show the doctors' wives had produced for them and that the gospel would be presented to them afterwards, I went to a candy store nearby and bought all the candy in the store and put it in bags. When the kids came, we gave each kid, one at a time, a candy and told them in Spanish that Jesus loved them. Nearly all trusted Christ at the end.

Castro had a spy follow me everywhere to be sure I didn't say anything bad about him or the government. The spy told me he was spying. He became a believer by the end of the trip but had to keep it secret because he would be killed if they found out. The last night we were there, after a week of miracles, I fell asleep getting extremely prideful again, like I had in Russia two years earlier. You would think I would learn my lesson by now, but I truly am weak in so many ways.

I lay on my bed in a room by myself again, thinking how lucky God was to have me. Again, Jesus woke me up with a horrible dream again, with sinful thoughts and deeds I had committed in the two years between Russia and Cuba flashing sequentially before my eyes. We commit a lot of sins we don't even realize we are committing. Then there are some we do justify and know as well. I guess as a psychiatrist, I should know that.

I woke up weeping again, and this time Jesus shared the other half of 1 Corinthians 1:27 with me about how God chooses the foolish things of this world to confound the wise. It was bad enough in Russia admitting to myself that I was weak without God in my life, but now I had to admit to myself that I was weak and foolish without God intervening.

Yet again, Jesus' intent was not to shame or condemn me but to just see the truth. The Apostle Paul said in Romans chapters 7 to 8 that sometimes, he does things he should not do, and other times, he fails to do the things he should but concludes that whole conversation by assuring us there is no condemnation for those of us who are believers. Jesus wants us to learn and grow from our experiences, even our sinful ones.

A Final Word to Pastors and Church Leaders:

Each of us is unique in both strengths and weaknesses, and God leads each of us in different ways. He gave each of us specific strengths and specific weaknesses too. With me, He has often led with dreams, but He leads others in a wide variety of various ways and circumstances.

Regardless of how He chooses to lead you, I want to encourage you to remember some of the things you have hopefully learned from this chapter. When you see your own weaknesses or foolishness, rather than beating yourself up, realize that being weak and foolish is what qualified you and me both to be used by God in the first place!

Remember what I shared about the word "acknowledge" in Proverbs 3:5–6—be looking around you for the hundreds of times He is there, never leaving or forsaking us, working behind the scenes, hugging us with one arm and leading with the other, wanting us to learn from our own failures. He counts our tears and places them in a bottle. I encourage you to find a prayer partner of the same sex outside of your own church. He doesn't have to live in Paris like mine does!

My prayer partner of the past twenty years, Jean-Luc from Paris, came to our home again in 2020 to spend some quality time with my wife and me. But he and I got together privately and spent hours thinking back to our births and trying to remember and admit every sin we had ever committed up to the present. It made us feel great!

James, the brother of Jesus, said in James 5:16 that if we confess our sins (faults) to each other, we will be healed. That would surprise lots of people but sharing sins with someone who shares his own back is very healing and relieving. We accept each other unconditionally. How much more does God accept us!

When you were a child and learned how to pray, you were probably thinking, at least unconsciously, "Dear Heavenly version of my earthly father"—but my God isn't a German immigrant, and your God isn't your father either. Make a pledge to yourself right now, writing down today's date in the back of your Bible, promising to be your own best friend and to make an effort not to say anything negative to yourself that you would not tell your best friend under the same circumstances.

Ponder that. You would tell your best friend the truth and show him grace. If you would say something different to yourself, then you are lying to yourself. Satan and demons are "accusers of the brethren." They don't need your help, but I'm sure they appreciate it! If you are upset with yourself about something, at least let it be the truth. If it is the truth, you would say it to your best friend. Jean-Luc and I do tell each other if something the other did is a really dumb thing to do or think, but we can say it in a loving and non-condemning way. We are wrapped in the robe of righteousness of Jesus, who took our place. It doesn't give us license to continue in our sins, so don't misinterpret that.

We treat many pastors in our Day Program who come and stay a few weeks and humble themselves by sharing things in group therapy with several other hurting people in the group. When they finish, they are stronger than ever before.

It is easier to empathize with suffering church members after you have recovered from your own anxiety or depression or personal failure. I know pastors who also have genetic disorders—bipolar disorder, OCD, even a schizophrenic—all of whom are happy and very functional on meds that correct the chemical imbalances they inherited. There is no such thing as "normal!" As Patsy Clairmont so wisely said in one of her book titles, *Normal Is Only a Setting on Your Dryer!*

CHAPTER 14

Honey Lake Clinic

Greenville, Florida

Karl Benzio, MD

Karl Benzio, MD, is a board-certified Christian psychiatrist who has held several health system clinical and leadership positions. Dr. Karl uniquely implements a faith-informed, Jesus-centered application of cutting-edge psychiatric science to not only successfully treat patients but also consult, teach, write, and serve as a frequent media guest expert and conference speaker addressing a wide range of behavioral health and social policy issues that impact individuals, families, and society.

He holds a BSE in biomedical engineering with focus in central nervous system imaging from Duke University, an MD from Rutgers-New Jersey Medical School, and had his psychiatry residency at UC Irvine. Dr. Benzio's expertise is in integrating brain physiology with psychological and spiritual principles into decision-making science with its endless application to every facet of psychological health and functioning for individuals, families, communities, and society.

Dr. Karl developed a unique cutting-edge BioPsychoSpiritual model focusing on the spiritual discipline of decision-making. His SPEARS tool not only reveals the causes of many issues but also unpacks and clarifies Bible-based, Jesus-centered, and scientifically synergistic spirit-mind-body treatment for all our psychological and spiritual struggles so we can access the psychospiritual healing and awakening Jesus taught, role-modeled, and died for.

A practicing psychiatrist since 1989, Karl has been blessed to help tens of thousands directly find healing while also learning so much from so many patients and colleagues. He was the first psychiatrist invited by Iraq's minister of health in 2007 into post-Hussein Iraq, leading a multidisciplinary team to consult and teach decision-making and treatment curriculum to Muslim Iraqi national healthcare providers and Christian churches, even though his curriculum is thoroughly Christian. He led a team facilitating healing workshops to mentors and children who were traumatized and tortured victims of Joseph Kony's ruthless abuses and atrocities in Uganda and Sudan.

He has given expert testimony for the US President's Bioethics Committee and numerous state legislatures on various social policy issues, including right of conscience, physician-assisted suicide, same-sex marriage issues, gender identity issues, pro-life issues, opioid epidemic, suicide, and other behavioral health complexities. He led a Behavioral Health Committee of unique Bux-Mont Katrina Relief Effort, where our county in Pennsylvania adopted Katrina devastated Hancock County, Mississippi, providing several millions of dollars financially and countless hours of professional expertise and labor services over several years. The effort was officially decorated and recognized by the US Congress and the Salvation Army as a template for relief/aid in future national catastrophes.

Dr. Karl's Life Change Radio Minute airs daily on over 425 radio stations. His Stepping Stones Daily Devotional integrates faith and psychiatry in a short practical and inspirational message read around the world and used by many churches and ministries (https://lighthousenetwork.org/stepping-stones/).

He served as the Pennsylvania state director of the American Academy of Medical Ethics from 2010 to 2019 and currently serves on the Focus on the Family Physician's Resource Council and is a content contributor to YouVersion, Bible App, Charisma, and iDisciple online resources.

Dr. Benzio was the founder of the Lighthouse Network in 2003, the cofounder and chancellor of Honey Lake Clinic in 2017, and founded and directs the Commission for Christian Psyche Excellence, a think tank charged with synergizing and advancing the Christian psychiatry movement that educates clinicians, develops treatment opportunities for service delivery, and researches the impact divine power has in psychospiritual healing.

Most importantly, Karl loves Jesus and the Bible, is married to his best friend, Martine, since 1991, is a father to three incredible daughters—Dominique, twenty-nine (husband Adam), Nicole, twenty-six (husband Connor), and Gigi, twenty-one—loves travel, psychologically intriguing TV shows/movies, anything about decision-making, pickleball, and sports, especially his beloved Pittsburgh and Duke teams.

Email: *KBenzio@HoneyLake.Clinic*
Website: *https://www.HoneyLake.Clinic* and
https://www.LighthouseNetwork.org
His Stepping Stones Daily Devotional sign-up is:
lighthousenetwork.org/stepping-stones/

Honey Lake Clinic

I'm so excited to share about Honey Lake Clinic, an amazing treatment center I was blessed to help start. But before I explain our unique integration of cutting-edge psychiatric science with biblical principles, I believe it's important to share some of my backstory leading up to Honey Lake Clinic. My story will not only help you understand and find treatment options for yourself and others in your life but also encourage you to be part of other people's healing.

Regardless of one's vocation, full-time ministry is God's calling for each of us, and hurting people are all around us. God's strategically placed you in their life as a lighthouse, providing safety and guiding them to healing. Be courageously open to the Holy Spirit. Allow Him to use your skills, education, and experiences (both good and bad) to help bring healing to whatever family, friends, church, neighborhood, workplace, community, volunteer organization, or any relationships you make. I did, and it changed my life and many others as well!

Background

My call to psychiatry started to dawn on me at the age of five when God laid on my heart the concept of "decision-making." Even at that tender age, I began to learn about and understand how to become a better decision-maker myself and help others become better decision-makers. Several years later, I realized a psychiatrist is an expert trained not only in why and how we make the decisions we make but, more importantly, the application of various therapies to help us become life-enhancing decision-makers. This led me to major in biomedical engineering at Duke University with particular focus on central nervous system (brain) imaging to equip me with great tools to become a psychiatrist.

I grew up in the church, saved as a little kid. But I only heard the Bible taught as either a history book pertaining to what happened 2,000 plus years ago or how my decision about Jesus was going to affect my eternal future. A pastor, Bob Thieme, floored me with his in-depth, eloquent, highly detailed teaching about the mind, emotions, will, Holy Spirit, decision-making, adversity, and how to progress to both psychological and, more importantly, spiritual maturity. And all his psychiatric material came from... *the Holy Bible!* This marked the first time I heard the Bible used to teach about my inner world other than condemning me for being a sinner.

Pastor Thieme had no medical or psychological degree, but his teachings powerfully discussed key aspects of psychological and brain functioning. I thought, if the Bible is that powerful, just think what viewing it through the lenses of psychiatric expertise could unleash! In that moment, God specifically commissioned me for my life's calling. He gave me a special assignment: to understand brain chemistry and how the mind functions so I could more clearly and practically articulate the healing powers the Bible teaches and bring this knowledge to the medical and treatment community who keep leaving God out of the healing process.

My personal world, on the other hand, was quite the opposite of my ministry calling, as my inner world was experiencing significant distress and turmoil. From kindergarten through third grade, I was taken out of class a couple times per week for speech therapy for a significant stutter and lisp. I struggled to start and finish words and sentences, so many other kids mocked or bullied me. Having to think of words I could get out without stammering made me overthink everything.

My struggles were compounded by frequent moves as youngster—living in four states, starting and stopping many schools, making and losing friend—all of which contributed to frequent bed-wetting till age fourteen and ongoing anxiety and depression. Even through these struggles, God blessed me academically, and I was highly decorated athletically, even performing on national TV in front of 70,000 people as a twelve and thirteen-year-old in the NFL Punt, Pass, and Kick contest. But with accomplishments comes pressure, and in high school, I found alcohol relieved my anxiety and social inhibitions. What I didn't realize was how it also compromised my decision-making in practically every area of life.

Despite mounting unfavorable consequences, high school was easy with many awards, privileges, and "power," affirming that my game-plan to achieve control while minimizing hurt was working. Unfortunately, Duke University was a lot harder, so my poor decisions and escalating alcohol misuse cost me a baseball scholarship and an Air Force ROTC full-tuition scholarship plus a generous living-and-book stipend. My grades started sinking, so I quit the baseball team—my first time quitting anything! I got caught cheating on a differential equations course exam, had a hearing in front of the Honors Review Board, and barely avoided being kicked out, but was placed on academic probation. I was drinking daily, my disruptive behavior was frequent, and I was involved in fights often. Playing replaced studying as I almost flunked out my junior year.

Stumbling out of Duke with a prestigious degree in biomedical engineering and killer MCAT scores but a non-competitive 3.0 GPA, I was rejected by my fourteen dream medical schools and waitlisted at my state school, New Jersey Medical School. My dream of being a psychiatrist seemed to be over. But in late August, three days before med school started, a giggly lady from the dean's office called. She didn't use the word miracle, but she did say this situation had never happened before. She was pleased to inform me that another incoming first-year student was unable to attend, the several names above me were no longer interested, and my name was next on the waiting list. She stated they had never gone through so many names on the waiting list, but if I wanted to enroll (and pay the hefty tuition), this new open slot was mine. Thanking God for miracles, I accepted.

You would think this whopper-sized miracle would catch my attention, and I would start to follow God, but as usual, I thought my way really did work. I thought I could do what I wanted and still get what I wanted. But now, with the stress, pressure, and workload of medical school, my insecurity, anxiety, mild depression, and need for control only worsened. So, my self-medicating behavior with alcohol increased, along with that of many of my peers. We even called our intramural basketball team the SIPs: Society of Impaired Physicians. Finally, life came to a crashing halt when halfway through medical school, not only did I get a DUI, but I was also arrested for six counts of aggravated assault. I landed in jail.

My decisions had been so destructive that God used jail to protect me from hurting myself and others. But more importantly, one comes face to face with oneself while behind bars. There is enormous shame but no way to hide. There Jesus spoke (not audibly but in my spirit) to me, saying, "Karl, you made Me your Savior when you were a kid, but you never made Me the Lord of your life. If you make Me the Lord of your life, I will teach you things about decision-making that will renew your mind and transform your life and help you transform other lives as well."

When I heard the Lord, I heard authority. When I heard authority, I heard author. Then I realized I had been trying to futilely and foolishly be the author of my own instruction manual for life. I thought I knew me, loved me, understood me, knew what was best for me, knew my needs, and knew my future more than anyone else, so of course, I should be the one to author my personal How-To book for getting the most out of life. I was smart enough to take a little of the Bible when it suited my needs, but the rest was from the world and my flesh.

At that point, I realized when someone designs or manufactures something, they don't make you guess how to get the most out of it. They write an instruction manual. Well, God designed my mind, and He was so merciful and kind to give me an instruction manual, the B.I.B.L.E.: "Best Instruction Book for Living Everyday!" I then read the Gospels, looking at all of Jesus' decisions, and started using the Bible as my personal instruction manual. I combined these discoveries with my psychological and brain science training and my own therapy. Over the next four years, not only did my personal life significantly turn around, but my professional life flourished because what I learned about decision-making became the core of the curriculum and therapy process I've used to help many others access the same psychospiritual healing of one's inner being or psyche.

Professional Life Prior to Honey Lake Clinic

My psychiatry residency at the University of California, Irvine, was one of the first places hit by managed care so I learned firsthand how insurances would radically change inpatient/residential behavioral health treatment. Post-residency, I helped a private Philadelphia suburban psych hospital adapt to a changing insurance system as I took over a chaotic adolescent inpatient program. I placed Christians in key nursing and therapist positions, we taught biblical principles of life management using secular terms, and the unit experienced a decorated turnaround. As I tried to infuse more overt biblical and Jesus elements, I got pushback, so I left.

I became the director of our local community hospital's psychiatric ER, inpatient unit, partial hospital program, and consultant to the medical units of the hospital. The department was successful financially, engaged in unique insurance at-risk contracts, and we were providing great care again using biblical principles. I was known as the psychiatrist who talked a lot about Jesus and what the Bible teaches. But again, I got some pushback when trying to develop a more overt Christian program. I felt God saying, "You learned what you needed regarding the administrative aspects; it's time to go full tilt with integrating science and Bible together."

I launched into private practice and was quickly full and successful. My science-faith integration was gratefully appreciated by patients, but I experienced firsthand many churches' leadership's fear of and anger toward psychiatry. Simultaneously, my secular mental health colleagues were leaving out the spiritual aspect of healing and mental health and had a low ceiling of success for years. So finally, acting on that commissioning as a teen, I started a non-profit ministry, Lighthouse Network, with the mission to reignite the Behavioral Health Revolution that Jesus started with His countercultural and revolutionary life and teaching. Being the Wonderful Counselor and Great Physician, Jesus ideally delivers psychospiritual healing beyond our wildest imagination.

Lighthouse Network had two main goals. First, educate the Christian church regarding the true science about the amazing psychological apparatus we call the mind that God intricately designed and wired into us. Understanding our minds allows us to be better stewards of our minds, as evidenced by fruit, produced by consistent godly decision-making. The second goal was to show the non-Christian treatment world the amazing psychological and physical healing that occurs when harnessing the divine power of God and applying the truths and life management principles in the Bible.

Christian psychiatrists are rare, so when Christians and pastors heard about my private practice, word spread quickly. I received many calls (pre-internet) from the region, then beyond. Even though I couldn't treat everyone, I had a hard time saying "no," so I would hunt and find a treatment option. Eventually, the Lighthouse Network Helpline became the largest Christian Behavioral Health Helpline in the world.

Teaching my unique SPEARS decision-making curriculum, which seamlessly integrates psychological and biblical principles, evolved into speaking at many Christian and secular conferences, missions trips to Kenya and Uganda, testifying in state legislatures, and visits to the White House to consult faith-based mental health initiatives and testify for President Bush's BioEthics Committee. In 2007, my most unique professional ministry was being the first behavioral health clinician from outside of Iraq to be invited into Iraq by the Iraqi minister of health after the fall of Saddam Hussein. Iraq is 99 percent Muslim, and they knew my curriculum was Christian, but they tried secular options, and their people were still dying of addictions and suicide due to the significant PTSD and depression from years of brutal dictatorship, abuse, trauma, and war.

As awareness of the curriculum and helpline grew, I developed a consulting niche by helping secular medical model addiction rehab facilities implement Christian programs and curriculum. On the other end of the spectrum, I helped Christian non-medical work-farm discipleship-type programs augment their spiritual curriculum by helping them improve the medical and psychological components. To me, the fastest and most robust healing occurs when all three spheres—spirit, mind, and body—are deeply addressed and integrated. In 2013, Dr. David Hoskins was growing his detox program to a residential rehab and wanted to implement Christian programming. Dave and I realized we had complementary skill sets, so we merged our two nonprofit organizations together under the name of Lighthouse Network.

Over the years, as our Helpline found many rehab programs for callers and as I developed Christian addiction rehab programs, only a couple of residential programs existed for callers who had no addiction but were struggling with significant mental health issues. Those struggling with significant life-interfering mental health concerns were limited to just two options. The most restrictive was a locked inpatient unit for three to six days, providing mainly safety management for the suicidal or psychotic patients but with minimal depth of therapy. The other option was partial hospital programs (also called a day treatment program), where a person lives at home with no professional supervision and goes to a clinic for several hours of intensive daily programming Monday through Friday for fourteen to forty-five days.

From my experience directing inpatient and PHP programs, I knew a level of care was missing. Most patients on a locked inpatient unit don't need the expensive, hospital-based, highly regimented, and restrictive level of care. Instead, I believed a relaxing Christian residential environment with loving, Christian staff delivering intensive psychological and spiritual therapy for thirty to ninety days would be transformative while requiring less staffing and restrictions and thus be less costly financially.

In 2016, while consulting to other programs, speaking, writing Stepping Stones Daily Devotionals, having a daily radio program, and doing radio and TV interviews, Dave and I got a call from Dave's father, Bob Hoskins, who runs OneHope, a major global ministry. Bob told us to go to the Honey Lake Resorts website, then asked if we could put a treatment center at this upscale hunting/fishing/destination wedding resort. He explained that a megachurch, Celebration Church in Jacksonville, Florida, bought a beautiful, peaceful retreat center. But being two hours from the church, the intended impact of various retreats for their congregants wasn't occurring, and for over a year, it was losing significant money each month. The pastor asked Bob his thoughts during a OneHope retreat at Honey Lake. Bob told the pastor that his son, Dave, and his partner, Dr. Karl, created Christian rehab programs around the country, and Honey Lake might be a wonderful place for one.

Right after New Year's Day, 2017, Dave and I went for a site visit, and after meeting with the Celebration Church leadership, I knew God had answered my prayer. Almost everything necessary for my dream to take the next step in Jesus' Behavioral Health Revolution, God provided. Twelve months is a usual timeline to put a large venture like this together as many local and state authorities need to be involved, give permissions, file paperwork, etc. Being in the Deep South of north Florida, a good old boys' network existed, and Dave and I were not part of that inner circle. But God opened doors and showed unmistakable and miraculous favor as we admitted our first patients less than four months later, May 1, 2017!

Honey Lake Clinic (HLC)

Our patients come from all fifty states and several countries due to the unique services we provide. Just driving under the beautiful Spanish moss canopy of Honey Lake Road, then entering through the old-school slow gates onto our peaceful, idyllic, out-in-the-country, 400-acre campus visually and physically transitions a person from a world of stressful chaos to an oasis of safety, opportunity, and hope. One of our young ladies called it the Honey Lake snow globe, as the blizzard of snowflakes is replaced by excessive outpouring of Holy Spirit particles peacefully insulating and permeating the entire property. Our patients arrive beaten down, stressed, belittled, and lost. We want them to know they are respected, honored, valued, and worthy in God's eyes. To that end, unlike a hospital or institutional setting, each patient's bedroom and the meeting rooms have a resort-like feel, while our spa provides massage, mani-pedi, facials, and hairstyling. The gym, pool, sauna, and game rooms offer great exercise, escape, relaxation, and stress-relieving activities. But before discussing the unique and powerful treatment provided, some basic but important logistics that guide the structure and delivery of treatment services will be described.

HLC Logistical Components

Many Christian substance abuse rehabs exist, but most of them are longer-term (nine to fifteen months) work farm discipleship programs that have minimal if any licensed professional clinicians to provide psychological or medical care. The Christian medical model rehabs view addictions as the primary issue, so they typically only dig minimally into the underlying psychological/psychiatric cause(s) of the addiction. Sadly, as I mentioned earlier, very few medical model non-locked residential facilities exist that treat those struggling psychiatrically but who have no addiction issue. Even more rare is a Christian facility to treat the non-addicted, mental health only struggler.

HLC is a unique, fully Christian-owned and staffed, non-locked program with residential accommodations on-site that are supervised 24/7 with clinical personnel. We also are a rare facility treating those struggling with a psychiatric/psychological issue without an addiction, as well as those with both a mental health diagnosis and an addiction (dual diagnosis). HLC is a medical model program, meaning we have licensed and board-certified clinicians with significant expertise, which is important for several reasons:

1. Our highly-trained clinical staff of psychiatrists, primary care physicians, psychologists, nurse practitioners, and master's level psychotherapists apply cutting-edge science and evidence-based treatments to address the medical and psychiatric issues while getting to the root of psychological and spiritual struggles so our patients experience freedom from their symptoms and/or addic-

tions to achieve their God-given potential and live victorious lives.

2. Our licensed and certified staff allow HLC to be credentialed by and accountable to various oversight accrediting organizations, including the Joint Commission on Accreditation of Healthcare Organizations (JCAHO), the Florida Department of Children and Families (for addiction services), and the Agency for Healthcare Administration (for mental health care). Frequent site visits and inspections by these agencies ensure the highest standards and protocols for care and safety for our patients and staff are being met.
3. Our licensed and certified staff and accreditations from the above agencies allow us to meet the medical/clinical services requirements of virtually all medical insurance companies. The importance of this is critical as it allows patients to access their insurance benefits to help pay the cost of treatment. Since most Christian facilities lack the requisite trained staff or state/national credentialing, they are not approved by insurance companies. By accessing insurance funding, HLC is able to afford and hire top credentialed, certified clinical staff while non-medical model facilities (although often less expensive) don't have the budget to afford this expertise or offer the full array of treatment modalities to their patients that HLC offers.

HLC has two separate treatment programs. Our adult program treats ages eighteen and up, and our female adolescent program treats young ladies ages thirteen to seventeen. About two-thirds of our patients have most of their stay covered by insurance, and the other one-third are self-pay. This is one reason why credentialing is crucial for many of our patients to access their insurance to cover their treatment. Our average length of stay for adults fluctuates around thirty-eight to forty days, with most staying thirty-five to fifty days, and it is around eighty-five to ninety days for our adolescent girls.

Regarding diagnoses and struggles, about one-third of our patients have some substance addiction with either illegal substances, prescription substances (opioids/pain meds, sleeping pills/tranquilizers, or stimulants), or, most commonly, alcohol and marijuana. The other two-thirds of our patients have a mental health issue with no addiction problems. The most common diagnoses our patients have disrupting their life are depression, PTSD, social anxiety, OCD, panic disorder, ADHD, bipolar, impulse issues, sexual struggles, anger, burnout, self-harm, and suicidal thinking or urges. Concurrently, many have a behavioral (or process) addiction to pornography, shopping, social media, video gaming, screens, eating, nonlethal self-harm, or gambling.

The levels of care HLC is licensed to provide include acute detox, residential and PHP for addictions, and residential and PHP for mental health. Patients live on HLC campus throughout their stay with us, and we have nursing staff, behavioral health technicians, and security on-site 24/7, with medical staff on-site during working hours and on call 24/7. Since we are not licensed as a locked inpatient unit, we are not able to restrain patients, lock them in a safe room, or give them medications against their will to calm them down. All our patients voluntarily sign in. No one is on an ordered commitment or admitted against their will. Patients also retain the power to sign themselves out against medical advice if they are not acutely dangerous to themselves or others. If they are acutely dangerous, we will pursue a commitment process, and they will be transported to a hospital and evaluated by a clinician to determine if a more restrictive supervised locked unit is needed to ensure their safety. We do admit many patients with suicidal thoughts and urges or who are hurting themselves in a non-lethal way. But, since we are not licensed as a locked inpatient unit, we won't admit anyone who is actively engaging in dangerous suicidal or self-harm behaviors or thinks they'd have trouble approaching staff to communicate dangerous urges to hurt themselves. We often receive patients transferring from psychiatric inpatient units once they've stabilized and have some control of those acutely dangerous urges and are ready for intensive treatment of the underlying issues.

Some of our patient criteria requirements are determined by our college campus-like layout. Patients need to physically be able to navigate around the campus. This fun and relaxing layout affords lots of opportunities, activities, and stimulation. Patients with significant psychoses in the form of hallucinations or delusions may have a difficult time not only with the expansiveness and stimulation of our open campus but also with the intensity and inner-world probing of our programming and content. So, unless the psychosis is under significant control, we usually don't admit someone with disruptive psychoses. A significant amount of our programming is in the form of groups that last fifty to sixty minutes, with some lasting 120 minutes. Patients need to have the capacity to manage themselves in a group format and the cognitive skills (exceptions for those who are detoxing from substances), to follow along and not be socially disruptive to the group format. Therefore, patients struggling with intrusive psychoses or cognitive issues like dementia, traumatic brain injury, or intellectual disability in the form of lower IQ would have trouble adapting to and benefitting from our program.

HLC Treatment Principles

Now let's discuss the treatment side of what HLC delivers. Most people enter those entrance gates feeling confused and overwhelmed, believing their mind/brain is too complex and beyond their understanding. They also aren't aware of how rich the Bible is with awesome psychological skills about living life well. Most have rudimentarily tried to apply the Bible in their pursuit of joy, peace, identity, and purpose, but efforts to change have only dug a deeper hole of frustration, despair, hopelessness, anger, or self-condemnation. Our goal is to pull back the curtain, like Toto does in *The Wizard of Oz*, to reveal that the mind and Bible aren't as overwhelming or complicated as Satan tricks us into believing. We demonstrate key psychological and biblical principles about how our mind works, why we make the decisions we make, who God really is, and how easy it is to have a rich relationship with Him while practically applying His teachings to manage our inner world as He designed us to.

When patients are significantly struggling, we know it didn't start yesterday. For most people, the seeds were planted years ago, with roots growing over time, eventually producing the present bitter fruit despite various attempts to change. Likewise, we know transformation doesn't occur overnight either, but rather is an ongoing process of equipping people with healthy psycho-spiritual skills and then consistently and intentionally practicing these skills within accountability and discipleship.

When a patient comes to us, the life they've been building is teetering, sometimes ready to collapse. People sometimes change the second-floor carpet or the kitchen cabinets, but foundation work is what is truly needed. Foundation work takes lots of time, energy, finances, work, and is filled with uncertainty and fear. What we do is help a person dig deep to their foundation, expose some of the spiritual and psychological cracks, fill them with Jesus cement and good psychological skills, and teach them how to assess for cracks in the future. Patients who commit to this process will leave with a more rock-solid foundation to rebuild a much stronger, sustainable life of excellence.

Core to our unique HLC DNA is not only our steadfast determination to look holistically at each person and their struggles, but we also comprehensively address all three spheres of physical, mental, and spiritual with significant depth. We believe the spiritual sphere to be the most important, but for spiritual maturity and wholeness to occur, our mind and our brain chemistry must function well also.

To address the physical sphere, every patient receives a physical exam by our primary care provider, and then appropriate lab work is ordered to make sure their body is working properly. Any non-psychiatric medical issues are attended to. We are a caffeine-free campus, minimize sugars, and serve a healthy diet. We advocate an eight-hour sleep schedule and help patients with fitness, nutrition, diet, and exercise. The patient's assigned psychiatric specialist performs a psychiatric evaluation to assess how the brain and mind are functioning. They unpack the patient's story, explore their struggles, uncover various symptoms, and help formulate a diagnosis. Detox protocols can be implemented if necessary. Psychogenomic (specific genetic) testing shows how the patient might respond to or metabolize certain psychiatric medications to help determine, if appropriate, a psychiatric medication course. Other physical options of treatment include supplements, rTMS (repetitive transcranial magnetic stimulation), neurofeedback, and Alpha stimulation.

Two key principles guide our psychiatric treatment of the brain. First, psychiatric medications or other psychiatric direct biological treatments alone never cure anyone. But they are great miracles God has provided in the natural realm to temporarily patch brain circuit malfunctions, thus soothing or lessening some disrupting psychiatric symptoms. As symptoms improve, we can absorb and apply more of the psychological and spiritual treatments that renew our mind as God designed the lasting healing process to work.

The second and more important principle in our HLC DNA is that decision-making is what alters our brain chemistry. I call decision-making *exercise* for the brain. When we make good decisions, our brain gets stronger, or as the Bible says, our mind is renewed. And just like when we do physical exercise with poor technique causing injury, whenever we make a poor decision, we injure our brain chemistry. So consistent Godly decision-making is the ultimate psychospiritual healing process. Therefore, the psychological and spiritual spheres are more important than the physical, but healthy biochemical hardware does make it easier to absorb and process information to determine and execute a good decision.

That brings us to the psychological sphere. When we become Christians, we are a new creation and have new potentials, but unfortunately, we don't get a brain transplant or a hard drive scrub or a memory bank mass delete. Most of us have experienced hurts, losses, and traumas, and we all have lots of misinformation stored in our memory banks about ourselves, God, others, and relationships. We've also developed some psychologically dysfunctional ways of dealing with our inner world, leading to faulty decisions that are usually more me-centered and not God-centered. The classic Romans seven struggle of Paul knowing what the right decision is, but not doing it, while also knowing what not to do, but doing it shines the light on how our inner baggage hijacks our decision-making process.

Each patient is matched with a primary psychotherapist whose major goal is to equip the patient with healthy decision-making skills. Most of the work entails unpacking a lot of deep-seated unconscious material that distorts the lenses through which we see ourselves, God, and life's circumstances so we can stop sabotaging our decision-making process. To replace our broken system, our therapists and all our programming push patients to identify all our inner thoughts and take them captive to the obedience of Christ, purging lies and misinformation and replacing it with God's truth. Also, understanding their personality style and temperament facilitates a lifelong process of ongoing equipping in emotional intelligence, conflict resolution, impulse control, forgiveness, attachment, intimacy, vulnerability, communication, and self-awareness skills.

Our therapists see their patients in individual sessions and in small process groups and accomplish the therapeutic goals by using many evidence-based psychotherapies, including EMDR, CBT, DBT, psychodynamic psychotherapy, inner child work, relaxation, mindfulness, art therapy, movement, psychodrama, motivational interviewing, meditation, and equine-assisted therapy. These modalities calm and slow the mind so we can much better understand the thoughts and emotions swirling inside and process them in a healthy way to be better stewards of that all-important decision-making process. Psychiatry specialists, special outside speakers, our pastoral team, and our nursing staff also play significant roles in reinforcing these mind-equipping principles.

That brings us to the most crucial sphere we address, the spiritual. Our first spiritual goal is to reeducate our patients as to who the God of the Bible really is because we all grow up learning and misapplying various attributes to God based on our troubled experiences and faulty earthly relationships. Teaching God's character, love, grace, forgiveness, and relentless fatherly pursuit of each patient allows God to be more desired and approachable. Then we teach, facilitate, and provide many opportunities to connect and communicate with God. Most of our patients come in as Christians, but some are not. Many connect to God for the first time at HLC as they put their faith in Christ for their salvation and are baptized in our pool!

The other spiritual goal is demonstrating how the B.I.B.L.E (Best Instruction Book for Living Everyday) is God's instruction manual instructing us on how to make the best decisions that lead to abundant life while avoiding the many "shortcuts" that lead to destruction. We often use the Immanuel Approach by helping the patient bring Jesus into the moment, thoughts, or memories to allow Jesus to guide their processing, emotions, and decisions. Our HLC mindset, the Bible (the best psychiatric textbook ever written showing why we do what we do and how to do life better using it), infiltrates all our sessions with therapists, psychiatric specialists, chapels, process groups, and psychological education and equipping.

As we teach the Bible, we are not content with just memorizing Bible verses—we always stress Bible application. Our desire for each patient is that they would allow their faith in God and His awesome biblical truths and principles to inform their psychological decision-making process in order to be consistent godly decision-makers. Thus, through the God-designed principle of neuroplasticity, their minds can be renewed and their lives transformed. Daily, we have a front-row seat witnessing how our patients apply these teachings and experience the miracle of a profound and deep psychospiritual healing.

The final and most often overlooked ingredient in our HLC special healing sauce is our loving Christian community of staff and patients. We are all designed to be in relationship and community. We all long for communities that are accepting, authentic, honest, loving, encouraging, forgiving, and non-judgmental but provide necessary correction and guidance in a loving way. A community in which we feel comfortable practicing our new skills and tools. Ideally, the church is such a community, but most people do not find it in their church, family, small group, etc. We commonly hear (especially from men) one of our patients comment in a group, "I can't believe I said that because I've never told anyone about (*fill in the blank*)." The love, acceptance, respect, and genuine care our staff has for patients, and especially how our patients share with each other, is a powerful bond through Christ and is an essential ingredient in the healing process. Many patients stay in touch with their peers after discharge through our online alumni program or through lasting friendships.

As you can easily see from the short glimpses of my personal testimony, God is the author of great comebacks. The turning point in my life was when I stopped writing my own story and instruction manual and started using His. That started the wild, exciting, beyond-my-wildest-dreams comeback journey I am still on, which keeps getting better with each season of ministry. Professionally, through my years of practice, treatment program development, and at HLC, I've seen tens of thousands of comeback stories, some from literal deathbed situations to now living psychospiritually rich and fulfilling lives.

Everyone needs help, and God has equipped many helpers to step in the gap and help people navigate a stormy time to get to the Promised Land of freedom, hope, joy, and peace, helping them reach their God-given potential. God has a plan for each one of us, we just need to excitedly and humbly offer up our fish and loaves, and He will amazingly multiply it in our lives and those around us. God is a redeemer and transformer of broken lives and relationships. Remember, decisions determine your life, so choose well!

Part 3: Focus and Future

CHAPTER 15

Mindset and Mission

Ministry must be both a mindset and a mission. Effectively serving others requires one to be intentional and dedicated. Thus far, we have outlined the needs for mental and relational health ministry, explored various ways to address it, and offered key resources for help. In this chapter, I want church leaders to be inspired to successfully get the ball down the field and into the end zone. We will examine several practical strategies which will hopefully lead many hurting people and relationships to victory. Let's start a mental and relational health ministry revival!

How do we specifically conduct mental and relational health ministry? Well, to borrow a line from an old movie about mental health, *What About Bob?*, we do well to take "baby steps." What follows is a progressively momentum-building incremental paradigm to accomplish the mission of helping the hurting to heal and find hope. The sequence below is not designed to be a one size fits all approach but can be utilized to create an effective mental health ministry mindset and mission in churches everywhere. Start small but pray large!

Here are ten specific suggestions any church can put into practice to boost the mental and relational health of their congregation:

1. Value Mental and Relational Health

To begin with, the value of mental and relational health must be recognized and reinforced in your church.[40] Just as good physical and spiritual health does not happen automatically or by accident, good mental and relational health is not something that naturally occurs in our fallen world. Physically and spiritually healthy people regularly make small, daily choices that contribute to and maintain their physical health. They intentionally value and care for themselves in a specific and prioritized manner. Yet even those who exercise healthy choices still become ill and injured. Consequently, we all need love, grace, forgiveness, and acceptance—especially when we are wounded and broken.

The same is true for our mental and relational health. Good mental health does not happen naturally or by accident! *Mentally and relationally healthy people make ongoing, specific choices that create and increase their mental and relational health* (e.g., nondefensively addressing their own issues, maturely regulating their emotions, proactively reducing their stress levels, increasing their coping skills, responding realistically to hurts and disappointments, maintaining loving and humble attitudes and actions, owning one's responsibility for conflicted relationships, accurately weighing the importance of life successes and failures, etc.).

Likewise, spiritually and emotionally healthy churches are intentional about the mental and relational health of their flocks. What we value and emphasize becomes important to us. As with spiri-

40 Stetzer, E. "How to assess the mental and relational health needs in your church" in Clinton, T. & Pingleton, J. (2019). *The Struggle Is Real: How to Care for Mental and Relational Needs in the Church.* Bloomington, IN: Westbow Press.

tual and physical health, even those who exercise healthy mental and relational health principles will still experience pain, pathos, and problems in a fallen world. But they will be better equipped to successfully and maturely cope, and they will be supported in their healthy church to find comfort and compassionate care.

Choosing to be laser-focused on valuing and developing the goal of becoming mentally and relationally healthy as a congregation can be absolutely life-giving. *Just as healthy sheep reproduce healthy sheep, churches that value health become healthy and reproduce healthy people.* A pronounced emphasis on becoming mentally and relationally healthy can open new and unexpected doors to evangelism, sanctification, and multiplication like perhaps nothing else in the church's ministry portfolio. As we have seen earlier, people are hurting now in unprecedented ways and in epidemic numbers—and they desperately need help. The fields are indeed ripe for harvest.

2. Proclaim the Truth

We all know that when we preach truth, lives are transformed. Just as truth is contagious, so, too, are healthy attitudes and actions. Yet the tragic truth regarding mental and relational health issues is that most pastors don't ever speak about them publicly. According to the landmark Lifeway Research study on mental illness in the church, two-thirds of American pastors seldom or never speak about mental and relational health topics.[41]

41 https://lifewayresearch.com/2014/09/22/mental-illness-remains-taboo-topic-for-many-pastors/

This is absolutely heartbreaking, as well as completely unacceptable. People matter. And people's pain matters. Knowing truth sets prisoners free and releases those in bondage. *Once more, we must end the silence, expose the secrecy, eliminate the shame, and erase the stigma surrounding mental and relational health disorders!* We are all human, and we all have pain and problems. We all are broken people in need of God's love, grace, and mercy.

Recall the statistics regarding mental and relational health issues referred to in Chapter 1. God is into numbers (He even named a book in His Bible by that name!) because while to many, statistics are cold and factual, to Him, they represent people. Again, the truth is that more people are hurting in more ways than ever before—that is an indisputable fact. And they all need love, prayer, understanding, acceptance, support, and help.

3. Lead by Example

We all know the most effective form of leadership is by example. Preaching is easy; practicing is hard. But let's dig down past the clichés. How does a servant leader best display their pastoral heart? By example. And that, my friend, takes guts. To end the deafening silence in the church about mental and relational health issues, we must courageously and boldly speak up and out and then live what we say.

It is bound to be controversial, but what would happen if a pastor wisely, prayerfully, and judiciously made themselves vulnerable by simply acknowledging some of their own pain or struggles in front of their congregation? I realize that many readers' blood pressure just shot up, but seriously, what would happen? Perhaps you may be tarred and feathered, run out of town on a rail, or shot at sunrise, but what if a pastor took the risk of being genuine and open about a part of their own pain in a mature, sensitive, appropriate, and humble manner?

Well, to be sure, that will likely make many in the audience initially uncomfortable or perhaps even feel threatened or insecure. And to reiterate, one must be prayerfully discerning about why, what, when, where, and how much to share of one's personal issues. It would be best to keep it generalized, brief, and without self-effacement or self-condemnation. It must be done for the right reasons—to be of help and inspiration to others—and above all else, it must do no harm for those hearing it (e.g., inadvertently causing new or immature believers to stumble, inciting gossip, justifying dysfunctionality or sinful laziness and irresponsibility, etc.). Furthermore, it must never degenerate into a substitute for one's own psychotherapy.

Self-disclosure is much like a sharp metal object: it can do great harm or facilitate deep healing. It has been said that the difference between a scalpel and a knife is motive. So definitely consider the risks. But also contemplate the very real benefits of being authentic, transparent, and relatable to your sheep. All pastors (and psychologists!) are broken people too. You may be amazed at how you instantly become more deeply credible, relatable, and lovable to your congregation when you let them know you hurt too.

Healthy self-disclosure simply normalizes one's own humanness. It is Isaiah 53:6 and Romans 3:23 in vivo. It isn't appropriate or helpful to indiscriminately spill one's guts from the pulpit as if in a confessional relationship. That would likely be harmful for some if not many of the hearers. But to humbly let people know that bullets may actually harm you, that you cannot outrun some speeding locomotives, and that you are no longer able to leap tall buildings in a single bound (sadly, over the years, I have lost several inches off my college vertical!) is liberating and refreshing. For them, and for you.

My favorite professor in graduate school remarked one day in class, "I wonder how many people in the church are kept away by the glare of our 'victory badge'?" *One of the most subtle and surreptitious dangers embedded within professional ministry is the phenomenon of pedestalization.* Take the risk to de-pedastalize yourself!

Whereas "the Teacher" commonly sat below his audience, in western Christianity, pastors typically stand on literal platforms above their congregations. What does that say about us? For those of us who are culturally image-conscious, we would do well to remember that Jesus was probably not clad in the latest GQ style, impeccably coifed, and pristinely manicured. He no doubt had body odor, manure on His sandals, an ungroomed beard, and dirt under His fingernails. But He loved purely and deeply, gently yet fiercely, and was approachable to everyone, even little kids.

Many pastors are lonely, disconnected, and isolated. One has to wonder if implicitly (not consciously or deliberately) coming across as literally and figuratively "above" one's flock causes them to be at least subconsciously placed on a pedestal. Quite ironically, then, that very dynamic functionally separates them from being able to relate, identify, and connect with their people and vice versa. It's lonely up on a pedestal.

Unfortunately, some church leaders become progressively inured and enamored with the pedestal and come across as proud, arrogant, unapproachable, and unable for their flock to identify with precisely because of the glare of their "victory badge." Remember that no one has it all together, no one is perfect, and no one is without flaws, faults, foibles, and failures.

The point is that pastors are human too. On his deathbed, Martin Luther, the great Protestant Reformer, had a small piece of paper in his pocket with the words "We are all beggars. This is true." Consequently, aren't we all beggars telling other beggars where to find bread? Jesus is the Bread of Life (John 16:35); we are merely baker's assistants!

4. Cultivate a Culture

Create a culture of compassionate caring. We are perhaps never more like Jesus than when we interact with others with a humble and loving attitude of compassion. Many of Jesus' healing miracles were preceded by Him being "moved" or motivated by compassion.

Compassion is nonjudgmental, nonpejorative, and nondiscriminatory. The church of Jesus should demonstrate that sort of culture in all ways to all people at all times. So how do we become focused on creating a culture of compassion?

It has been famously stated that if we fail to plan, we plan to fail. We must be intentional about the identity of our churches. Identity is simply who and what we are. Identity precedes and, to a large extent, dictates function. Don't be casual, trendy, or random as you consider crafting the "brand" or identity of your church.

Become real, honest, and intentional about being known as a broken church for broken people! How can the Holy Spirit not bless and move in a church that deliberately markets itself to the downcast, downtrodden, and down-and-outers of society? Churches comprised of societal sophisticates aren't likely to compete for those hurting souls, but aren't they the ones for whom Jesus died? Look for ways to specifically be sensitive to hurting people and offer them love, grace, mercy, and redemption. *Make the gospel visceral, vibrant, and vital.*

5. Preach Biblical Examples

The Bible is filled with real-life examples of persons struggling with dysfunctional marriages and families, addictive issues, and significant emotional problems. Doing a sermon series on mental and relational health issues and Bible characters who struggled is relevant, realistic, relatable, and redemptive.[42] Scripture never sanitizes or whitewashes its' heroes. People in scripture aren't polished and slicked up—what you see is what you get. People connect to and identify with genuineness.

For those who typically preach expositionally, it may seem unusual or uncomfortable to do topical series or character studies. But please prayerfully consider educating, equipping, and empowering your people with some specific tools and principles which can be applied in their personal lives and relationships immediately. Perhaps you could consider preaching

---

42 One hundred sixteen different mental and relational health issues that people commonly struggle with are directly addressed within the context of scripture along with dozens of character sketches and other practical tools to help hurting people in a unique study Bible: Clinton, T, Hindson, E., and Pingleton, J. (2019). *The Care and Counsel Bible*, Nashville, TN: Thomas Nelson.

these on Sunday evenings or for mid-week services. This will make the Bible come alive in unmistakable, tangible ways in people's lives and relationships.

Often Christians, at least subconsciously, tend to think that characters in God's Word are somehow super holy, paragons of virtue, morally faultless, and shining examples of spiritual excellence. That was usually very far from the case. The inspired Logos makes abundantly clear that the ground at the foot of the cross is level.

Looking for stories to preach about personal issues of adultery, substance abuse, incest, murderous rage, sexual addiction, suicidality, anxiety attacks, psychotic delusions, depressive despair, obsessive thoughts, along with a myriad of other problems and pathologies? Look no further than in the inspired words of scripture!

The Bible directly addresses all of these and more—without silence, secrecy, shame, and stigma. Unpack the stark, blunt, unvarnished reality of scripture for people to be able to relate to and connect with. Far from being sacrilegious or dishonoring of the Holy Spirit-breathed very Word of God, your flock discovers how biblical truth tangibly validates their broken and pain-filled lives in down-to-earth ways. You may be astounded at the power and witness of the Word, perhaps like never before, and might wonder why you took so long to share it with your parishioners!

Dr. Ed Stetzer said it this way:

> However reluctant pastors may be, individual and family members of the mentally ill are anxious to

recognize the elephant in the room and remove the taboo status. If a church is going to be transformational in society, it has to address needs, and a church that only talks about certain needs is no better than a church that only preaches about certain topics. In the same way that all of the Bible is inspired and deserves to be preached, all of the maladies of humanity deserve to be brought to light under the gospel of Jesus, where healing can be found and encouragement received.[43]

6. Conduct Seminars and Workshops

A very powerful way to address mental and relational health needs in the church is to offer practical training on such topics as marriage, parenting, developing a healthy Christian identity, stress management (particularly around holidays), and so on. Meeting people's needs where they live is successful and fulfilling ministry. People need—and will appreciate—reliable and useful information on how to live their lives and relate to their loved ones more effectively.

Don't feel overwhelmed about all the work and preparation for these kinds of presentations. One of the most positively received ministry endeavors I have ever had the privilege of participating in was wondrously creative yet refreshingly simple and required no prep.

A good friend of mine, Dr. George Westlake, who was a lead pastor of a megachurch (Sheffield Family Life Center in Kan-

43 Stetzer, E. in Clinton, T. & Pingleton, J. (2019). *The Struggle Is Real: How to Care for Mental and Relational Health Needs in the Church*. Bloomington, IN: Westbow Press, p. 6.

sas City, Missouri), approached me with the novel idea of us conducting a topical question and answer session in the main auditorium on a Friday evening. Everyone received a three-by-five-inch card and a pencil when they arrived and were encouraged to write down any question they liked and anonymously pass it to an usher. Then we addressed them (but not from the stage—we sat in front of it!). For hours—with no break. The questions just kept coming.

The first time we focused on marriage from a biblical and a psychological perspective. The following month we tackled parenting. Those first two times, around 10:00 p.m., nursery workers interrupted us to tell us people's children were exhausted and needed to go home, and we needed to stop. In future months, we added some female staff and therapists to the panel to provide more perspectives as we addressed other topics. The anonymity and personal freedom of the format allowed people to voice concerns regarding sexuality, intimate relationships, and personal problems they may never have been free to do otherwise due to their shame and stigma. This format is super simple and is truly low-hanging fruit. And the positive feedback about the impact on people's hearts and lives was astounding. I have replicated this idea in other churches, with similar results and responses.

Consider inviting trusted, mature Christian mental health professionals to partner with you for these events if there are none in your congregation. Have them develop and present topical workshops in their area(s) of clinical specialty relevant to your congregation. Open the seminars up to and market them throughout your whole community. Offer Friday evening and Saturday marriage conferences/retreats. Consider partnering with other churches as well. In doing so, you will verify to your city that you are a difference-maker in people's lives—a hospital, not a museum.

7. Offer Support Groups

Again, churches are filled with real people who have real problems and need real help. The Greek word "allelon," translated into English as "one another," appears over one hundred times in the New Testament. The strong and explicit emphasis within the body of Christ is that we are an interdependent, interpersonal organism. Each part affects and impacts the whole. We are instructed to love, accept, bear with, pray for, encourage, confess to, serve, honor, live harmoniously with, greet, and forgive one another—among many other things.

Small groups were the norm of the early church. A few years ago, I had the privilege to stand in the ruins of what archeologists firmly believe was the Apostle Peter's house. It was truly amazing to realize that some of the first Christians went to church in that room just a few yards up the hill from the Sea of Galilee in the little village of Capernaum. Oh, to have been able to witness those early services and how those Jesus' followers shared with and no doubt supported one another as they worshipped in the sociohistorical context of persecution, suffering, and uncertainty.

Small clusters of people naturally lend themselves to the potential development of warm, intimate connection and close, personal sharing. We are relational beings created and destined for relationships. The church of Jesus should be the paragon of how to get along with and support others. Spiritual intimacy and sharing lead naturally to interpersonal connection.

A helpful starting point for any church to be intentional and deliberate about mental health ministry is to begin a recovery ministry. Christianity is all about recovery, both implicitly and explicitly. For those grappling with issues beyond normal "spiritual" struggles, groups designed for that purpose are the perfect place for them to share. Several specific types and models of recovery groups were outlined in the previous chapter.

Spiritually and emotionally mature laypersons are naturally well-suited to emerge as facilitators of small groups. With proper training and supervision, lay counselors functioning within a lay counseling ministry can be a viable, helpful resource for any church.[44] Well-trained lay counselors can facilitate much healing and help for persons suffering from grief and loss, substance abuse, sexual addictions, divorce, etc.

Be intentional about publicizing your support groups within the church and within your community. Placing your groups and their locations and meeting times in your bulletin, on your QR codes, on your social media, and on your website will normalize people's struggles. Such visibility will naturally serve to be a source of comfort and encouragement to those who are hurting and their families. Don't be surprised when support groups and your "marketing" efforts about them organically become outstanding disciple-making and evangelization mechanisms.

---

44 For a detailed analysis of the practical benefits of developing a lay counseling training program in the local church, as well as specific models of how to organize and oversee them, see the excellent presentation by lead pastor and clinical psychologist Dr. Siang-Yang Tan, "How to Develop an Effective Lay Counseling Ministry" in Clinton, T. & Pingleton, J. (2019). *The Struggle Is Real: How to Care for Mental and Relational Health Problems in the Church*. Bloomington, IN: Westbow Press.

8. Create a Resource Center

Establish a mental and relational health resource center in your church offering useful books, videos, websites, and referral network information. The visible presence of these resources speaks silently about your congregation's awareness of and sensitivity to those with mental and relational health needs. People will feel accepted, supported, and cared for by realizing their church's leadership is being thoughtful, considerate, and proactive in offering help in a tangible and visible way to those who are hurting.

Consider delegating the leadership of the resource center to a caring and committed volunteer or small group of volunteers. Obviously, retired bookstore managers or librarians would be ideal, but see who has a burden or calling for this ministry and let them grow into it! It can be in a small space off the lobby and open a half hour before and after service or through the week as needed. The point is to start small and grow as the response and need warrant.

You don't have to have a huge church or a commercial quality full-fledged retail bookstore to get the mental health resource initiative running. The main takeaway is that the local church provides an abundance of helpful tools to make available to hurting individuals, couples, and families. It is important to vet/approve the materials by a committee authorized by the board or other leadership group to ensure clinical quality and doctrinal orthodoxy.

There will be an initial financial outlay involved in the startup of a quality resource center. Pitch the idea to people you believe may have a vision and/or a burden so they can enjoy the blessing of helping others. Donors like to give to missions and ministries they believe in. A generalized reality of most church cultures is that the ministry initiatives that receive the necessary commitment and allocation of time, money, and volunteer resources are those that matter most to senior leadership. Jesus was clear that before we build a tower, we need to consider the cost (cf. Luke 14:28). Becoming a church, which is a beacon of light shining out to hurting people in your community, is truly a wise and perpetual investment in God's kingdom.

9. Partner and Collaborate

Reach out to and connect with various Christian mental health clinics and agencies, rehabilitation centers, addiction recovery programs, crisis pregnancy centers, treatment programs for troubled teens, maternity homes, and the like. Ask them how your church can serve and support them. Put them on your church prayer list or chain. Feature one program or center in your bulletin or on your video screens every month. Have children make crafts or write cards in Sunday School as an outreach project which can be sent to encourage people who are going through treatment. Consider organizing volunteer construction teams to help a mental health ministry facility with a remodel or expansion project. Ask your parishioners for other ideas about how they want to get involved.

Determine that your congregation will become a literal Aaron and Hur to come alongside and support such ministries in the battle against human suffering, addiction, and dysfunction. Direct personal involvement and meaningful volunteer commitments with such programs and treatment centers will sensitize and endear people to those ministries. Consider partnering with other churches across town. Who knows what other organic and creative ideas will be inspired?

It has been wisely and correctly stated that a rising tide floats all boats. *A kingdom ministry and mission mindset require that we focus on collaboration instead of competition.* It is fascinating to see how churches who invest in other ministries flourish themselves. Take up offerings to sponsor mental health ministries. Conduct fundraisers for them. Encourage donors to scholarship needy people's treatment. Many pastors have become jaded or even cynical about other ministries bleeding their church dry financially. But churches need these ministries, and these ministries need the church. Generous people will themselves be blessed—abundantly—both here and in eternity (Proverbs 11:25).

10. Practice Hospitality

Several years ago, a friend of mine wryly noted that depression is not a "casserole disease." What he meant by that was that in the church, people naturally and routinely reach out to persons with physical problems. We can comfortably pray for aunt Mabel's lumbago, grandpa Mortimer's gout, or cousin Myrtle's rheumatism. And we supply them with tangible expressions of love, help, and support—as we should (including casseroles!).

Fortunately, I have never had any of those diseases—for which I am grateful. But what about being kind, thoughtful, and helpful to those suffering from mental and relational health issues? Etymologically, the term "hospitality" is derived from the word for the place where we send people who are seriously infirmed or injured. Hospitals offer a full range of interventions and services designed for the care, comfort, and correction of critical conditions. Do most churches even pray for someone wrestling with panic attacks, sexual addiction, eating disorders, or severe mood swings? Much less reach out to them in kind-hearted, generous, meaningful, and gracious ways to make them feel accepted and cared for?

When was the last time you heard (or preached) a sermon on hospitality? There is a plethora of scriptural teaching about the subject. Paul tells us to "Share with the Lord's people who are in need. Practice hospitality" (Romans 12:13, NIV). Hebrews reminds us, "Do not forget to show hospitality to strangers, for by so doing some people have shown hospitality to angels" (Hebrews 13:2, NIV). Peter bluntly (imagine that!) addresses our attitude about demonstrating altruistic caring by commanding us to "Offer hospitality to one another without grumbling" (1 Peter 4:9, NIV). And John concludes by teaching that "We ought therefore to show hospitality to such people so that we may work together for the truth" (3 John 1:8, NIV).

Examine these passages: we are exhorted to practice, show, offer, show. These are all verbs! Let's do the work of ministry—even, maybe especially, for those struggling with mental and relational health disorders. The struggle is real indeed.

CHAPTER 16

Self-Harm and Suicidality

Suicide. Perhaps there is no more chilling and ominous word in the English language. Few words evoke more intense visceral reactions or painful human emotions. It epitomizes a scourge of broken hearts, wasted potentials, overwhelming helplessness, and prematurely extinguished lives.

Suicide is a widespread, complex, and controversial topic spiritually, socially, and psychologically. If people are honest with themselves, most would admit they have, in a vulnerable moment, at least briefly entertained fantasies or fleeting thoughts of what it might be like to escape their painful circumstances, unrelenting suffering, and/or overwhelming distress. All of us experience desperation, hopelessness, and despondency in life at some time(s) and to a certain degree(s). And ever since Genesis chapter 3, all of us humans are all broken.

Unsurprisingly, God's Word is not silent, secretive, shame-inducing, or stigmatizing about human problems, not even when it comes to the disturbing topic of suicide. The Bible doesn't whitewash or sanitize its characters or gloss over their struggles. In fact, Scripture lists seven people who took their own lives: Abimelech (Judges 9:52–54); Samson (Judges 16:23–31); Saul and his armor-bearer (1 Samuel 31:1–5); Ahithophel (2 Samuel 17:23); Zimri (1 Kings 16:18); and most notoriously, Judas Iscariot (Matthew 27:3–5).

Furthermore, several of God's chosen leaders—including Elijah, David, and Jonah—grappled with intense suicidal thoughts and feelings. Many biblical passages poignantly describe sorrowful lament, intense loneliness, confusing meaninglessness, extreme desperation, excruciating agony, and abject hopelessness.

Briefly explained, suicidality exists along a progressively escalating continuum of universal human angst—from painful emotions (despair) to obsessive thoughts (suicidal ideation) to destructive actions (suicide attempts). Church leaders will do well to carefully and wisely attend to these dynamics among their flock.

Not everyone who talks about suicide will attempt suicide and not everyone who attempts suicide talks openly about it beforehand. Thus, it is imperative to take seriously every threat of suicide, however implicit or vague. Even if you suspect someone is just pleading for help or dramatically seeking attention, don't underestimate the danger and casually dismiss them.

There is a significant difference between various types of suicidal threats, gestures, and even attempts. For example, studies show teenage girls express suicidality the most frequently but with the lowest potential lethality. Conversely, older males talk about it and threaten it the least but have the highest rate of any population of completed suicide.

But make no mistake: Suicide does not discriminate. People of any age, gender, or ethnicity can be at risk for attempting suicide—which can be destructive even when it is not fatal. Some who survive a suicide attempt end up with brain damage or other life-altering injuries.

As was outlined in Chapter 1, the statistics regarding suicide are catastrophic. Over 130 people die every day in the United States by self-murder—one person every eleven minutes. Suicide is nearly triple the number of homicides in this country. It is the tenth leading cause of death in America and is the second-highest form of death for people ages ten to thirty-four. One point four million people attempt suicide every year, 3.5 million make a formal plan to commit suicide, and 12 million think seriously about suicide every year. Rates of completed suicides have escalated dramatically—over 35 percent—since 1999. Tragically, about twenty-two US military service veterans end their own lives every day. Globally, over 1,000,000 people die by their own hands annually.[45]

Suicide and suicide attempts and even suicidal ideation exert serious emotional, physical, and economic impacts. People who attempt suicide and survive may experience extensive injuries that can have long-term effects on their health as well as on their relationships. Typically, they also experience depression and other mental health issues. A bit of good news, however, is that over 90 percent of people who attempt suicide and survive never go on to die by suicide.

Suicide and suicide attempts also affect the health and well-being of friends, loved ones, co-workers, and the larger community, particularly the church community. When people die by suicide, their surviving family (including church family)

45 https://www.cdc.gov/suicide/facts/index.html

and friends may experience shock and bewilderment, anger and outrage, guilt and responsibility, depression and anxiety, and may even experience thoughts of suicide themselves. The financial toll of suicide on society is also costly. Suicides and suicide attempts cost this country over $70 billion per year in lifetime medical and work-loss costs alone.[46]

A most unique and poignant feature of suicide is the deleterious and destructive impact upon those who are left behind. Besides, the immediate family, churches, schools, and entire communities are shocked and saddened by the senselessness of suicide. Among adolescents, a classmate's suicide may lead to a city-wide copycat deluge of more suicides.

Suicidal Signs and Symptoms

A significant number of people with suicide ideation keep their thoughts and feelings a secret and show no sign that anything is wrong. Suicidal behavior is complex with no single or universal cause. Although many different factors can contribute to a person's suicidal struggles, there are several shared characteristics. Most usually, a person who experiences or could experience suicidal thoughts and behaviors will exhibit a few or many of the following signs or symptoms:

- feeling or appearing to feel trapped or hopeless;
- feeling intolerable emotional and/or physical pain;
- being preoccupied with violence, dying, or death;
- having mood shifts, either happy or sad;
- talking about revenge, guilt, or shame;

46 https://www.nimh.nih.gov/health/statistics/suicide

- experiencing agitation or a heightened state of anxiety;
- experiencing changes in personality, routine, or sleep patterns;
- increasing the use of drugs or alcohol;
- engaging in risky or reckless behavior, such as driving carelessly or taking drugs;
- getting their affairs in order, making a will, giving things away;
- experiencing depression, panic attacks, or impaired concentration;
- isolating themselves, withdrawing from family and friends;
- talking about being a burden to others;
- experiencing psychomotor agitation, such as pacing or wringing the hands;
- saying goodbye to others as though it were the last time;
- experiencing a loss of enjoyment in previously pleasurable activities, such as eating, exercise, social interaction, or sex;
- expressing severe remorse and self-criticism;
- expressing regret about being alive or ever having been born;
- talking about wanting to die or wanting to kill themselves;
- talking about feeling empty, hopeless, or having no reason to live;
- actively planning or looking for a way to kill themselves, such as searching for lethal methods online, stockpiling pills, or buying a gun;

- making potentially lethal threats or having murderous feelings toward others—some people who are homicidal may pose risk for a homicide-suicide.

Suicidal Risk Factors

Suicide does not discriminate. Anyone at certain times or under certain circumstances can be at risk. Suicidal behavior is complex, and there is no single cause. Many different factors may contribute to someone making a suicide attempt. But people most at risk tend to share specific characteristics. The main risk factors for suicide are:

- depression, other mental disorders;
- substance abuse disorder;
- certain medical conditions, particularly those with grave or terminal implications;
- traumatic brain injury;
- chronic pain;
- relationship loss, rejection, divorce;
- death of a loved one, impacted grief;
- significant financial problems, prolonged unemployment;
- history of prior suicide attempt(s);
- history of being victimized by bullying;
- identifying as LGBTQIA+ with no family support;
- family history of a mental disorder or substance abuse;
- family history of suicide;
- family violence, including physical or sexual abuse;
- having guns or other firearms in the home;

- having recently been released from prison or jail;
- being exposed to others' suicidal behavior, such as that of family members, peers, or celebrities.

Many people have some of these risk factors but do not attempt suicide. It is important to note that suicide is not a healthy or functional response to stress. Suicidal thoughts or actions are a sign of extreme distress, not merely a harmless plea for attention, and should never be ignored.

Often, family and friends are the first to recognize the warning signs of suicide and can be the first step toward helping an at-risk individual find treatment with someone who specializes in diagnosing and treating mental health conditions.

Suicidality is extremely complex. Treatments and therapies for people with suicidal thoughts or actions will vary with age, gender, physical and mental well-being, and with individual experiences.

Self-Harm

Another disturbing, growing, and terrifying mental health problem involves self-harm, primarily in the form of what is commonly known as cutting. Self-harm or self-injury means hurting oneself on purpose. This is often a subconscious effort to cope with or blunt one's otherwise unmanageable emotional turmoil and distress. The most common method is cutting oneself with a sharp object. But any time someone deliberately hurts themself is classified as self-harm. Some people feel an impulse to cause burns, pull out their hair or pick at their wounds to prevent healing. Extreme injuries can even result in broken bones. By far, the most frequent demographic of persons who inflict self-harm is teenagers and young adults.[47]

Cutting is a practice that is understandably frightening and frustrating to parents. It is generally not a suicide attempt per se, though it may look and seem that way. In extreme cases, self-injury can indeed result in the loss of one's life. Cutting is self-injury—the person is literally making cuts or abrasions on his or her body, usually the arms and legs, and in areas where clothing usually obscures. It's difficult for many people to understand cutting because it seems to be blatantly masochistic. But for a rapidly escalating number of kids, they use cutting in a misguided and dysfunctional effort to control, blunt, or cope with their emotional pain.[48]

The practice of cutting has long existed in secrecy. Cuts can be easily hidden under long sleeves or pants. But in recent years, movies and television programs have popularized, if not normalized, and even romanticized it—prompting greater numbers of teens and tweens to experiment with it. Many persons attribute the recent widespread incidence of cutting to the rise of the Goth culture, which introduced and popularized it.

Make no mistake: hurting oneself—or thinking about hurting oneself—is a clear sign of emotional distress. A person's uncomfortable emotions may grow more intense if they continue to use self-harm as a coping mechanism. In addition, the scars and disfigurement often left over from the wounds are a source of shame and embarrassment later in life. They may also

---

47 https://www.mayoclinic.org/diseases-conditions/self-injury/symptoms-causes/syc-20350950

48 https://www.nami.org/About-Mental-Illness/Common-with-Mental-Illness/Self-harm

risk infection from a wound or even a fatal injury if the self-damage is severe. Drinking alcohol or doing drugs while hurting oneself directly increases the risk of a more severe injury than was likely intended.

Self-harm occurs most commonly during the teenage and young adult years, though it can also occur later in life. Persons at the highest risk are people who have experienced trauma, neglect, or abuse. For instance, if an individual grew up in an unstable family, cutting or other forms of self-injury might have become an adaptive and functional coping mechanism or the only way they knew to silently scream for help.

The urge for a person to hurt themselves may start with overwhelming anger, frustration, or pain. When a person is not sure how to deal with emotions, or they learned as a child to hide or suppress their feelings, self-harm may feel like a cathartic release. Sometimes, injuring oneself stimulates the body's endorphins or pain-killing hormones, thus temporarily elevating a person's mood.

Or, if a person doesn't feel many emotions, they might cause themself literal physical pain in order to feel something "real" to replace a state of emotional emptiness or numbness. Finally, cutting and other self-harming behaviors can serve to blunt one's otherwise intense emotional distress, thus concretizing or objectifying their internal pain in an externalized and self-controlled way when they are feeling out of control in abusive or exploitative situations.

Once a person injures themself, they may experience fear, shame, and guilt. If their shame leads to intense negative feelings, that person may be apt to hurt themself again. The behavior can thus become a dangerous self-perpetuating cycle and a long-time habit. Some people even create rituals around it.

Self-harm isn't the same as attempting suicide. However, it is a symptom of emotional pain that should be taken seriously. Furthermore, self-injury can be unintentionally fatal if drastic enough. If someone is hurting themself, they may be at an increased risk of feeling suicidal. It's important to find treatment for the underlying emotions.

Self-Harm Signs and Symptoms

Common signs and symptoms of self-injury may include:

- Scars, often in precise patterns;
- Fresh cuts, scratches, bruises, bite marks, or other wounds;
- Excessive rubbing of an area to create an abrasion;
- Keeping sharp objects on hand for no apparent reason;
- Wearing long sleeves or long pants, even in hot weather;
- Frequent reports of accidental injury;
- Chronic difficulties and dysfunctions in interpersonal relationships;
- Behavioral and emotional instability, impulsivity, and unpredictability;
- Frequent statements of helplessness, hopelessness, and/or worthlessness.

Self-Harm Risk Factors

Most people who inflict self-injury are teens and young adults. This phenomenon usually begins in one's preteen or early years when their emotions are often labile and exacerbated by raging hormones, peer pressures, loneliness, and conflicts with parents and/or other authority figures.

Certain factors may escalate the risk of self-harm in this vulnerable population, including:

- friends who self-injure;
- trauma history, including being emotionally, physically, and sexually abused;
- low self-esteem, high levels of self-criticality;
- social isolation and alienation, including rejection from friends and peers;
- unstable, dysfunctional family system;
- mental health issues such as depression, anxiety, eating disorders, and personality disorders;
- substance abuse.

So how do we effectively minister to those struggling with thoughts, feelings, and impulses of self-injury and suicidality? As with most things, first, we must acknowledge the reality and magnitude of the issues. It is imperative that in ministry, we always respect hurting people and take their feelings, concerns, and situations with the utmost importance and personal dignity. What follows are some key ministry directives to help those suffering with these challenging issues. Although there are significant differences between suicidality and self-harm, for ministry purposes, the following directives apply to both.

Prevention

It has been correctly observed that prevention is always much easier and more effective than cure. There is perhaps no realm in which this adage is truer than that pertaining to suicide and self-harm. Although it is not always possible to get upstream from a person's private self-destructive tendencies and temptations, there are some important ways to minister prophylactically.

To begin with, *we need to become healthy ourselves and model that health* to our families and congregations. This means learning about these topics so we can speak knowledgeably. It may also mean sharing lessons from our own experiences. As with most things in life and ministry, we simply cannot give what we do not possess. During an in-flight emergency, airline passengers are supposed to put on their own oxygen masks before helping others get theirs in place. Similarly, we'll be unable to teach and serve effectively if we neglect ourselves. Yet many Christians, especially pastors, feel guilty about caring for their personal needs. They endeavor to somehow love their neighbor better than they love themselves, which is functionally impossible! An incontrovertible law of God's universe is that a stream cannot rise higher than its source. Healthy and appropriate self-care is indispensable. Ministry is fraught with unique stressors, endemic loneliness, and frequent discouragement. Many times, charity needs to begin at home. Above all, we must guard and care for our hearts and teach our flocks to do the same (Proverbs 4:23). *A church cannot be healthier than its leadership.*

We need church leaders to address suicidality and other mental and relational health issues directly, specifically from the pulpit. This means learning about these topics so we can speak knowledgeably. It may also mean sharing lessons from our own experiences. In a 2014 LifeWay Research survey, 23 percent of Protestant senior pastors reported personally struggling with mental illness. Yet 66 percent of pastors said they seldom preach or teach about mental illness.[49] To do so means people will be comforted to know they are not the only ones suffering and struggling. These may be the most powerfully impactful, personally relevant, and persuasively life-changing messages a pastor ever preaches. You will likely not find such homilies online! The most effective sermons are the ones that the pastor practices. Church leaders exercising healthy, appropriate self-care loudly proclaims people's worth and value eloquently. *A church cannot be healthy if it doesn't specifically address the scope of human need.*

We need to reach out. We must courageously and compassionately shine light, speak truth, and spread salt into our darkened, deluded, and decaying world. Recall that healthy people, couples, families, and churches talk out—not act out—their feelings. Knowing truth liberates. We need biblically and clinically sound teaching and preaching about the reality of mental and relational health issues. We need to be correctly informed about the stark realities of being tempted to despair during dark and difficult times. We all need to internalize and appropriate the love, grace, mercy, forgiveness, and redemptiveness of Jesus Christ. And we need to be assured of compassionate love and support as we talk out—not act out—those painful

49 Cisney-Ellers, J. & Ellers, K. (2019). *How to develop an effective suicide awareness and crisis response ministry.* In Clinton, T. E. & Pingleton, J. P., *The Struggle Is Real: How to Care for Mental and Relational Health Needs in the Church.* Bloomington, IN: Westbow Press

feelings. Purpose to become a safe person and for your congregation to become a safe harbor for hurting people to be able to receive care and counsel from that trustable environment. *A church cannot be healthy if it is not emotionally safe.*

We need pragmatic strategies to hopefully prevent suicides but also specifically minister to loved ones victimized by suicide in tangible and helpful ways. Again, 132 people in the US end their own lives every day. Your church needs to know how to minister with excellence to these very real needs. Remember that people in crisis, those tragically suffering, and those wounded by trauma are generally very receptive to the Gospel. Let's not miss these crucial opportunities to end the silence, expose the secrets, eliminate the shame, and erase the stigma surrounding suicide and other mental and relational health issues. *A church cannot be healthy if it is not equipped to effectively minister to specific human needs.*

Intervention

What should you do if you think someone is depressed or suicidal? As uncomfortable or awkward as it may be, start by kindly and compassionately asking how the person is doing emotionally. Don't be passive and dismissive. Be bold and proactive as you ask the Holy Spirit for guidance and direction as to how you can be better sensitized to hurting people and compassionate with them.

Of course, this is easier if you have a relationship with the individual. An old adage suggests the best time to plant a tree was twenty years ago, and the second-best time is now. The same principle applies here. The best time to build a relationship with a person in crisis is before the crisis, but the second-best time is today.

Many pastors are understandably hesitant to inquire about a parishioner's mental health. Leaders may worry about embarrassment or hurt feelings, but navigating an awkward moment is far easier than preaching at the funeral of someone who died tragically, prematurely, and unnecessarily.

Asking in a loving, empathetic, non-judgmental way if a person has entertained thoughts of suicide can not only yield valuable and essential information, but it can also make a fearful, anxious, depressed, and overwhelmed person feel accepted, understood, and valued. Being sensitive to the hearts of hurting people is quintessentially Christlike.

Keep in mind that temptation is not a sin—even the temptation to end one's life. However, a person who acknowledges suicidal thoughts needs help. They may feel paralyzed by guilt for having such struggles or fear judgment and condemnation for opening up about them.

If someone is threatening or suspected of being even slightly suicidal, assess the crisis by considering three key questions:

1. *Do they have a plan?* Fleeting or even obsessive suicidal thoughts are of significantly less concern than having a clearly developed method for suicide.
2. *Do they have available means to end their life?* Is it realistically accessible (e.g., weapons, medications, etc.), and is it realistically lethal?
3. *How lethal is the threat?* Horizontal cuts on the wrist are of far less immediacy than taking bottles of pills and some-

one talking about purchasing a gun is in less immediate danger than a person holding a loaded firearm.

When someone cannot or will not assure you, family members, and loved ones he or she will not act on suicidal thoughts and feelings, you must take appropriate and immediate action. If the individual will not agree to seek help, call 9-1-1 and/or the national suicide hotline, which is 9-8-8. In many cases, a suicidal person must be hospitalized involuntarily (laws regarding involuntary hospitalization vary by state, but please do the morally and ethically correct thing—not just the legally correct thing). It is much better to safe than sorry.

One key to ministering effectively to those struggling with suicidal ideation is to understand their distorted thought processes. Research reveals that suicidal people almost universally hold the irrational belief that committing suicide is the best or even the only way out of their predicament. Additionally, most suicidal individuals erroneously believe no one will miss them if they are gone. Thus, emotionally overwhelmed people often irrationally conclude there is no hope and no help, no one cares, and nothing can change their dire situation.

People need to realize suicide never resolves anything. They need someone to lovingly guide them into the truth that ending their life is never the best, much less only option. It has been ironically observed that suicide is a permanent solution to a temporary problem. In actuality, suicide never solves anything and creates an often multigeneration legacy of shame and pain. I have worked with dozens of people over the years with persons whose grandparent committed suicide—and that is a currently haunting problem for them many years after the fact. The reverberations of that egocentric decision will cascade throughout the entire family system for years.

It has also been said that suicide is the ultimate act of self-centeredness. That is also true. Having someone compassionately give them a reality check can offer them a different perspective than the one in which they are overwhelmed with in their excruciating circumstances.

Suicidal people need both pastoral care and mental health care. Personally shepherd them (more about how to make an effective referral is discussed in the next chapter) as they obtain the level of professional treatment they need, from outpatient psychotherapy to inpatient stabilization. Lonely, hurting people need meaningful, safe, and potentially redemptive connection with other people.

Seek education on how to respond effectively to a suicidal crisis. Just as EMTs practice CPR and other emergency interventions regularly so they do not panic in a dire situation, you should develop a plan and regularly review it. Build trusted therapeutic referral relationships in your community. Familiarize yourself with national referral hotlines. Know the procedures in your local hospital community for both voluntarily and involuntarily placing someone for treatment.

Be there for hurting people, keep them safe, and stay connected with them.

Aftermath

Tragically, suicide is not always prevented. When a suicide happens, grieving family members and friends, and the community as a whole, may be surprisingly receptive to the loving care, concern, and compassion of your congregation. The first order of Christian ministry is to be compassionately sensitive to meeting hurting people's needs.

People are often most open to the love of Jesus when they are experiencing brokenness. Yet the tremendous silence, secrecy, shame, and stigma of suicide can make ministry challenging.

Suicide is devastating for those who are left behind. In addition to the grief that immediate family members experience, suicide shocks and saddens churches, schools, and entire communities. A young person's suicide may even lead to a citywide copycat deluge of more adolescent suicides.

What can pastors and ministry leaders do? Suicide is a crisis of enormous proportions, with traumatic ramifications that will eventually impact even the smallest churches. How do we lovingly lead with compassion, care, and comfort in such times? How do we help those we serve come to grips with the anguish, turmoil, guilt, outrage, confusion, and heartache suicide leaves behind?

In Mandarin (which has no letters or alphabet but rather characterized word pictures), there is no discreet word picture for the word "crisis." Rather, there is a fusion of two different characters: the one for "danger" (we get that one) and the one for "opportunity" (which is typically less readily apparent in a crisis situation). When people in the congregation are in crisis, look for opportunities to love and serve them at the point of their pain, agony, and often abject suffering.

Many times, there are perplexing and haunting questions regarding the eternal destination of the deceased following a suicide. This is an extremely sensitive and valid concern. Yet this is not a time for arrogantly and brashly splitting theological hairs or coldly pronouncing legalistic judgment. The truth is we humbly do not know everything, and we certainly do well to realize that judgment is above our pay grade.

This is a time to defer to and direct their focus on the loving Father and assure the family and friends of His unfailing comfort, kindness, love, understanding, grace, mercy, and forgiveness. Simply put, God loved that person more than we did and therefore is more concerned about their eternal well-being than we are. The Apostle Paul said we currently "see things imperfectly, like puzzling reflections in a mirror," and what we know is "partial and incomplete" (1 Corinthians 13:12, NLT). Being mere mortals is intrinsically humbling. That is one of the many reasons for which we need to possess, exercise, and demonstrate faith.

We need pragmatic strategies for ministering to people in their sorrow, whether they are wrestling with mental illness, experiencing a relational problem, or grieving the loss of a loved one. The suffering, wounded, and traumatized are vulnerable to isolation and despair, but they are also often receptive to the gospel.

Let's not miss opportunities to walk alongside the brokenhearted, demonstrate the compassion of Christ, and point people to the One who offers hope and healing.

As with other traumatic grief situations, diligently and intentionally exercise best practices of pastoral care and ministry to the distraught loved ones. Bear in mind they are likely experiencing an overwhelming roller coaster of painful emotions, including guilt, shame, outrage, futility, helplessness, and unrelenting sorrow. Remember that one-year anniversaries of grief events are traumatic, hard, and lonely. Reach out, support, encourage, listen, empathize, and pray for and with them. And keep on doing it. They will need it.

CHAPTER 17

Referrals and Resources

Providing hope, health, and healing to the hurting in an informed and capable manner is a valuable and specialized form of ministry no less important than any other way in which pastors serve their congregation. Whether addressing mental and emotional issues ourselves or on behalf of members of our flock professionally, the salient question becomes: "To whom can I turn for help?"

This is a crucial concern that must be considered carefully and cogently. This chapter addresses the need for making an effective referral, the 'art' of making an effective referral, the 'science' of making an effective referral, and the pastor's role after making the referral. Finally, a list of helpful ministries, organizations, and treatment options are included for those in need.

The Need for Making an Effective Referral

As was mentioned earlier, studies pertaining to persons seeking help for their mental and relational issues consistently verify that the vast majority of Americans reach out first to a pastor, priest, or rabbi. Although most probably didn't sign up for this duty (and colossal responsibility), pastors and other church leaders are by default the gatekeepers or "first responders" for most people seeking help or guidance regarding a mental health concern, a suicidal crisis, a severe relationship problem, or a major life trauma. Yet most pastors are not trained to know how to nor have the bandwidth to adequately help navigate their sheep safely through the proverbial rocks and reefs in the storm-tossed waves of their seas of despair and despondency.

Sometimes the best way I can help someone as a clinical psychologist is to refer them to another mental health professional who is more specialized or experienced in a certain arena and consequently can likely help them better than I. It not only provides great personal relief at times to recommend someone else more specifically trained, experienced, or specialized in a certain area but great professional satisfaction to know that suggesting the client see Dr. Smith down the hall or Dr. Jones down the street is the best way I can help them. That is truly a win-win for all concerned. It is not only good old-fashioned common sense; it displays the best clinical practice along with the highest professional ethics. Again, no one can help everyone. We need to collaborate. And we often need to refer. But how, when, and to whom?

Meeting congregants' mental and relational health needs can be done in a variety of ways. As we have seen in the previous chapters, addressing these crucial ministry needs can also be conceptualized along a continuum of care. Some churches offer specialized training in lay counseling; many offer various support groups, some have counseling professionals on staff, some have professional "in-house" counseling centers, some contract with "out-house" counseling centers in the community, then there are specialized treatment programs, residential rehabilitative centers, partial day treatment programs, and full in-patient psychiatric treatment facilities. The more ministry tools we have in our ministry toolbox, the more effectively we can minister to hurting people and relationships.

The "Art" of Making an Effective Referral

I believe that knowing how to make an appropriate and effective referral can be thought of as part art and part science. Your aid in facilitating a parishioner's understanding of the various forms of professional assistance available can be valuable and encouraging at a time when people often feel highly vulnerable, confused as to where or to whom to turn, and how to access those services. It's a big, scary world out there. Whom can they safely trust? Who is best qualified and experienced?

Once you have established a strong collegial working alliance with a good, solid, spiritually and emotionally mature therapist (more about that later), often the tricky part becomes how to successfully hand off your church member to them. Many times, your sheep may feel abandoned or rejected by thinking you don't care for them or don't want to help them yourself. In this scenario, it is essential to emphasize to the person/family that often, the best way you can care for them is to recommend someone else—a trained specialist in their particular area of need—who has the time, talent, and training to help them better than you can. This "artful" skill requires you to be direct, definite, delicate, and diplomatic.

The potential for making a referral can be part of a broader conversation about the limit of the number of pastoral counseling sessions you will facilitate as well as any other restrictions you may place on counseling (e.g., same-gender counseling, conflicts of interest, issues which transcend your expertise and training, lack of time, etc.). The necessity of making a professional referral should be considered when:

- Significant clinical symptoms manifest themselves.
- Thoughts/temptations of self-harm are disclosed.
- Thoughts/temptations of harm to others are disclosed.
- Your involvement becomes emotionally inappropriate, and you are no longer able to remain objective.
- You clearly know that you are beyond your level of competency.
- You're reaching your pastoral counseling session limit and have begun to feel in over your head.
- Your instinct tells you that something is going on the person(s) have not revealed, or you feel uneasy, but you can't articulate what or why.
- The Lord's Spirit is leading you to refer this person/couple/family.

Make the need for referral clear. Explain why you believe it to be in their best interests and make sure to follow up with them later to see if they contacted the clinician and how the process is going. A good referral is crucial to good counseling. Being open and direct helps proactively reduce the silence, shame, and stigma that many in the church still have regarding counseling or psychotherapy and mental illness and relational problems. That applies to the appropriate use of antidepressants and other medications too. Many Christians still believe they just need to have more faith, get the sin out of their lives (as if they actually can!), or somehow get tougher and pull themselves up by their bootstraps (which, if you actually think about it, defies the nature of gravity!).

Please use the utmost in discretion in discussing the need for a referral. The church can feel like a notoriously public and exposed place, particularly to someone beset and burdened by shame. Hurting people already feel exposed, vulnerable, and as though everyone else can look through them to see the embarrassing personal problems with which they are struggling. Your discussion about the need for a referral should be done in private and with the utmost respect for the person or family's dignity, worth, and self-respect.

Do your homework on both the best available resources in the community, which can be of support to the hurting person(s) involved and the most workable strategies for anticipating and responding to their potentially resistant attitude or mindset toward receiving help. Then before your conversation with them, prayerfully consider how to be the most sensitive to their unique concern(s). Keep in mind that it's not that people don't want relief from their suffering (unless they are very masochistic!); it's that change is hard, scary, uncertain, and generally requires a lot of difficult work. They may have tried several ways to work on their issues as their hope has dissipated. Furthermore, asking for help may not only feel humbling and humiliating to the hurting person(s), it may activate deep-seated feelings of guilt, inadequacy, failure, and ineffectualness, all of which are hard to face in the best of circumstances.

In asking the Holy Spirit for discernment and direction on how you can wisely steer the conversation, consider enlisting the wise and caring support of another trusted, mature church leader, deacon, or elder, while at the same time being careful not to make the person(s) feel ganged up on. And always, if there is an imminent danger or threat of suicide and/or harm to others, please call 911. Don't risk a tragedy or another statistic; this is where the old adage of being safe rather than sorry holds true.

Please be mindful that our culture is still, in some respects, confused and/or ignorant about the nature and dynamics of emotional, mental, and relational dysfunction; in other ways, it humiliates those who suffer with these (e.g., media/sitcom depictions and labels of "crazy," "wacko," "nutcase," or "funny farms," "psycho wards," etc. to disparage and denigrate persons with such pain). Your role is both instrumental and invaluable in helping to sensitively and compassionately normalize the incidence and universality of typical human struggles. Everyone hurts. All relationships experience conflict. Everyone fails at times. Addictions and harmful habits are human. Most people's resistance to receiving help is based on fear, pride, shame, stigma, or some combination thereof. Be gentle, understanding, accepting, and kind.

Remind yourself and them that nearly 44 million US adults suffer from a diagnosable mental illness each year... that's one out of every four to five people! Address it. Communicate about mental health with your congregation. Don't over-spiritualize it. There is much ministry to do. Keep shepherding! And concerning those parishioners you have referred for help, set and maintain healthy boundaries regarding their treatment by asking them in general ways how the counseling process is going. It may also be helpful to ask their permission to consult with their clinician and have them sign the requisite release of information form to do so.

Many clinicians find that working together with a referring pastor makes each of their respective roles easier and more productive. Feedback from the clinician about the therapy is very important to help you stay alongside persons whom you refer for help, not only to offer them ongoing quality pastoral care, prayer, and support but to ensure that they do not feel discarded or forgotten. Likewise, feedback from you about medication compliance, social interaction and relational functioning, supportive structures, and other pastoral observations can be vital information for a clinician to better help your sheep. If you do not live in an area that has mental health professionals who meet all the above criteria, then avail yourself of various national referral networks, which can more than likely yield positive results (see end of chapter for several). Many state licensing boards have eased restrictions on telehealth/video therapy due to the pandemic, in most cases greatly reducing the geographical challenges involved in matching hurting people with the best providers suited for their needs.

The "Science" of Making an Effective Referral

Several factors are important in prayerfully selecting a person, agency, clinic, treatment facility, or another resource from which we seek guidance and assistance for ourselves, our family members, or our parishioners when their problems transcend the scope of our expertise or training. Among other things, we wonder if the therapist will be safe, trustworthy, and respectful of our congregant's issues. Will they treat these concerns with care, compassion, and confidentiality? Will they be nonjudgmental, accepting, and sensitive? Can I trust them as an uplifting ally to my ministry, or will they be an undermining adversary to it? And most importantly, are they doctrinally orthodox, and do they know what they're doing theologically as well as psychologically—i.e., will they lead a client astray or to the path of life?

Consequently, it is imperative that you first make a concerted effort to develop a close and healthy working relationship with one or more reputable Christian counselors in your area in order for you to make referrals with confidence and assurance. Take them out for breakfast or lunch. Get to know them personally so you may say with confidence and integrity to a parishioner that you would not hesitate to refer a friend or loved one to this particular clinician. Here are some key "fruit" to look for in selecting a good referral for Christian counseling:

- Does the therapist possess and manifest a personal and growing relationship with Jesus Christ?

- Does the therapist possess and demonstrate a genuine sense of caring, compassion, and concern for people who are hurting?
- Does the therapist base their work on a biblical worldview and value system?
- Does the therapist express a desire to be seen by you as a trusted colleague in ministry, and are they open to consulting with you on the client's behalf provided the appropriate (legally required per HIPAA regulations) release forms are signed to maintain a healthy confidentiality boundary?
- Does the therapist have the appropriate professional training, credentials, experience, and state licensure as a certified mental health professional?

Once we realize the need to make a referral and have convinced our church members of that, the question then becomes: "What sort of mental health professional is best suited for their need?" There are several types of professional credentials reflecting various levels of training and expertise, ranging from master's level professional counselors, marriage and family therapists, and social workers to doctoral-level psychologists and psychiatrists. It isn't unusual to find the mental health care field somewhat confusing. So, for clarity, what follows are the fundamental differences between various kinds and levels of clinicians:

- *Counselors and Marriage and Family Therapists* (individuals with a minimum master's-level training in child, individual, and/or marriage counseling).
- *Social Workers* (persons with master's-level training in counseling along with specialized emphasis on incorporating community resources in their assistance to hurting persons and families).
- *Psychologists* (individuals with doctoral-level training who specialize in diagnosing, assessing, and treating mental health disorders by means of psychological assessment, counseling, and psychotherapy).
- *Psychiatrists* (medical doctors with specialized training in the diagnosis and treatment, including primarily pharmacologic treatment, of mental disorders).

Despite all this awareness and your best efforts, do not be surprised if your congregant misperceives your well-facilitated referral as pejorative and rejecting. Be sensitive to the likelihood that the swirling currents of shame and stigma run deep, and parishioners who are facing mental and/or relational challenges are probably used to feeling criticized, judged, and abandoned. Gently but firmly normalize the universality of people's pain and problems, and assure them they are loved, accepted, and cared for by you and their church family.

One practical way to practice what is preached is to listen to suggestions from the person or family as to how they can best be helped. After appropriate resources are sought out and referral(s) are made, there may be other obstacles preventing or precluding the hurting person from getting the care they need.

Many hurting people lack the financial resources to receive the treatment they need and so will benefit from a benevolence fund or financial assistance. Others may need childcare during appointments, regular meals, or transportation to appointments. Pray for provision. Enlist help from others. Utilize community resources. Start ministries to serve those needs. Evaluate how your church can make a bigger contribution to persons with similar problems. Tailor programming to target those issues. Dedicate a trained volunteer or team of volunteers to serve faithfully and consistently alongside a hurting person, couple, or family to ensure structural support, follow-through, and continuity of care. Seek out and appropriate relevant community resources and connect hurting people to them. Preach, practice, and teach compassion and empathy; in your sermons, come down hard on temptations to indulge in the wildly popular "church" sins of gossip, judgment, and rejection.

After the Referral

Be committed to ongoing shepherding and pastoral care. Making a referral doesn't mean you wash your hands of the person(s). Quite the opposite; in some respects, that's when the hardest work begins! It is essential that after resources are sought out and referrals are made, a pastor or other church leader continues to regularly reach out to, meet with, and personally serve the individual, couple, or family. Many hurting people avoid relationships, so it's fairly common (and sadly easy) for those persons to fall through the proverbial cracks.

The pastoral role changes once a referral to a clinical professional takes place. The pastor's involvement might change to being that of spiritual guide, offering support and wisdom while attempting to honor the clinical process that is developing. In addition, the parishioner now holds the privilege of confidentiality and must sign a release to allow the therapist to speak with you regarding their care. For various reasons, patients are often reluctant to sign blanket releases of confidentiality—even when they trust the good intentions of the pastor. In these cases, it is typically best to honor their boundaries and simply come alongside in whatever way seems appropriate.

Please continue to lovingly pastor persons as they work through their challenges; such is a crucial element of the high and holy calling of a minister of the liberating gospel of Jesus Christ. He lived and died for everyone; scripture never hides or whitewashes our brokenness. All of us are created in and reflect the *imago Dei* and thus are of equal worth and value at the level foot of the cross, regardless of our psychiatric diagnoses! Because at the end of the day, as well as at the end of our lives, whatever we have done to the "least" of these...

Resources

Many types of mental health-oriented care support groups and ministries are a functional integration of a more modern understanding of mental illness and mental health with what the church has historically referred to as pastoral care or care ministry. Church leaders such as clergy, deacons, elders, and lay ministers have responded to the emotional and relational needs of the church body throughout history. This is a beautiful example of God's call to "love one another" (John 13:34). The following care support ministries are simply examples of how this integration has been applied in a practical and effective manner.

National Suicide Prevention Hotline: 9-8-8 (24 hours per day, available in both English and Spanish)
National Child Abuse Hotline: 800-422-4453
National Child Trafficking Hotline: 888-373-7888
National Domestic Violence Hotline: 800-799-7233
National Referral Networks for Christian Counseling and Care:

- Focus on the Family—https://findacounselor.focusonthefamily.com/;
- Lighthouse Network—https://lighthousenetwork.org;
- American Association of Christian Counselors—https://connect.aacc.net;
- Find Christian Counselor—https://findchristiancounselor.com.

Celebrate Recovery

Celebrate Recovery is a Christ-centered twelve-step-type recovery program oriented toward those who are struggling with various addictions and compulsive behaviors. Their motto is that they help people deal with their hurts, habits, and hang-ups. Celebrate Recovery (https://www.celebraterecovery.com) was founded by Pastor John Baker of Saddleback Church in 1990 and typically includes a time of both teaching and instruction, as well as a small-group support component made up of individuals experiencing similar forms of addiction or emotional distress. Although Celebrate Recovery is typically thought of as a church-based addiction recovery program, the model has been applied to various types of mental health issues, including anxiety, depression, anger management, disordered eating, abuse recovery, etc. Celebrate Recovery can play an important role in people's emotional and spiritual healing, and for many, it is an important adjunctive component of their ongoing work in Alcoholics Anonymous, psychotherapy, and pastoral counseling.

Divorce Care Ministries

The process of going through a divorce is considered the second-highest life stressor, ranked just behind the death of a spouse. Divorce can carry a unique set of emotional concerns for Christians who may have been taught a variety of messages about how God feels about divorcing one's spouse. These uniquely Christian perspectives on divorce, accompanied by frequent feelings of guilt, anxiety, depression, and even suicidal feelings, make divorce care ministries a vital ministry to any congregation. Divorce care ministries, such as DivorceCare (https://www.divorcecare.org), follow a recovery type model that includes readings, instruction, and support group components. Some, such as DivorceCare for Kids (https://www.dc4k.org), provide extended care and support to the entire family system. Given the profoundly disruptive nature of divorce, ministries such as these can provide a safe, constructive, and accepting environment that facilitates healing and growth.

Fresh Hope

Fresh Hope is a peer-to-peer Christ-centered wellness approach to mental health recovery based upon six tenets that empowers people to connect both their faith and recovery principles. This approach both empowers and encourages individuals to live full and rich lives in spite of their diagnosis.

Developed by Pastor Brad Hoef as a result of his own experience with a severe mental health issue, this small group dynamic has been helpful to people across the country and around the world. The goals of Fresh Hope are:

- To equip and empower individuals (and their loved ones) who are affected by a mental health diagnosis to live a full, rich, and purpose-filled life in wellness and wholeness (mental, physical, and spiritual) through participation in local Fresh Hope groups, which are Christ-centered peer support groups, as well as online forums, educational opportunities, and faith-based mental health resources.
- To provide ongoing assistance to individuals and their families during times of transition by providing Mental Health Navigators in local communities who are certified peer support specialists and certified wellness coaches.
- To challenge the Christian church to address the mental health crisis in their community, challenging them to provide a "compassionate, understanding, safe and supportive place" for those who struggle with mental health issues. This includes understanding that many mental health challenges are due to the brain's improper function and are not character flaws, moral failures, or a spiritual weakness.

- To advocate on both the state and national levels for continued mental health reforms to repair the issues that are "broken" in the system.
- To provide peer-run wellness centers in the local communities as a positive place of encouragement, connection, empowerment, and learning.
- To join with other organizations and voices in tearing down the thick walls of cultural stigma regarding "mental illness."

Their website contains further information about their ministry and includes clear information about how to develop a Fresh Hope group in your church: https://www.freshhope.us.

Mental Health Grace Alliance

In 2011, Mental Health Grace Alliance ("The Grace Alliance") was founded to create practical and grace-filled resources for those living with mental health challenges. Mental Health Grace Alliance curriculums utilize a whole-health (i.e., holistic) approach, integrating evidence-based science (neuroscience, psychology, biomedical, etc.) and biblical scriptures/faith experience for mental health recovery (resilience).

The amazing impact from the Grace Alliance programs and training were published in four journals, with results showing:

1. Participants saw reduction of mental health symptoms.
2. Participants were aided in overall mental health recovery.
3. Participants experienced a renewal of their faith.
4. Training increases confidence and skills to respond and minister to mental health challenges.

Mental Health Grace Alliance has reached twenty-five countries with thousands utilizing the resources and hundreds of Grace Alliance groups. Their website is https://www.mentalhealthgracealliance.org.

Grief Recovery Ministries

Ministering to those who are grieving is an important and frequent part of ministering to a congregation. Pastors are commonly called to care for those who are grieving the loss of a loved one. Typically, however, the grieving individual needs care and follow-up long after the pastor or ministry leader has moved on to more urgent issues. Church-based grief recovery ministries, such as GriefShare (https://www.griefshare.org), can be an effective way to minister to the emotional and mental health needs of those who are grieving. GriefShare can be a staff or lay-led program that includes a weekly video-based instructional time followed by a small-group discussion. Programs such as these can be vital to the grieving individual and family, are often low in cost, and require very little training or time commitment from pastoral staff.

Marriage Mentoring

An approach to decreasing the likelihood of divorce among congregants might begin with a well-developed marriage mentoring ministry. Beyond the church and professional marriage counselors, there are very few institutions or individuals prepared to encourage, support, educate, and walk alongside those who may be struggling in their marital relationship. Marriage mentoring ministries, such as the Center for Marriage and Relationships (http://cmr.biola.edu/resources/mentors/) or Marriage Mentoring (https://www.marriagementoring.com), provide structured, effective content and mentoring relationship models to pastoral or lay ministers in a church ministry context. These programs are typically workbook-based and combined with an ongoing mentoring relationship with a mature couple in your congregation. The mentoring couple is not expected to provide all the answers to the mentee couple but simply to walk alongside and share from what they have learned about marriage and relationships. Marriage mentoring can be a tremendous blessing to young or struggling couples in your church context and indirectly strengthen the marriages of mentoring couples as well.

National Alliance on Mental Illness

Although not a Christian organization, NAMI exists to offer support and assistance to those suffering from all types of mental illness and to support their families and loved ones (https://www.nami.org).

CHAPTER 18

Tips and Tools

Launching a counseling ministry can be a daunting and intimidating task. Questions inevitably swirl around important practical operational considerations such as fee structure, ethical and legal standards, business and accounting operations, and more. Unfortunately, these crucial administrative factors in the delivery and provision of counseling services are rarely addressed in graduate school; thus, many counselors are left to recreate the proverbial wheel.

Based on what type of model of counseling ministry is preferred as described in the previous chapters, or a perhaps a hybridized combination of two or more, there are some significant and universal basics that must be addressed. What follows are some key practical issues involved in the organization and implementation of an effective Christian counseling ministry.

Legal-Organizational Structure:

Many churches choose to make their counseling center/program an extension of their 501(c)(3) not-for-profit tax-exempt entity, including substantial fiduciary and pragmatic advantages. The board of the ministry must formalize this, which is usually a simple and straightforward process. Others may opt to make the center a limited liability corporation (LLC). It is best to determine the unique goals and needs of the ministry and seek legal counsel accordingly.

Liability Insurance Coverage:

For licensed mental health providers to receive third party (health insurance companies and Medicare and Medicaid programs) reimbursements, they are required to obtain malpractice insurance. The minimum professional liability coverage required in most states is $1,000,000 per occurrence/$3,000,000 aggregate. Many church insurance policies have umbrella options, riders, or other features that may offer some additional protection. It is essential to insure in order to ensure fiscal stability and peace of mind. Fortunately, it is rare for churches and for mental health professionals to be sued for malpractice, but it is prudent to be cautious, nonetheless.

Ethical Standards:

Whereas all professional organizations have ethical guidelines and standards to be adhered to, as Christians, our ethical standards should be circumspect and above reproach. The overarching and altruistic biblical basis of love should be preeminent in all a believer says and does throughout their entire life, much less as reflected in the way they care for hurting and vulnerable people. By far, the most comprehensive and thorough code of ethics in the helping professions has been created by the American Association of Christian counselors and may be found here: https://www.aacc.net/wp-content/uploads/2020/06/AACC-Code-of-Ethics-Master-Document.pdf.

As with most things, prevention is easier—and cheaper—than cure. Healthy boundaries and ministry practices are a Christian counselor's best friends.

Record Keeping:

It is essential for the practice of effective and ethical psychotherapy to keep accurate and confidential documentation of each session. This not only helps guide and structure the treatment process but acts as the most effective safeguard against malpractice suits and is the best way to guarantee consistent quality service delivery. Back in the "old days," everyone wrote their case notes by hand after each session and kept them in a locked filing cabinet secured in a locked room.

In the digital age, various secure software programs are available for full record-keeping and so much more. One of the best is https://www.therapynotes.com, which not only provides online password-protected note keeping but also bills insurance, keeps accurate client financial records, does scheduling, and offers a secure platform for video therapy/telehealth.

Fees and Charges:

The cost of counseling services can vary widely depending on the credentials and experience of the therapist, the type of services offered, and the geographic area. Generally, health insurance companies will pay a significant portion (less deductible and co-pay) of what is determined to be "reasonable and customary" fees.

Some Christian counseling centers may opt to not get involved with insurance companies and offer their services free or for a donation. I strongly suggest that churches do charge clients something regardless of their financial circumstances. Research validates the commonsense conclusion that people tend to not value what they have no investment in. All seasoned therapists know that the number of "no show" clients who miss appointments is drastically reduced when fees are charged if they do not cancel beforehand.

But it is true that mental health services are quite expensive. For those who do not have health insurance, it can be cost-prohibitive. Consequently, many counseling agencies offer what is called a "sliding scale," often based on one's ability to pay. Because for a large portion of my childhood, I was raised in poverty, I have always been sensitive to and accommodating with people who are uninsured and cannot afford professional psychotherapy. I strongly suggest that church leaders implement an ongoing scholarship program for deserving uninsured persons to supplement the partial fees they are charged. Conducting fundraisers, donor appeals, and requests for helping underwrite the care for deserving persons is just good ministry.

Several years ago, I was working with a person who stated they were very poor and could only afford five dollars per session (and since I was in a group practice that worked on a 70/30 split of collected fees, I only received 70 percent of that fee!). After several sessions in which she casually remarked about or referred to things and lifestyle choices I couldn't afford, I looked out the window following our session one day and watched her drive away in a new Mercedes. After working through my feelings of being duped and betrayed, I confronted her with the obvious. Embarrassed by her lie, she reacted defensively and quit, obviously not properly motivated or ready to work on real character change and growth.

Since then, I have recommended that uninsured persons wanting a fee reduction or scholarship bring some form of accountability in return for that accommodation. There are many kinds of scholarship applications and forms out there to determine reduced fees for counseling. But the simplest and most equitable way I know of to do this is to have them bring in their 1040 income tax statement from the previous year and charge them 1 percent of their gross annual income. For example, if they earned $32,178 the previous year, their fee becomes $32. That usually works. A few people may protest that formula, but it never ceases to amaze me how much money people will spend on exotic coffees, theater tickets, personal grooming, electronic toys, and other nonessential items. At the end of the day, people need to value themselves.

Many practices these days do not bill insurance but operate on a cash or pay-as-you-go basis. In those cases, the therapist or counseling center may issue a "Superbill" receipt to the client, which they can turn in to their insurance company for reimbursement. The "Superbill" contains the therapist's license number and credentials, date of service, charge, amount received, and the necessary diagnostic and procedural codes verifying the delivery of professional mental health care services. This procedure is also often used when a client has an HMO policy that permits out-of-network provider exceptions.

Forms and Procedures:

To reiterate, some of the most important tools of the trade are never taught in grad school. Chief among these are methods of conveying and gathering crucial information that is essential for the psychotherapy process to be successful. These include legally required disclosures of exceptions to confidentiality, regulations surrounding the Health Insurance Portability and Accountability Act (HIPAA), mandated abuse and neglect reporting procedures (for children, disabled, and elderly persons), procedures involved in duty to warn (of potential danger to oneself and/or others), client rights, office and accounting practices, appointment policies, intake forms, and so on.

It is important (and legally required) to address these fundamental dynamics of the counseling process with clients. Perhaps the simplest and most efficient way to do so is by having them read and sign various forms attesting to their having read the above information. I always go over the disclosure information at least briefly with each client(s) and address any questions they have. Be sensitive to the likely response people may have of feeling overwhelmed by all the paperwork and legalities. Make these forms available to be downloaded off your website and electronically transmitted if the client desires (or have them come thirty to forty minutes early) so that they can familiarize themselves with the information and complete them before the initial appointment.

Clinically, by far the most important document is the intake form. It is that person's voluntary disclosure and description of the issues they present to their therapist. For me, this is one of the best diagnostic tools in existence. By answering comprehensive questions about their life, the information they share (or choose to not reveal—which is likewise diagnostically significant) speaks volumes about their personality, pathology, relationships, history, strengths, insights, self-awareness, and specific areas of distress. I go over it in detail, preferably prior to the first appointment, and then with them in the initial session. The information derived from their answers on that form helps me get to know them much better, faster, and deeper than I ever could without it. It is truly indispensable.

~~~~~~~~~~~~~~~~

My heartfelt prayer is that this book launches a clarion call for the church universal to minister directly and effectively to the billions of people worldwide who suffer from mental and relational health concerns. *I passionately implore you to spread this message*—share it with your families and friends, your ministry colleagues and associates, and your denominational and professional circles. Pray, serve, lead, discuss, and advocate for those with mental and relational problems. We need to start a mental and relational health revolution in the church.

Again, churches are filled with real people who have real problems and need real help. We are commanded to "Carry one another's burdens and in this way you will fulfill the requirements of the law of Christ [that is, the law of Christian love]" (Galatians 6:2, AMP). Let's do it!
~~~~~~~~~~~~~~~~

INTAKE FORM:

Jared P. Pingleton, Psy.D
Licensed Clinical Psychologist
"Restoring Lives, Renewing Relationships"

Confidential **INTAKE FORMATION** **Please Print Clearly**

Name: ______________________________ Birthdate__________ Age: _____ Gender: M / F

Address: ______________________________ Social Security Number: ______________

City: ______________ State:_____ Zip:________ Home Phone:__________ Cell:__________

Email: ________________ List persons with whom you are now living, their ages and their relationship to you:

____

____

____

Calls or e-mail will be discrete, but please indicate any restrictions: ______________________

Occupation: ______________________________ Education level: ______________

Employer: ______________________ Length of employment:__________ Work Phone:__________

Were/are you a member of the armed services?_______ If so, when:__________ What branch?______________

Spouse's name: ______________ Birthdate:__________ Social Security Number: __________

Spouse's occupation: ______________________ Education level: ______________

Spouse's employer: ______________________ Length of employment:________ Work Phone:__________

Was he/she a member of the armed services? _______ If so when?__________ What branch?______________

Emergency contact: ______________ Relationship:__________ Phone(s):______________

REFERRAL

How did you find out about us? ______________________________________

Name of referral source: ______________________ Phone:______________

If applicable, may we have your permission to confidentially contact this person to thank them for the referral? YES NO

PHYSICAL HEALTH

Current health status (circle one): Excellent Good Fair Poor Date of last physical exam: ______________

Clinic or physician's name: ______________________ Phone:______________

What serious illnesses have you had and when? ______________________________

Hospitalizations (reason/diagnosis/dates): ______________________________

Describe any current physical problems/illness: ______________________________

Are there medical or physical issues/problems that interfere with your well-being? If so, briefly describe: ______________

____

List any medications you are now taking and their purpose (including nonprescription medications like sleeping pills, diet pills, etc.):

MEDICATION	PURPOSE	DOSAGE
____________	____________	____________
____________	____________	____________
____________	____________	____________
____________	____________	____________

Prescribed by: ____________________ If applicable, may we contact your physician in order to coordinate care? YES NO

List current or past history of alcohol use for you and/or family members: ____________________

List current or past history of drug use for you and/or family members: ____________________

List current or past history of any nervous and/or mental disorder for you and/or any family members: ____________________

____

List current or past history of legal difficulty or trouble with the law: ____________________

PROBLEM INFORMATION

Briefly describe what brings you into counseling: ____________________

____

____

____

____

____

Briefly describe the history and development of your concern from onset to present: ____________________

____

____

Why are you coming for counseling now instead of a few months ago or a few months from now? ____________________

____

What are your goals for counseling – what do you wish to accomplish? ____________________

____

What specific concerns or anxieties do you have about counseling? ____________________

____

Rate how strongly you want to change your problem: (do not want to change) 1 2 3 4 5 6 7 8 9 10 (desperately desire change)

Have you been to counseling before?______When?____________With whom?____________________

If so briefly describe your experience ____________________

Current stressors (please describe how the following areas are stressful for you):

Marriage/home ____________________

Children/parents: ____________________

Work/school: ______

Financial: ______

Social: ______

Spiritual: ______

Sexual: ______

Other: ______

Major present stress: ______

Date and place of last vacation: ______

FAMILY BACKGROUND

Father's name: ______ If deceased, date and cause: ______

Age: ______ Occupation: ______ Education level: ______ Health: ______

Describe his personality, attitude towards and relationship with you, past and present: ______

______

______

Mother's name: ______ If deceased, date and cause: ______

Age: ______ Occupation: ______ Education level: ______ Health: ______

Describe her personality, attitude towards and relationship with you, past and present: ______

______

______

Parents' marital status: ______ Briefly describe your parents' marriage: ______

______

How did they handle conflict in their relationship? ______

______

If divorced, when did it occur and what was your reaction to it? ______

______

If one or both of your parents remarried, when did it occur and what was your reaction to it? ______

______

Step-father's name: ______ Age: ______ Occupation: ______

Describe his personality, attitude and relationship with you, past and present: ______

Step-mother's name: ______ Age: ______ Occupation: ______

Describe her personality, attitude and relationship with you, past and present: ______

If you were not brought up by your parents, who raised you? ______

Between what years? ______ Who took care of you as an infant? ______

How were you disciplined as a child and by whom? ______

Siblings (list names, ages, marital status, occupation and place of residence): ______

____

____

____

Give your impression of the home atmosphere in which you grew up, including how people got along? ______________

____

____

____

How was love expressed in your parents' home? ______________________________________

How was anger expressed in your parents' home? _____________________________________

What was their attitude toward sex and was there any teaching about it? ____________________

Were you or your siblings ever physically and/or sexually abused, assaulted or neglected? ______________

Age of first sexual experience: _________ History of unsafe sex and/or promiscuity: ____________________

MARITAL HISTORY

Marital status: __________How long did you know your spouse before engagement? ___________ Length of engagement: ________

When did your relationship become sexualized? __________Did you cohabit before marriage? ________ For how long?___________

Date of marriage: ________________List names and ages of children/stepchildren and indicate which (if any) are from a previous relationship: ____

____

____

Describe the strengths of your marriage: ____

____

Describe the conflicts in your marriage: ____

____

Describe your relationship with your in-laws: ____

Date(s) of previous marriage(s)/divorce(s): ____

RELIGIOUS/SPIRITUAL IDENTIFICATION

Describe the religious training you received growing up and how God was viewed by your family? ______________

____How important are spiritual concerns to your life? _______________

How would you describe your current spiritual life? _____________________________________

____

Denominational affiliation: ________________________ Average monthly worship attendance ___________________

Do you want your therapist to integrate Christian spirituality into your counseling process? YES NO

SYMPTOM CHECKLIST (please check all that apply)

_____ I am dissatisfied with my life and want a change

_____ I am dissatisfied with the current state of my family life, and/or my interpersonal relationships in general

_____ I am dissatisfied in my relationship with my spouse or significant other

_____ I am dissatisfied with, confused about, or have questions regarding the sexual part of my life

_____ I am dissatisfied with my body

_____ In the past few weeks or months I have thought about how I could end my life

_____ Have you ever thought about ending your life or had a plan to harm yourself?

_____ Have you ever made an attempt to end your life?

I have recently experienced:

_____moodiness _____change in sex drive _____resentment _____mental confusion or disorientation

_____unusual anger or irritability _____change of appetite _____stomach trouble _____decreased energy or motivation

_____anxious feelings _____unusual fatigue _____bowel disturbances _____feelings of helplessness

_____inability to relax _____difficulty sleeping _____racing thoughts _____feelings of sadness, loss or grief

_____loneliness _____nightmares _____apathy/hopelessness _____inferiority feelings

In the last few weeks or months in order to try to feel better about my life, I have done the following:

_____binge eating/purging_____ignored my normal responsibilities _____worked more than usual

_____drank alcohol _____not gotten out of bed or had poor hygiene _____used pornography or erotic material

_____used illegal drugs _____isolated myself from people _____acted sexually in an unusual way for me

_____misused prescribed drugs _____constantly surrounded myself with people _____harmed myself by cutting, burning, etc.

In my lifetime I have experienced:

_____the loss of a loved one _____an abortion _____living with someone who was/is addicted

_____a traumatic event _____divorce of my parents _____abandonment/exploitation by important people to me

_____physical abuse or assault _____divorce of my own _____being unloved by important people to me

_____sexual abuse or assault _____the loss of someone by suicide _____being fired from a job

_____the death of a child _____an addiction of my own _____ something else significant to me _______________

____

Form completed by: _________________________________Date:_____________ Is above information true and accurate? _____

About the Author

Rev. Jared Pingleton, PsyD

Dr. Jared Pingleton is a Christ-follower, husband, father, and grandfather. He is also a third-generation minister, clinical and consulting psychologist, professor, author, and international speaker who is passionate about communicating Jesus' love, mercy, and grace to a hurting and conflicted world. A respected leader in the Christian mental health field, Jared has been in professional practice since 1977, offering help, hope, and healing to thousands of individuals, couples, families, and churches.

Dually trained in theology and psychology, he has been a professor at several Christian universities and seminaries, served on the pastoral staff of two large churches (where he founded and directed church-based community counseling centers), and has authored, co-authored, or edited several books, including:

- *The Care and Counsel Bible* [consulting editor];
- *The Struggle Is Real: How to Care for Mental and Relational Needs in the Church;*
- *Making Magnificent Marriages;*
- *Marriage: Its Foundation, Theology, and Mission in a Changing World;*
- *Be Strong and Surrender: A Thirty-Day Recovery Guide;*
- *Addiction and Recovery Handbook;*
- *Praying With Jesus: Reset My Prayer Life;*
- *Christian Perspectives on Human Growth and Development;*
- *An Integrative Analysis of Psychological and Christian Concepts of Relational Maturity.*

Jared earned Doctor of Psychology and MA degrees in clinical psychology from Rosemead School of Psychology, Biola University; an MA in counseling from the University of Missouri-Kansas City; and a BS in psychology and biblical studies (summa cum laude) from Evangel University. He did additional graduate studies at the University of Kansas and at the Assemblies of God, Talbot, and Fuller Theological Seminaries.

Dr. Pingleton currently maintains an active speaking schedule and a private psychotherapy and consulting practice. He served for several years as the Director of Mental Health and Ministry and as Vice-President of the American Association of Christian Counselors and as the Director of Counseling Services at Focus on the Family, respectively. Prior to that he was in private practice for thirty-six years.

Dr. Pingleton has extensive national and international media experience—appearing as a guest, host, or co-host on hundreds of television and radio programs and in many leading print publications. He maintains several professional affiliations, volunteers on the boards of several ministries, has received six "Who's Who" awards (including "Who's Who" in America) along with several other national recognitions, and is a popular national and international speaker and conference leader.

Jared and his precious wife, Linda, have four stellar sons, four amazing daughters-in-law, and five adorable grandchildren. In addition to spending fun and meaningful time with his family, he enjoys sports of all kinds (he is an ardent Kansas City Chiefs, Kansas City Royals, and Kansas Jayhawks fan), travel, mountain climbing, vintage automobiles, landscaping, hiking, antiques, classical music, and coin collecting.

All of Dr. Pingleton's resources can be found at a discount on his website: http://www.drpingleton.com, as well as contact information about having him speak or conduct workshops and seminars.

CPSIA information can be obtained
at www.ICGtesting.com
Printed in the USA
JSHW032241311022
32397JS00002B/2